Tour of Occitanie by rail

Take the Occitanie Rail Tour

CONTENTS

- **4** 10 great reasons to travel by rail
- **8** Occitanie Rail Tour: Fabulous Journeys by rail
- **10** Holidaying by rail
- **11** Bike and train
- **12** The liO network in practice

14
FABULOUS JOURNEYS BY RAIL

- **16** The Causses of Quercy line (Brive - Rodez)
- **28** The Lozère line (La Bastide-St-Laurent - Marvejols)
- **34** The Cévennes line (Langogne - Nimes)
- **42** The Mediterranean line (Nimes - Perpignan)
- **60** The Catalan country line (Perpignan - Villefranche-de-Conflent)
- **66** The Yellow Train line (Villefranche-de-Conflent - Latour-de-Carol)
- **74** The Pyrenees line (Latour-de-Carol - Toulouse)
- **86** The Lot and Dordogne line (Toulouse - Brive)
- **96** The Bastides and most beautiful villages line (Toulouse - Villefranche-de-Rouergue)
- **102** The Cathedrals line (Toulouse - Rodez)
- **108** The Aubrac line (Béziers - Saint-Flour)
- **118** The Pont du Gard and Rhône line (Nimes - Pont-Saint-Esprit)
- **128** The Camargue line (Nimes - Le Grau-du-Roi)
- **134** The Côte Vermeille line (Perpignan - Portbou)
- **146** The Canal du Midi line (Toulouse - Narbonne)
- **154** The Piémont line (Toulouse - Lourdes)
- **168** The Gers line (Toulouse - Auch)
- **174** The Canal des Deux-Mers line (Montauban - Agen)
- **180** The Tarn line (Saint-Sulpice-sur-Tarn - Mazamet)

187
THEMATIC EXCURSIONS BY RAIL

- **188** Rugby towns
- **196** UNESCO World Heritage sites
- **205** Index

10 GREAT REASONS TO TRAVEL BY RAIL

The train can be anything but humdrum travel. Quite the contrary, rail offers the possibility of making unexpected discoveries! Abandon your preconceptions and come and savour the pleasures of rail travel. Here are some reasons why.

I minimise my carbon footprint

Did you know that transporting travellers by train generates 8 to 20 times less CO_2 than travelling by car? Travelling without contributing to wrecking the planet has become a priority!

No more traffic jams

We can all remember going on or returning from holiday and being stuck on the motorway, with the feeling of wasting time rather than making time. Taking the train means controlling your travel time and taking it easy! No more getting stuck in your car behind a tractor, a truck, or a motorhome!

I make the most of my travel time

On liO trains (regional trains), you may not be travelling at high speed. But so what! The time spent on the train is all part of the holiday!

I arrive fresh and raring to go

On the train there is no stress, no fatigue. I can rest, reflect, read, play cards, or simply take it easy!

I can watch the world go by

The big advantage of the liO train lines proposed in this guide is that they pass through all kinds of wonderful landscapes. It's not just the cows that watch the trains passing by; we too can watch the cows grazing in the fields!

I can take the whole clan
Do your kids get restless in the car? Take the train: for them it will be a real adventure! Don't forget how much fun this means of transport can be for little ones...

I can meet people
On the liO trains, you can meet all kinds of people: whether frequent travellers, or tourists just like you. It's an opportunity to exchange tips on the region!

I can go when I like
There are no bookings required for the liO trains! So I can set off on the day and at the time that I want. Except on the very busy lines in the summer, I will always find a seat.

I can move around

On the train, there's no need to stay stuck in your seat. If I get pins and needles, I can stand up, and go walk around. You might sway from side to side a little, but you quickly learn to keep your balance!

I can take my bike on board

On liO trains, there are spaces reserved for bikes. So I can get on the train with mine. On certain trains, it is possible to book, and on others – if it isn't high season – you're sure to be able to find a place to hang it from a rack or park it in the dedicated area.

OCCITANIE RAIL TOUR: FABULOUS JOURNEYS BY RAIL

Lapeyrere Sébastien - CRT Occitanie

Such a beautiful, vast and varied destination, Occitanie South of France is always a great place for travelling, and particularly for travelling by rail. As the stages unfold, its treasures are unveiled. From unexpected discoveries to offbeat encounters, from unique experiences to friendly moments, taste the pleasures of responsible tourism, so rich in sense and value. All along the line, Occitanie offers you great moments of freedom and shared pleasures from which you'll emerge transformed.

Here, it is the seasons that set the pace, and it is in slow mode that you need to travel to perceive all the nuances of landscape, discover the extent of the cultural wealth on show, and make the acquaintance of the passionate individuals who live in the heart of these landscapes and who fashion them. In Occitanie, lifestyle, friendliness, and hospitality are by no means vain intentions. Indeed, an expression has been forged to encapsulate this overarching concept: "Occitality"!

The region is vast, needless to say, and the variety of the landscapes in this area of southern France never ceases to amaze. Vast swathes of countryside, traversed by the Canal du Midi, the Canal de la Robine and the Rhône canal at Sète; criss-crossed by the Way of St James pilgrimage trails, with their scatterings of churches, abbeys and small stone bridges; irrigated by spectacular hewn valleys ideal for canoeing or abseiling. Mountains that are the playground, summer and winter, of outdoor enthusiasts, skiers and hikers, but also for lovers of high-altitude villages and castles perched on outcrops. There is of course the Mediterranean: on the Côte Vermeille ("Vermilion coast"), or at Sète, flanked by ponds and lagoons, and at Thau, Leucate or Bages-Sigean; a perfect seascape for lazing on the beach, feasting on fresh fish and shellfish in the ports, diving, nautical activities, or discovering the surrounding wildlife. And then there are the towns and cities! Regional capitals, historic cities, cultural metropolises, as dynamic as they are beautiful and festive: Toulouse, the "Ville rose" ("pink city"); Narbonne, with its Archbishop's Palace; Lourdes, the "holy"; Montpellier, the "wise"; along with Auch, the "Gascon"; Nimes the "Roman"; or Montauban the "Artist"... Occitanie is all this and more: a multitude of experiences, to be renewed from season to season: snowshoeing on Mount Lozère, hiking on the Aubrac plateau, paragliding around the Millau viaduct, cycling on the towpath of the Canal du Midi, scuba diving off Collioure, wine tasting at vineyards and a summer cruise in a scow in the Lot... And always discovering something new, exciting, passionate, fun.

In this guide you will find suggestions for "Fabulous Journeys". To book or to find out more, please contact the tourist offices or the service providers referred to herein.

www.voyage-occitanie.com

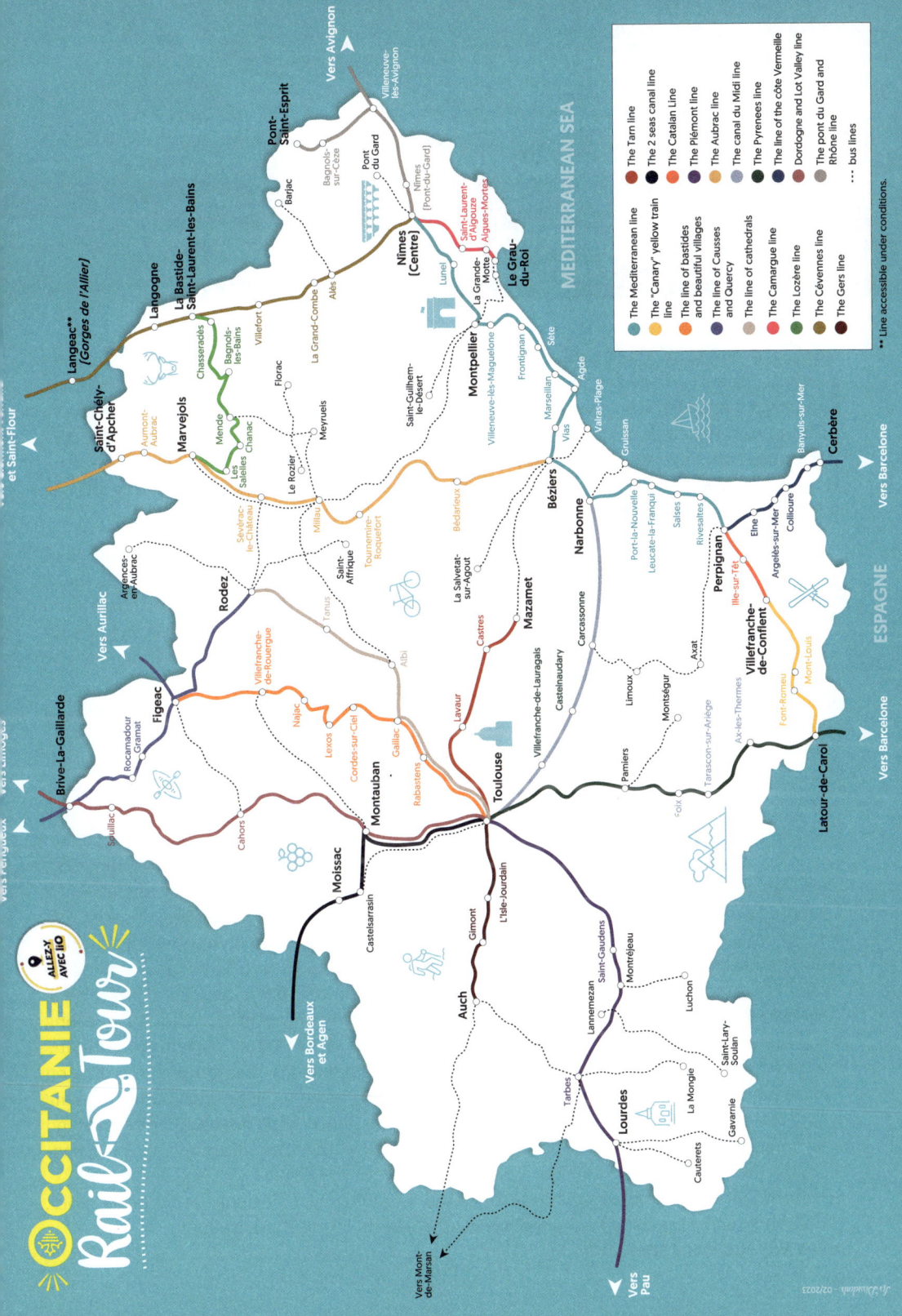

HOLIDAYING BY RAIL

Here we explain to you how we have devised this guide, for hassle-free and away-from-it-all holidays by rail. It is aimed at everyone who would like to discover Occitanie without travelling by car.

GETTING TO OCCITANIE

By rail
SNCF lines serve Toulouse and Montpellier from most major French and European cities (Madrid, Barcelona, Milan, Brussels, Amsterdam...). Occitanie is traversed by two high-speed rail lines: the Perpignan-Figueras (Spain) line, and the LGV Méditerranée. Several high-speed lines are planned or in production: between Montpellier and Perpignan and between Bordeaux and Toulouse.

By air
There are 10 airports (9 international) for flying into Occitanie. The biggest ones are Toulouse-Blagnac (around one flight every 30 minutes) and Montpellier-Méditerranée. You can also land in Carcassonne, Tarbes, Perpignan, Nimes, Béziers, Rodez, Castres and Brive.
In addition, Toulouse and Montpellier offer direct links to several European cities: Berlin, Frankfurt, London, Madrid, Brusels, Amsterdam...

CHOOSE YOUR LINE

Depending on how much time you have
Our rail tours last between 4 and 15 days, counting one day for each stopover (a stopover being a stop at one of the stations on the line). You can of course remain longer in a town where there's a lot to do and see. It's up to you to determine your programme!

As the fancy takes you
For each stopover station, we propose a walk around town, a monument, or an iconic museum to visit. In addition to these cultural visits, we offer suggestions for some enjoyable open air activity, such as an easy hike and/or bike ride. And, to combine pleasure with practicality, for each stopover you will also find recommendations for accommodation less than 20 minutes' walk from the station, a restaurant, a shop where you can buy provisions for a picnic or purchase local produce, along with cosy spots for an afternoon break and for enjoying an aperitif at the end of the day. That should cover all bases!

TRAVELLING LIGHT

You are going to be travelling by train, getting on board and alighting at least once a day. Forget the big bulky suitcase and opt for a backpack. Take just what is strictly necessary, without forgetting, depending on your destination, your swimwear and comfortable shoes for walking.

WHEN YOU GET THERE

When you get to the departure station, buy the ticket to your first stopover (you will need to buy a ticket for each stage of the tour). There may be a ticket office or a distributor, or both, depending on the station layout. A bank card is therefore a must. When you get to your destination, the first thing to do is drop off your luggage: there are no longer any left luggage facilities in stations, so go to your hotel to leave your bag there. Enjoy your stay!

BIKE AND TRAIN

The rail tours that we propose in this guide are most often accompanied by bike rides or excursions. Below are a few tips on how to combine train and bike.

Take your bike with you or rent one!
On certain stages, we propose bike rides, and sometimes having a bike with you can be useful for getting to your hotel. Your bike can go with you on the train (see below). If you don't have one, we tell you where you can rent bikes, if possible close to the railway station. Be aware that bike hire companies often require a deposit. Consider taking your cheque book with you.

TRANSPORTING YOUR BIKE

For information about transporting your bikes on the train, consult the SNCF website: www.sncf.com/fr/offres-voyageurs/voyager-en-toute-situation/velo-a-bord. The instructions to follow differ according to the train type.

Intercity and TGV trains
www.sncf-connect.com.
Non-dismantled bike – On most Intercity trains and on certain TGV lines, a space is reserved for transporting standard non-dismantled bikes. Booking is mandatory (€10 per bike) and must be done at the same time as buying the travel ticket.

A rule to be respected for everyone's comfort and safety: if you are travelling with a non-dismantled bike, avoid peak times. Remember that you are responsible for your bike throughout the duration of the trip.
Dismantled bike – A bike that is dismantled and stored in a carrier case with maximum dimensions 120 × 90 cm is considered hand luggage. You can travel with it free onboard all Intercity and TGV trains.
Ouigo: special case – In this type of train, to travel with a bicycle, it must be dismantled and stored in a suitable case (see above), and the baggage option duly paid (€5).

liO trains
liO trains are accessible for bikes, free of charge and without booking, in a dedicated area, subject to available space (6 bikes per carriage). Look out for the bike pictogram indicated on the outside of the door to the carriages equipped with a bike rack system. Make sure you arrive at the station at least 10 minutes in advance to give yourself sufficient time. In busy periods, the guard may ask you to take the next liO train. Bike traffic forecasts: www.ter.sncf.com/occitanie/services-contacts/voyager-avec-son-velo/embarquer-son-velo.

THE LIO NETWORK IN PRACTICE

liO, the regional public transport service for Occitanie, accompanies you throughout your tour. Below you will find some useful information.

THE NETWORK

liO is the single regional public transport service comprising different modes of transport for the entire Occitanie region. Its network consists mainly of regional trains, called liO trains, and intercity coaches, called liO coaches. In this guide we mainly propose tours by train, but which sometimes require a coach to be taken when there is no railway for a given stretch. Each time we indicate which liO train or liO coach to take.

GET CONNECTED!

Looking for traffic news and train times, or buying a ticket? Go to: lio-occitanie.fr

PRICE DEALS

Family travel
The "AvantagiO' Tribu" deal offers reductions on the price of your tickets depending on the number of travellers: 30% off for a group of 3; 40% off for a group of 4; 50% off for a group of 5.

Small prices
€1 ticket – At the initiative of the Region, single incentive-based pricing has been in place since the end of 2022 for 18-26 year-olds: on the first weekend of each month, rail tickets cost €1 for any journey in Occitanie (except in July and August).

For young people : "+=0 " Formula – The more you travel the less you pay: 50% reduction for 0 to 10 trips per month, free travel after +10 trips, then bank the surplus beyond 21 trips. Reserved for those aged 18-26.

LibertiO' Jeunes -50% ticket for young people – This allows people aged 26 or under to travel for half price by liO train or coach, anywhere in Occitanie, every day.

Offers for everyone, all year round
"Avantagi'O" tickets (limited in number) allow you to travel for €1 on all liO lines, for tickets going on sale 10 days before departure. "Avantagi'O Futé" tickets adapt the price of your ticket according to the distance covered: €3 (up to 40 km), €5 (from 41 to 80 km), €10 (from 81 to 200 km), €15 (beyond 200 km).

ACCESSIBILITY

"Accès Train liO" (liO Train Access) is a free service, to be booked in advance, for assisting people with disabilities. It is available in 51 of the region's stations. To book the service (a minimum of 48h before departure) and consult the terms and conditions, go to the site:
www.ter.sncf.com/occitanie/services-contacts/accessibilite-assistance/acces-train-lio

EVERYONE HAS THEIR OWN WAY OF LIVING IN OCCITANIE, AND FOR ALL THERE IS .liO

Download the new app liO Occitanie.

On the Cévennes line.
Laurent Boutonnet/Région Occitanie

Fabulous journeys by rail

All these rail journeys can start out from Montpellier or Toulouse. You can get from one city to the other in 2h05 by Intercity train or TGV, with trains departing every hour.

Villefort viaduct, on the Cévennes line.
Patrice Thebault/Région Occitanie

THE CAUSSES OF QUERCY LINE

From Brive-la-Gaillarde, the line leaves behind the verdant "Causse Corrézien" to join the rugged contours of the landscape around Rocamadour. It traverses the arid Causse de Gramat, ensconced between the river Célé, which it meets near Figeac, and the Dordogne. Handsome Causse farms, with their archetypical slate roofs, will accompany you along the way. Then, all at once, Rodez – on its hill overlooking the Aveyron river – hoves into view.

⭐ FROM BRIVE-LA-GAILLARDE TO RODEZ - 10 DAYS

- **Non-stop trip:** 2h30
- **Frequency:** 7 liO trains/day
- **Timetables:** www.ter.sncf.com/occitanie/se-deplacer/fiches-horaires
- **Non-stop ticket price:** from €27.30
- **Onboard services:** bicycle transport authorised
- **Line connections:** Lot and Dordogne line from Brive-la-Gaillarde, Cathedrals line from Rodez

📷 Where best to sit to admire the landscape? On the right of the train, in the direction of travel.

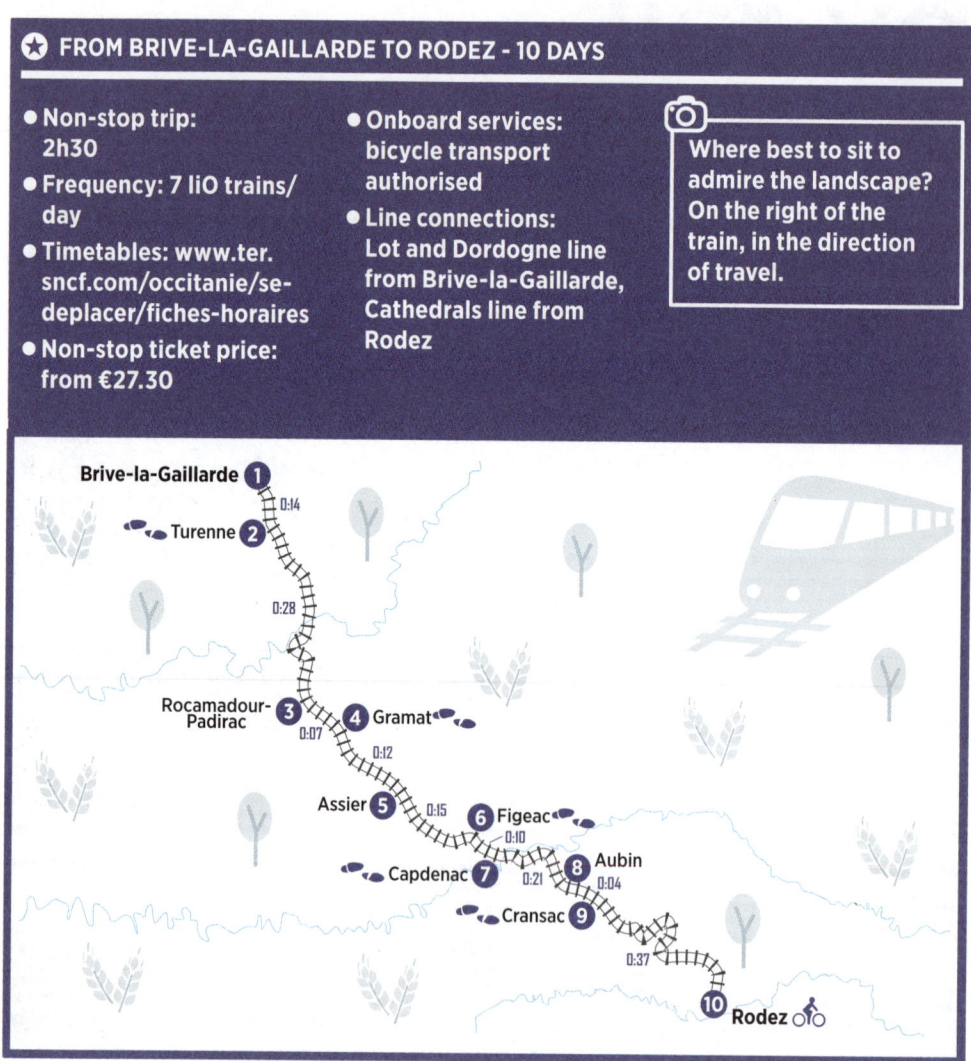

FABULOUS JOURNEYS BY RAIL

Figeac.
Patrice Thebault/CRT Occitanie

1 BRIVE-LA-GAILLARDE

To recharge your batteries. Brive "the courageous", which was so well able to defend the walls it had erected, is a dynamic and welcoming town, whose heart beats to the clamour of its rugby stadium. It is also the wealthiest town in Corrèze. This can be seen in its townhouses, museums and monuments, built in sandstone, and whose warm patina is highlighted in the rays of the setting sun. Last but not least, it is where writers converge for the Book Fair in early November, to throw the spotlight on their beloved Corrèze.
Tourist office - pl. du 14-Juillet - 05 55 24 08 80 - www.brive-tourisme.com.
Book fair - foiredulivredebrive.net.

A bed for the night. In the historic town centre, 5 minutes from the station, Le Miel des Muses is a charming hotel, installed in an old hardware store, with spacious rooms each bearing the name of a variety of wine grape. The design and the wooden decor make for a warm and intimate atmosphere. Small rooftop pool, jacuzzi and steam room (€25/h).
A little further away (17 minutes walk), Le Quercy hotel is also ideally situated. Near the banks of the Corrèze, the rooms of this modern hotel are spacious and well appointed. Continental or American-style breakfast.
Le Miel des Muses - 21 r. J.-Jaurès - 05 55 23 79 65 - www.lemieldesmuses.fr - - 10 rooms, €89/140 - €13.
Hôtel Le Quercy - 8 bis quai Tourny - 05 55 74 09 26 - www.hotelduquercy.com - 48 rooms & 1 suite €105/120 - €13.

Art for all tastes. The 17 rooms of permanent collections in the Labenche museum attract a varied public. In the basement are kept the geology and paleontology collections. On the ground floor, you can admire the Art Nouveau furniture designed by Pierre Selmersheim (1869-1941), as well as Debussy's quarter-top piano, a stained glass window with the Noailles coat of arms, and a late 17th century Aubusson tapestry. The rooms on the first floor present collections of history, art and archaeology.

The second and third floors are devoted to the popular arts and traditions.
Musée Labenche - 26 bis bd Jules-Ferry - 📞 05 55 18 17 70 - www.museelabenche.fr - May-Sept. : 10 a.m.-12:30 p.m., 1:30-6 p.m.; Oct.-Apr. 2-6 p.m. - €5.

Dining. In its long dining room, Amédélys serves up contemporary cuisine according to the seasons, where Limousin beef and duck reign supreme. The dishes are accompanied by carefully chosen wines, all reasonably priced. At La Table d'Olivier, a locale that is all beams and bare stone, with contemporary furniture and designer lighting, Pierre Neveu prepares a bold and refined cuisine using fresh produce. Attractive presentation of dishes, efficient and friendly service. You were advised to book ahead.
Amédélys - 9 r. de l'Hôtel-de-Ville - 📞 05 55 74 42 09 - www.amedelys.fr - closed Sun.-Mon. - Lunch deals €9/15 - menus €22/30.
La Table d'Olivier - 3 r. St-Ambroise - 📞 05 55 18 95 95 - closed 2 wks end Aug.-start Sept., 3 wks Jan., Mon.-Tues., and Wed. lunchtime - lunch menu in wk. €32 - menus €55/80.

For a picnic. Major regional market, every Tuesday, Thursday and Saturday, Georges-Brassens market hall.

Sweet snack. Are you partial to freshly squeezed fruit juices, homemade cheesecake or hot chocolate? Then get to the Django! There is a really nice atmosphere to be enjoyed in this pleasant eatery decorated with furniture picked up in flea markets. You'll appreciate taking time out there.
Le Django - 4 pl. des Patriotes-Martyrs - 📞 05 19 07 68 80 - le-django.eatbu.com - Tues.-Sat. 8:30 a.m.-6 p.m.

Aperitif time. In the heart of Brive, here is the ideal spot for enjoying a drink and watching a rugby match. There is always a buzz in the air!
Café des Halles - 12 pl. de la Halle - 📞 05 55 87 53 65 - Tues.-Wed. 10 a.m.-midnight, Thurs.-Sat. 10 a.m.-1:30 a.m.

From farm to fork. At the end of August, Brive-la-Gaillarde takes on the appearance of a giant farm, when the Livestock Festival comes to town. You will see how the livestock farmers of the region go about their business, with more than 700 animals on show (cattle, sheep, poultry, pigs and horses). And if you're feeling peckish you can try some of the specialities on the tasting stands.
Info: www.brive-tourisme.com.

② TURENNE

➔ **The station is situated outside the town centre. To get to the town centre by public transport, take the bus at the station exit (lines LR3 or LR4) and get off at the Le Bourg stop (5 min).**
Info: transports.nouvelle-aquitaine.fr.

Higher and higher. A castle keep that reaches towards the sky, perched houses that seem to tumble around the castle's remains... Here is the spectacular town of Turenne! Stronghold of the Huguenot Viscount Henri de La Tour d'Auvergne, Marshal of France and hero of the Thirty Years' War, the town remains proud to have been the capital of the ancient viscounty, a true State within the State. While simply strolling around the village streets is an attraction in itself, do not miss the opportunity to visit the Château de Turenne. Of this ancient 14th century keep, only the guard room is open to visitors, with its broken barrel vault. Facing the keep is Caesar's tower. Climb to its top (go on, you can manage it!) and you will be able to admire the fabulous views all around. After the effort: the reward!
Tourist office - av. du Sénateur-Labrousse - 📞 05 55 24 08 80 - www.brive-tourisme.com.
Château de Turenne - 📞 05 55 85 90 66 - www.chateau-turenne.com - Jul.-Aug.: 10 a.m.-7 p.m.; Apr.-Jun. and Sept.-Oct.: 10 a.m.-noon, 2-6 p.m.; rest of the year: contact for details. - €5.50, free for under 10s.

A bed for the night. This fine stone building receives its guests in a decor from the early 18th century. Each room bears a woman's name. Breakfast is served under the arches of the old "White Penitents" refectory, where you can also dine. You can enjoy its large garden with

Rocamadour on the cliffside. MartinM303/Getty Images Plus

a view of the château. You can also purchase local delicacies in the "Échoppe à Doudou" gift shop.
Le Clos Marnis - Le Clos Marnis - ✆ 05 55 22 05 28 - closmarnis.online.fr - 5 rms. €69 (volume discount) ☕ - set meals on reserv.

Dining. Before or after visiting the castle, you will receive a warm welcome here in a beautiful (and pleasantly cool) vaulted room, or on a pleasant terrace when the weather permits. This very reasonable pizzeria also offers salads and traditional dishes.
Les Capucins - av. Joseph-Brugel - ✆ 05 55 24 43 11 - www.facebook.com/pizzeriales capucins - closed Mon. evening and Tues. - pizzas €13/15, lunchtime special (except Sun.) €12.

👣 **We're not even tired!** If the climb to the château is not enough for you, the tourist office has suggested circuits and paths to satisfy your desire to stretch your legs some more. Take for example the discovery itinerary (4 km - 1h30): it takes in every must-see part of the village. After this, Turenne will be like an open book for you!

③ ROCAMADOUR-PADIRAC

➔ The station is well outside the centre of Rocamadour. The only solution is a taxi! The ride will cost around €20.
Taxis AB Plus - ✆ 05 65 38 70 54.

A breathtaking gem. Miraculous crag, steeped in history, faith and legends, sanctuary of the Black Virgin, place of pilgrimage: Rocamadour is all of these. It is also one of the most extraordinary sites you could ever visit. The old dwellings, towers and oratories seem attached limpet-like to the steep cliff 150 m above the Alzou canyon, dominated by the castle's fine keep and the seven chapels and churches.
Tourist office - L'Hospitalet - ✆ 05 65 33 22 00 - www.vallee-dordogne.com.

A bed for the night. Ideally located at the foot of the castle, close to the Stations of the Cross and the lifts leading to the village of Rocamadour, this family-run hotel offers excellent value for money. Cosy and comfortable

Excursion out of Figeac

Padirac Chasm

➔ In season, liO 876 coach line links Figeac station to the Padirac Chasm ("Gouffre de Padirac"), with stops at Gramat and Rocamadour. 4 return trips/day, daily in Jul.-Aug. and w'ends only in Jun. and Sept. - €2. *Info:* www.lio-occitanie.fr

The Padirac chasm was officially inaugurated in 1899, ten years after the speleologist, Édouard Alfred Martel, discovered the passage. To date, the length of the known network is 42 km (26 miles). Ready to take the plunge? A visit to this vertiginous chasm, its mysterious river and the vast caverns decorated with gigantic limestone concretions is a must for anyone discovering the Causse de Gramat. Two lifts with parallel staircases descend into the 32 m-diameter chasm to the scree cone formed by the collapse of the original vault. From the bottom of the cone, at a depth of 75 m, the view of the walls covered with stalagtite flows and vegetation and of the sky above is striking. Stairs then lead down to the underground river, 103 m below ground level. After the descent to the bottom of the chasm, you travel 500 m by boat and then 400 m on foot.

A flotilla of flat-bottomed boats offers an enchanting ride on the surprisingly clear waters of the "flat river". The guides then act as gondoliers for the duration of this underground crossing. Although the depth of the river varies from 50 cm to 4 m, the water temperature is constant (11°C), as is that of the cave (13°C). At the end of the journey, you can admire the "Grande Pendeloque" (Great Chandelier) stalactite of the Lac de la Pluie ("Rain Lake"). This gigantic stalactite, the tip of which almost reaches the surface of the water, is only the final pendant of a string of concretions 60 m high. In the Lac des Gours, a series of pools, separated by natural limestone dams ("Gours" meaning dams), divide the river and the lake into fabulous pools, under a 6 m high waterfall.

The Salle du Grand Dôme, impressive for its height (94 m), is the most beautiful and largest of Padirac Chasm: a viewpoint halfway up allows you to observe the rock formations and calcite flows that decorate its walls.

☏ *05 65 33 64 56 - www.gouffre-de-padirac.com - from Apr. to start of Nov. - times: contact for details - booking advised - €19.50 (4-12 year-olds: €14.50) - take warm clothing and waterproofs.*

Padirac Chasm.
K. Thomas/Blickwinkel/age fotostock

rooms, buffet breakfast with view, garden for relaxation and a warm welcome.
Hôtel Le Relais Amadourien - rte du Château - ☏ 05 65 34 39 19 - www.relais-amadourien.com/fr - 28 rms. €65/90 - 🍽 €9.90.

Take-off imminent. After visiting the pilgrimage town and discovering its wealth of treasures, here is something else to visit. Close to the ramparts is a breeding and reproduction centre for diurnal and nocturnal birds of prey. Some 100 chicks are born there every year! The aviaries are tailored to ensure the well-being of the animals, hence the reduced visibility for the visitor. A care unit takes in injured birds and then releases them back into their natural environment. You will also have the privilege of witnessing a splendid flight demonstration.
Rocher des Aigles - rte du Château - ☏ 05 65 33 65 45 - www.rocherdesaigles.com - closed from start Oct. to end Mar . Jul.-Aug.: 10 a.m.-8 p.m.; Apr.-Jun. and Sept.: 2-7 p.m., School & Pub. hols. 10:30 a.m.-7 p.m. - €11 (under 13s: €7).

Dining. For a quick lunch, this bright and cosy brasserie with its contemporary decor has a superb terrace from where you can admire the cliff in its entirety, facing the village of Rocamadour. A light menu with local flavours will stave off your hunger pangs. Friendly welcome, quick and efficient service.
Envies de Terroir - rue de la Couronnerie - ☏ 05 65 33 67 38 - enviesdeterroir.site-solocal.com - closed evenings, Wed. and 11 Nov.-15 Feb. (except Christmas hols.) - €25/35.

Marvellous cavern. Discovered in 1920, this cave located under only 8 m of rock presents some beautiful mineral formations. Some of its wall paintings date back 20,000 years. They show negative handprints, punctuations, some horses, a big cat, and a stylised deer. The cave is located in the heights of Rocamadour, a ten-minute walk from the centre.
Grotte des Merveilles - village de l'Hospitalet - ☏ 07 88 26 84 78 - www.grottedesmerveilles.com - guided tour (45min) from mid-Jul. to end Aug. : 10 a.m.-6 p.m., dep. every h; from start Apr. to mid-Jul. and from end Aug. to mid-Sept.: every day except Fri. (except school hols.)

10:30, 11:30, 2:15, 3:15, 4:15 and 5:15; rest of the year: contact for details - closed from start Oct. to start Apr. - €8 (under 11s: €5).

Head in the clouds. Every year in late summer an astonishing ballet takes place in the skies of Rocamadour: 30 or so hot air balloons take off twice a day. A feast for the eyes!
Montgolfiades - www.rocamadouraerostat.fr.

 ## GRAMAT

Fairs' central. Capital of the Causse that bears its name, Gramat hosts a large trade fair each Friday morning. You will of course be able to discover the market hall and taste the delicious local produce. But a stroll through the narrow streets will reveal another facet: a town dedicated to horses, with stud farms and horse races in August.
Tourist office - pl. de la République - ☏ 05 65 33 22 00 - www.vallee-dordogne.com.

A bed for the night. It is a 12-minute walk from the station to this pleasant, newly renovated hotel. The rooms are clean, comfortable and very well equipped.
Hôtel Le Centre - pl. de la République - ☏ 05 65 38 73 37 - www.lecentre.fr - 18 rms. €85/99 - 🍽 €12.90.

Dining. Let yourself be won over by the homespun cuisine of the British chef running the kitchen of this pretty family house, hard by the station. When the weather is fine, you can enjoy a leg of farm lamb from Quercy braised with preserved lemon on the terrace, beneath the chestnut trees. Tête de veau is often on the menu, which changes every three months.
Le Relais des Gourmands - 2 av. de la Gare - ☏ 05 65 38 83 92 - www.relais-des-gourmands.com - closed Sun. eve. and Mon. (exc. in Jul.- Aug.) - lunch deal: €25 - Gourmet and Gastronomic menus €39/47.

For a picnic. Market on Tuesday and Friday mornings, in the hall.

In their wild state. Specimens of the local flora – downy oaks, dogwoods, Causse ash – can be found alongside various animal species, most of which are European, and which live here in semi-liberty. To kill two birds with one stone (so to speak!), a 3 km marked trail will allow you to discover these animals while taking a pleasant walk.

Parc animalier de Gramat - *25 min walk from the station, along the D14* - ✆ *05 65 38 81 22* - *www.gramat-parc-animalier.com* - *Jul.-Aug.: 9:30 a.m.-7 p.m.; Apr.-Jun. and from start Sept. to end of Autumn hols.: 10 a.m.-6.30 p.m.; rest of the year: 1:30-5:30 p.m.* - *€14.50 (under 11s: €12).*

⑤ ASSIER

In the age of nobility. Jacques de Genouillac, known as "Galiot", a figure of the French nobility during the Renaissance, wished to set himself up in an estate worthy of his rank. He did so by building a majestic edifice, of which unfortunately only the west wing remains. Its architecture and sculptural programme are fully in line with the early Renaissance transition: medieval and classical facades, spiral and ramped staircases, sloping roofs, and domed towers. In addition to the castle, make sure to spend a moment visiting Assier church, whose exterior frieze presents the exploits and titles of Galiot de Genouillac on 75 sculpted panels.

Tourist office - *pl. de l'Église* - ✆ *05 65 40 50 60* - *www.tourisme-figeac.com.*

Assier Castle - ✆ *05 65 40 40 99* - *www.chateau-assier.fr* - *May- Aug.: 10 a.m.-12.30 p.m., 2-6:30 p.m.; rest of the year: enquire in advance* - *€4.*

Dining and overnighting. This pleasant B&B has comfortable rooms, overlooking the garden, Assier castle, and the market square. The owners will delight you with their high-quality home cooking. It's a 10 minute walk from the station.

Orlaya - *pl. de la Halle* - ✆ *05 81 24 70 82* - *www.orlaya.fr* - *3 rms. €65/85* ☕ - *set meal dinner: €28.*

⑥ FIGEAC

Stand-out architecture. An architectural marvel steeped in a prestigious past, Figeac's medieval streets wind their way through a multi-faceted topography. You never tire of discovering the sloping alleys, with their bends and turns, their staircases, and their sandstone walls, where each door and each window testifies to the care taken in their restoration. In the heart of the town, it feels good to take the weight off your feet at a terrace table in one of the squares of the preserved sector, or maybe you'll decide to call at the Champollion museum, dedicated to Figeac's most famous son.

Tourist office - *pl. Vival* - *hôtel de la Monnaie* - ✆ *05 65 34 06 25* - *www.tourisme-figeac.com.*

A bed for the night. Located on the left bank of the Célé river, 5 minutes from the station, the public baths were transformed into a hotel in the 1970s. Well-appointed rooms and terrace-bar at water level.

Hôtel des Bains - *1 r. du Griffoul* - ✆ *05 65 34 10 89* - *www.hoteldesbains.fr* - *19 rms. €59/90* - ☕ *€8.50.*

Discover the world of calligraphy. On the ground floor, the exhibits chart the life of Jean-François Champollion, a man fascinated by the cult of the dead and the Egyptian Pantheon, and his work as an Egyptologist (sarcophagi, clay tablets, etc.). On the various floors, you get to discover the history of writing from around the world: the birth of writing, from the reed pen of the scribes to the invention of the alphabet, and the evolution of the book, from parchment to computers. A fascinating place, not to be missed.

Musée Champollion - *Les Écritures du monde (World writing)* - *pl. Champollion* - ✆ *05 65 50 31 08* - *www.musee-champollion.fr* - *Jul.-Aug.: 10:30 a.m.-6:30 p.m.; Apr.-Jun. and Sept.-Oct.: daily exc. Mon. 10:30 a.m.-12:30 p.m., 2-6 p.m.; rest of the year: daily exc. Mon. 2-5:30 p.m., 24 and 31 Dec. 2-4 p.m.* - *closed from mid to end Jan.* - *€5.*

Dining. In the heart of the medieval city, you can dine in the former guard room of Viguier castle, with its high ceiling and painted beams, and its fireplace with sculpted mantle. La Dînée du Viguier serves fine classic cuisine: lobster

Figeac the medieval.
ChrisAt/Getty Images Plus

carpaccio with vegetables, Quercy pie (foie gras, morels, truffles).
Working hard at the oven of La Racine et la Moelle, chef Julie concocts modern and tasty dishes. Served up without fuss and always cooked to a tee. A friendly atmosphere and as natural as the fine selection of wines (the establishment doubles as a wine store).
La Dînée du Viguier - 4 r. Boutaric - ☎ 05 65 50 05 05 - closed Mon.. - lunch deal €29 - €49/85.
La Racine et la Moelle - 6 r. du Consulat - ☎ 09 83 53 81 58 - closed Sun.-Mon. - menu €36/50.

For a picnic. Saturday morning markets at Place Barthal, Place Vival, Rue de la République, Place Carnot, Place Champollion and Rue du 11-Novembre.

Fancy a dip? This big 14-hectare leisure centre on the banks of the Célé, north-east of Figeac, is a 20-minute walk from the centre. There is a large lake, a playground and a water sports centre.

Domaine du Surgié - Figeac-Surgié - ☎ 05 61 64 88 54 - www.domainedusurgie.com - May, Jul.-Aug. and Sept.: 8:30 a.m.-7:30 p.m..

The stage is set! This festival is open to diversity, to the discovery of new talent, and giving great figures of the theatre a fresh showcase. It is one of the highlights of the cultural calendar in the Lot. Partnership with the St-Céré festival.
Festival de théâtre - www.festivaltheatre-figeac.com - from end Jul. to start Aug.

👣 **Aiguille du Pressoir circuit.** This short hike takes in a section of the Way of St. James pilgrimage route. All along the way, you will be able to contemplate Figeac's architecture at your leisure.
4.5 km - 1h30 circuit - easy. Sheet available from www.tourisme-lot.com.

⑦ CAPDENAC

→ The station is out of town, 2.5 km to the east of Capdenac-le-Haut, on the opposite side

of the Lot. The only option: a taxi from the station or from Figeac (7 km away). It should cost from €15 to €20.
Allô Taxi Figeac - 📞 *06 07 19 00 17.*

A little Higher. The place is also called Capdenac-le-Haut ("High Capdenac") to differentiate it from its neighbour, lower down: Capdenac-Gare ("Capdenac Station"). This hilltop village was originally a Gallo-Roman site. Perched on a rocky outcrop at a bend in the Lot river which it overlooks, this strategic location offers beautiful views over the Lot valley. The citadel, which retains some of its fine, ancient streets, is perched atop its promontory, steep-sided on all sides except the north. Setting off from the North gateway, called the "Comtale" gateway, the rue de la Peyrolerie fringes the village to the east, from where can be heard the hum of Capdenac-Gare down at the river side. The beautiful southern gateway, part of the ramparts, preserves the last vestiges of the 13th and 14th century walls and citadel. At the far end of Place Lucter, there is also a superb panorama of the Lot valley and the river's snaking path to Faycelles.

Tourist office - pl. du 14-Juillet - 📞 *05 65 64 74 87 - www.tourisme-figeac.com.*

Dining and overnighting. This 15th century village inn, fully restored, faces the medieval keep of Capdenac which overlooks the Lot valley. Its rooms are soberly decorated and local dishes are served up in the restaurant with a great deal of courtesy.
Le Relais de la Tour - pl. Lucter - 6 km south-east of Figeac - 📞 *05 65 11 06 99 - www.lerelaisdelatour.fr/home - closed for the autumn and Feb. hols.* - 🍴 - *11 rms. €85/100* ☕ - *lunch deal: €11.50 , menu: €24/34.*

Sweet snack. Enjoy a break in this friendly crêperie overlooking the Lot valley.
L'Oltis - r. de la Commanderie - 📞 *05 65 34 05 85 - 10:30 a.m.-9:30 p.m., Sat. 10:30 a.m.-11 p.m. - closed Mon.-Tues.*

👣 **Count the steps.** A vertiginous staircase with 135 steps, hewn into the cliff above Capdenac-Gare, leads to two pools built in Roman times, in a cave where the fresh crystalline water bubbles in the shadow of the rock.

Capdenac.
D. Gammert/dpa-Zentralbild/age fotostock

Fontaine des Cent-Marches - pl. St-Andrieu - obtain the access code from the tourist office - €2.50 (under 18s: €2) joint ticket with castle keep, situated pl. Lucter.

8 AUBIN

➜ **No accommodation near the station: a stage to be done in the day from Capdenac.**

Stage halt. This village is dominated by a fort built at the end of the 2nd century by the Roman general, Claudius Albinus. You can easily plan a stop here between two trains to visit its Mine Museum, located only 8 minutes walk from the station, and then spend the night in Cransac or Rodez. Among its other curiosities, there is the church of Notre-Dame, essentially a Gothic edifice, but which shows some traces of the earlier Romanesque building. It houses a 13th century lead baptismal font and a polychrome wooden Christ, an interesting 12th century Romanesque sculpture.

Dining. Before or after visiting the museum, here is an address with varied menus based on fresh produce from regional producers. Home-made cold cuts and cheese.

Café-restaurant Le Musée - 15 r. Henri-Barbusse - ☏ 05 65 64 66 41 - lunch deal: €13.50, menu: €15.

Mine of information. This museum is located in the heart of the Aubin-Decazeville coalfield, where the last underground mines closed in 1965. In a large room there are archives, photographs, models, clothing and tools on display, evoking the work of the miners (both men and women – for coal extraction – and even children until 1874). You can also find out about their festivals and parades, with a very rich collection of banners and flags. Afterwards, a guided tour leads to a gallery with wooden supports, reconstructed by former miners. Thrills are guaranteed with a realistic simulation of a coal gas explosion! The visit ends in the audiovisual room, with films recounting the history of the "Black country".

Musée de la Mine Lucien-Mazars - allée du Musée - ☏ 05 65 43 58 00 - www.museede-lamine-lucienmazars.fr - Jul.-Aug.: daily exc. Mon. 10 a.m.-noon, 2-6 p.m.; Jun and Sept.: daily exc. Sun. 2-6 p.m.; Apr.-May and Oct.: Tues., Thurs. and Sat. 2-5:30 p.m. - free entry.

9 CRANSAC

Three names. The history of the town is marked by three major periods, each linked to the richness of its subsoil. Built at the foot of a "burning mountain", "Cransac-les-Eaux" was known until the 19th century for its curative waters. Two sources were reputed at the time for their virtues, particularly in the treatment of liver ailments. It then became "Cransac-les-Mines" when, from 1880 to 1962, the industrial revolution led to mining being introduced here. Galleries were dug and some thirty mine shafts were opened. After the closure of the last mine in 1962, "Cransac-les-Thermes" returned to being a spa town. An establishment was inaugurated in 1963, with the natural gases being channeled to the thermal baths. The facilities are used to treat osteoarthritis and rheumatism and attract those seeking spa cures and therapies.

Town Hall - pl. Jean-Jaurès - www.cransac-les-thermes.fr.

Tourist and spa tourism office - L'Envol - pl. Jean-Jaurès - ☏ 05 65 63 06 80 - www.tourisme-paysdecazevillois.fr.

Dining and overnighting. A 15-minute walk from the train station, this pleasant hotel-restaurant is set in an old mining house nestled in the middle of a 2-hectare natural park, with swimming pool. In terms of cuisine, priority is given to the local produce of Aveyron. In season, estofinade, a typical dish based on dried cod, potatoes and eggs, can be enjoyed on advance booking.

Hôtel du Parc - 11 r. du Gén.-Louis-Artous - ☏ 05 65 63 01 78 - www.hotelduparc-cransac.com - 32 rms. €65/98 - ☕ €11 - 🍴 - menu: €30.

Another mine of information. This is where to go for a potted local and social history of the place: numerous documents (postcards, official notices, newspaper cuttings) and

THE CAUSSES OF QUERCY LINE

objects have been patiently collected by the miners of Cransac so that the mine (closed in 1962), which was the main activity of the town for 120 years, is not forgotten. Three tableaus reconstitute the development of the mining operation over the years (1850, 1900 and 1950).
Les Mémoires de Cransac (Memories of Cransac) - On the 1st floor of the tourist office - ☏ 05 65 63 06 80 - www.tourisme-conques.fr - May-Oct.: 9:30 a.m.-noon, 3-6 p.m., Sat. 9:30 a.m.-noon, 2-5 p.m.; rest of the year: contact for details. - €3.50 (under 12s free).

"Open-cast hiking". From the spa centre, a hiking trail leads to the Vaysse forest, an expanse of robinia trees that have reforested a succession of open-cast mines at the end of their activity. A guide *(€4)* is on sale in the tourist office.

⑩ RODEZ

→ The station is situated outside of the centre. To get to the cathedral, take the bus at the station exit (line D) and get off at the Cathedral stop (4min, 5 stops).
Info: www.agglobus.rodezagglo.fr.

Bike hire. Formulas for hire or guided rides. Possible delivery.
Aveyron on a bike - ☏ 07 60 10 84 99 - www.aveyronavelo.fr - Jul.-Aug. 9 a.m.-12:30 p.m., 2-6 p.m.; rest of the year: contact for details. - Mountain bike, road bike or electric bike from €25 to €55/day.

Black is black... On its hilltop 120 m above the Aveyron river, Rodez offers one of the most beautiful views of the region, from the dry plateaus of the causses to the wet hills of the Ségala. In the heart of a sparsely populated region, the town has become a must-see destination for visitors from all over the world. In the midst of its lively old streets, you will discover its wonderful red stone cathedral. Obviously, and above all, people come to tread in the footsteps of the town's native son, Pierre Soulages (1919-2022), and admire his works in the museum that bears his name *(see box insert p. 107).* Art enthusiasts are also drawn to the Fenaille museum: occupying the townhouse of Maurice Fenaille (1855-1937), a wealthy industrialist and patron of the arts (notably Rodin), this popular museum is dedicated to history, archaeology and art.
Tourist office - 10-12 pl. de la Cité - ☏ 05 65 75 76 77 - www.rodez-tourisme.fr.
Fenaille Museum - 14 pl. Eugène-Raynaldy - ☏ 05 65 73 84 30 - www.musee-fenaille.rodezagglo.fr - Jul.-Aug.: 10 a.m.-6 p.m.; rest of the year: daily exc. Mon. 10 a.m.-1 p.m., 2-6 p.m., w'end 10 a.m.-6 p.m. - €11 (under 18s free) - ticket giving access to the Soulages museum.

A bed for the night. Just a stone's throw from the cathedral (2 minutes' walk from the bus stop), the Hôtel du Midi has simple and practical rooms, quiet on the courtyard side and with double glazing on the street side. The kitchen serves up traditional dishes as well as the inevitable aligot. In the same area, the Mercure Cathédrale also offers pleasant modern rooms. This 1930s hotel has retained its Art Deco mosaics on the facade and floor, as well as its solid wood staircase and paintings by Maurice Bompard.
Hôtel du Midi - 1 r. Béteille - ☏ 05 65 68 02 07 - www.hotel-du-midi.net - ✕ - 34 rms. €60/70, €60/pers. in 1/2 board - ☕ €9 - 1 appart. €90/130.
Hôtel Mercure Cathédrale - 1 av. Victor-Hugo - ☏ 05 65 68 55 19 - www.all.accor.com - 36 rms. €143/194 ☕.

Reaching for the heavens. It took almost 300 years to build one of the largest gothic cathedrals in the south of France (107 m long, 36 m wide, and 30 m-high vaulted ceiling). The construction of the astonishing pink sandstone cathedral of Notre-Dame-de-l'Assomption began in 1277 following the collapse of the choir and bell tower of the previous building a year earlier. Half a century later, the apse and two choir bays were completed. In the 14th century, a transept and two bays of the nave were added, and in the 16th century the whole building was completed. The austere appearance of the main facade, without a door, recalls its defensive vocation. Remarkable for its detached position from the cathedral, the magnificent bell tower, built on a massive

Soulages museum, designed by RCR associates at Passelac & Roques, and the cathedral. Ch. Guy/hemis.fr

14th century tower and 87 m high, has six floors. It is 28 m higher than the bell tower of Villefranche-de-Rouergue, despite the latter being meant to rival that of Rodez in height! _Cathédrale Notre-Dame_ - 9 a.m.-5:45 p.m. *(sometimes earlier in winter)* - *guided tour of the clock tower by booking at the tourist office* - €8 *(6-17 year-olds: €6)*.

Dining. In the Soulages Museum, the Michel Bras' Café offers a gustatory journey. The menus are composed of classics (stuffed eggs, rack of pork with cabbage), but revisited with brio by Michel Bras, who has left his 3-star restaurant in Laguiole in the hands of his son. A tip: be sure to book in advance! If you're looking for a quicker meal option, head to the Côté comptoir *(no bookings required)* where you can feast on their Niwan (a kind of garnished waffle). _Café Bras_ - av. Victor-Hugo - jardin du Foirail - 05 65 68 06 70 - www.cafebras.fr - *rest.: Wed.-Sun. lunchtime & Sat. evening; menu €39 - Côté comptoir: Wed.-Sun. noon-6 p.m.; meal deal €13*.

Sweet snack. On two floors, this friendly establishment in the old part of Rodez offers salads, toasties and sandwiches for lunch, as well as pancakes, waffles and home-made pastries in the afternoon. Large choice of coffees, teas and ice creams to enjoy on the pleasant terrace in fine weather.
Le Petit Moka - pl. des Maçons - 05 65 75 63 34 - *daily exc. Sun.-Mon. 9:30 a.m.-5:45 p.m.*

Urban loop. The tourist office has established an easy pedestrian circuit of around 2 km (1h30). The loop takes in all the town's main monuments and museums.
Info: circuit can be downloaded from www.rodez-tourisme.fr/brochures; adult or child audioguide for hire from the tourist office (€5).

Getting away from it all. At the gates of Rodez, it is also possible to go for an e-bike ride via a guided tour.
Aveyron on a bike - 07 60 10 84 99 - aveyronavelo.fr - *from €35/pers. (1h30), cycle and equipment included.*

THE LOZÈRE LINE

This journey begins in La Bastide-Puylaurent, on the Ardèche and Lozère border, a land of forests and pastures. The train then heads for Mende, a town where paths and cultures meet. After discovering its historic heart and its thousand-year history, we continue on our way towards the perched village of Chanac, not far from the Tarn Gorges, to finally reach the royal town of Marvejols, nestled in the Colagne valley.

✪ FROM LA BASTIDE-SAINT-LAURENT TO MARVEJOLS - 4 DAYS

- Trip with a stopover in Mende : 2h
- Frequency : 2 liO trains/day and 2 liO coaches/day for the La Bastide-Mende link, 1 liO train/day and 2 liO coaches/day for Mende-Marvejols stopping at Chanac
- Timetables: www.ter.sncf.com/occitanie/se-deplacer/fiches-horaires
- Ticket price: from €3
- Onboard services: bike transport authorised in the liO trains
- Useful to know: be aware that from Mende, not all trains stop at Chanac
- Connected lines: Cévennes line from La Bastide-St-Laurent; Aubrac line from Marvejols

Where best to sit to admire the landscape? On the right-hand side, in the direction of travel.

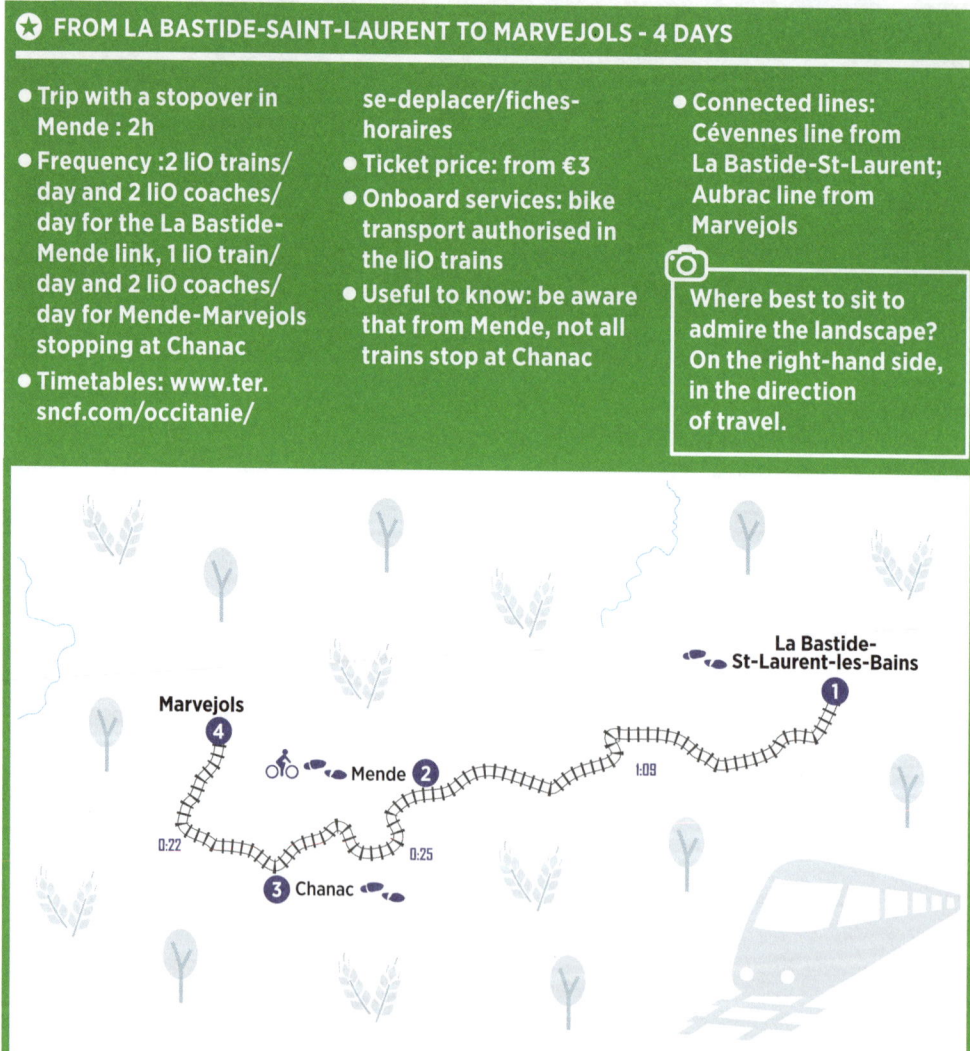

Mende. P. Jacques/hemis.fr

❶ LA BASTIDE-ST-LAURENT-LES-BAINS

➔ **The station serves the town of La Bastide-Puylaurent.**

Nature stage. On the border of the Ardèche and Lozère, La Bastide-Puylaurent was created in the 19th century during the construction of the Paris-Nimes railway line. It is a pleasant, cool summer resort located in the high valley of the Allier, whose slopes are covered with woods and pastures.
Tourist office - ✆ 04 66 46 12 83 - bastide-puylaurent.fr.

Dining and overnighting. A former coaching inn, close to the station and in the heart of the village, the Grand'Halte is an unpretentious and friendly family hotel-restaurant. The rooms are simple, a touch old-fashioned, but clean and well-equipped. Traditional restaurant.
Hotel-restaurant La Grand'Halte - r. des Tilleuls - ✆ 04 66 46 00 35 - from Easter to Nov.1 - www.hotel-lagrandhalte.fr - 20 rms. €65/67 - 🍴 €8 - ✖ €15/30.

Hike to Notre-Dame-des-Neiges. At the entrance to the village, take the "Le Cévenol" hiking path then the path to the right in the direction of the Abbey of N.-D.-des-Neiges (2h circuit). It's a bit of a climb, but a beautiful view awaits you at the entrance to the Trouée de la Borne! The Cistercian abbey, founded in 1850, is isolated in the midst of coniferous and beech woods, in a mountain corrie, sheltered from the winds that sweep across the high plateaus of the Vivarais. It was here that Charles de Foucauld, explorer and priest (1858-1916), did his novitiate, from January to June 1890. Robert Louis Stevenson, during his famous travels with his donkey, also passed through here.

❷ MENDE

➜ The train station is a 10-minute walk from the centre, to the south, on the opposite side of the Lot.

🚲 Bike hire. Electric mountain bikes for hire a 13-minute walk away from the station.
Lozère Découverte - 5 pl. René-Estoup - ✆ 06 49 42 13 38 - www.lozere-decouverte.com - eMTBs from €40 € per 1/2 day.

Lose yourself in its beauty! Contained within its ring of boulevards, the capital of Lozère - the least populated department of France - retains the appearance of a town sheltered in the lee of its imposing cathedral. You will happily lose yourself in its narrow and winding streets, lined with old houses which, to the gaze of the attentive passer-by, will discreetly reveal a beautiful wooden door, a noteworthy gate or an oratory. Take the rue de l'Arjal, where you can admire a beautiful corbelled timber-framed house (No. 20) and a 15th century house with mullioned windows (No. 16), before arriving at the Place du Griffon, whose fountain was used to clean the streets. Look for the Rue de la Jarretière, the narrowest street in the city, which leads to the Place au Blé. As the name suggests, this is where grain was sold. At No. 7 rue d'Aigues-Passes there is a 17th century house with false balusters on the windows. Mandrin, the famous 18th century brigand, is said to have hidden a fabulous treasure there. Lastly, to the north of the old centre, there is Notre-Dame bridge, very narrow and built in the 13th century, which has repeatedly withstood terrible flooding of the Lot thanks to its wide-open main arch.
Tourist office - pl. du Foirail - ✆ 04 66 94 00 23 - www.mende-coeur-lozere.fr.

A bed for the night. A 9-minute walk from the station, the Hotel de France is a charming former coaching inn located in the heart of the city, with spacious, comfortable, bright and nicely renovated rooms. A little further away, the well renovated Hotel du Commerce offers modern and comfortable rooms in the historic centre and good value for money.

Hôtel de France - 9 bd Lucien-Arnault - ✆ 04 66 65 00 04 - www.hoteldefrance-mende.com - ✖ - 31 rms. €110/120 - 🍽 €12.
Hôtel du Commerce - 2 bd Henri-Bourrillon (opposite the tourist office) - ✆ 04 66 65 13 73 - www.lecommerce-mende.com - 10 rms. €61/66 - 🍽 €9.

Impressive bell tower. Several churches preceded the present cathedral, the building of which took place mainly in the 14th century under Pope Urban V, but which has undergone many subsequent modifications. Indeed, when Captain Merle took over the town in 1579, he spared only the bell towers (early 16th century), the northern side walls and the apse chapels. The cathedral had the largest bell in Christendom (weighing 20 t): the "Non Pareille". All that remains is the enormous 2.15 m-high clapper, situated under the organ (17th century), next to the Bishop's bell tower. This tower, the "Clocher de l'Évêque", is 84 m high and has a fine colonnade in the upper parts inspired by the Italian Renaissance, which contrasts with the sobriety of the Canons' bell tower ("Clocher des Chanoines"). The cathedral was restored in the 17th century.
Cathédrale N.-D.-et-St-Privat - pl. Urbain-V - 9 a.m.-7 p.m. (outside of church services) - free entry - in Jul.-Aug., possibility of climbing the bell tower, on reservation at the tourist office.

Dining. As its name suggests, La Cantine cultivates a vintage spirit – handmade crockery, relaxed but attentive service – as well as also favouring organic and local produce.
The food at the Hotel de France is also very good: braised sweetbreads, Lozère filet of beef... The chef concocts fine market cuisine with a focus on local produce, and the skilled and motivated team makes dining here a particularly pleasant experience. A fine place to eat!
La Cantine - 25 r. du Collège - ✆ 04 66 32 86 12 - www.restaurant-la-cantine.fr - closed Sun. eve.-Mon. - lunchtime deal: €17/23, menus: €21/28.
Hôtel de France - 9 bd Lucien-Arnault - ✆ 04 66 65 00 04 - www.hoteldefrance-mende.com -

Fabulous Journeys

Robert Louis Stevenson Trail: hiking in the Cévennes

➔ To get to Le Pont-de-Montvert from Mende: liO 251 coach to Florac, then liO 261 coach - in Jul.- Aug. only.
Info: www.lio-occitanie.fr

With or without a donkey, there is a great adventure to be had on the Robert Louis Stevenson Trail, or GR® 70 long-distance footpath, in the heart of the Cévennes National Park. Two days, two stages, to walk 50 km in the footsteps of the Scottish writer and his donkey, Modestine. You are now ready to set off along the trail, with backpack and route map in hand, starting out from Le Pont-de-Montvert, a charming village set between Lozère and the Cévennes. En route for Florac, your first stopover. Along the way, you cross the Cham de l'Hermet plateau, descend into one valley, then another, before taking a breather in the village of Cocurès on the banks of the Tarn. Then it is on to the village of Bédouès, marked by its perched collegiate church built by Pope Urban V. After 28 km of hiking, you get to Florac, and a welcome first stopover! The smallest sub-prefecture of France has plenty of charm, and plenty of bustle to boot, with all the hikers seeking accommodation for the night, and a table for dining, to recover from this long day of walking up hill and down dale. The second day's stage will be easy and shorter, through the Tarnon valley and the Miment gorges, but no less enchanting. Admire the scene formed by the resplendent colours of the heather and the romantic ruins of the castle of St-Julien-d'Arpaon. And here you are already at Cassagnas, the end of your hike, the village where the shuttle bus will take you back to your starting point.

2 days, 1 night - half-board accommodation €40, return shuttle €15 - in spring and summer.
Contact: Pont-de-Montvert tourist office.

Robert Louis Stevenson Trail.
M. Dupont/hemis.fr

closed Sun. lunch, Sun. eve. and Mon. lunch - menu: €39.

For a picnic. Here you will find good products directly from the farms and workshops of the region: cold cuts, meat, cheeses, breads, jams, honey, fruit juices… All you could want for preparing a good picnic with local produce and picking up a souvenir at the same time.
La Maison des paysans de Lozère - 1 pl. René-Estoup - 📞 04 66 41 08 34 - 10 a.m.-1 p.m., 3-7 p.m. - closed Sun.-Mon. (Sun. in Jul.-Aug.).

🚴 **3, 2, 1, get peddling!** At the tourist office, several maps are available indicating 11 mountain bike circuits and trails with the "FFC" (Fédération française de cyclisme) label, with varying levels of difficulty. An MTB park (3 runs for all levels) has also been set up in the undergrowth, on the Causse de Mende.
Mende Cœur de Lozère - pl. du Foirail - 📞 04 66 94 00 23 - www.mende-coeur-lozere.fr.

Loops. A nature trail is lined with panels presenting the fauna and flora of the Causse. Among the key stops, don't miss the St-Privat hermitage (small chapel and cave) and the panorama from the Mont-Mimat cross, which offers an exceptional view of the town of Mende. 4.5 km (2h) or 10.2 km (4h30) loops.
Causses nature trail - dep. place du Foirail. Come equipped with suitable walking footwear and water. No difficult passages, but it is a forest environment, so no prams or pushchairs!

➔ **Attention: from Mende, not all trains stop at Chanac. Make sure to check the destination of the line you are taking.**

③ CHANAC

➔ **The station is a bit out of the way, north of the town, a 15-minute walk away, on the other side of the Lot river.**

In its keep. The tower and the site of the remains of the medieval castle warrant a stop in this village perched atop its natural rocky promontory. High above the old town stands the keep (follow the sign for "La Tour"), the only vestige of the feudal castle, and former summer residence of the bishops of Mende. Don't miss the church of St-Jean-Baptiste to admire the gilded and carved wooden altarpiece (17th century) surmounted by a baldachin.
Tourist office - quartier de la Vignogue - 📞 04 66 48 29 28.

Dining and overnighting. An 18-minute walk from the station, you will find this small, simple hotel, which is perfect for a stopover. In the restaurant, everything is home-made using local produce. On the menu: salads, cold cuts, local meats or solid seasonal specialities (tête de veau, calf sweetbreads, lamb sweetbreads…). Half or full board is available.
Le Relais des Causses - pl. de la Mairie - 📞 04 66 48 20 14 - restaurant-hotel-chanac.fr - 10 rms. €70 - ☕ €7 - 🍴 menu: €16/21.50 - closed Sun. eve.

On the banks of the Lot. Every year, during the Whitsun weekend, the "Lozère trail" comes to Chanac to offer exceptional foot races. Besides this, you can check out the Visorando website for details of a medium-difficulty hike (12 km, 4h15) towards the hamlet of Villard, for a different view of the town and a climb up on to a plateau.
Le Villard from Chanac - www.visorando.com.

④ MARVEJOLS

➔ **The station is a 15-minute walk from the centre.**

A royal town, former capital of Gévaudan. Although the small medieval city of Marvejols seems a tranquil enough place today, its fortified gates still seem to resound with the cries of its tormented past. Declared a royal town in 1307 by Philippe le Bel, Marvejols sheltered Protestants in 1586, which led to its destruction by Admiral de Joyeuse. Today, times are more clement, and the town nestles serenely in the beautiful Cologne valley, at the crossroads of the great natural spaces of the Lozère, and gateway to the Aubrac Regional Natural Park, the granite massif of the Margeride, and the Lot valley.
Tourist office - porte du Soubeyran - 📞 04 66 32 02 14 - www.gevaudan-authentique.com.

Marvejols.
Ch. Boisvieux/age fotostock

THE LOZÈRE LINE

A bed for the night. An 18-minute walk from the station, on the threshold of the town centre, this is a convenient hotel-restaurant with functional rooms. Warm welcome guaranteed. Hôtel de l'Europe - 11 pl. Barry - ✆ 04 66 47 16 35 - www.hotel-marvejols.fr - 35 rms. €60/95 - ⚏ €10 - ✕ €15/28.

Fortified gates. Marvejols has three fortified gates which command the northern, southern and eastern entrances to the old town. The Soubeyran Gate (North gate), guarded by the statue of Henri IV, who helped rebuild the town, can be visited: from the top of its 68 steps, there is an exceptional view over the town's flagstone roofs. The statue of the Beast of Gévaudan, the work of sculptor Emmanuel Auricoste (1908-1995), who also created the statue of Henri IV, takes centre stage on the Place des Cordeliers. The other two gates are the Theron and Chanelles Gates, the latter formerly called the Hospital Gate. Stroll within the confines of these three gates and discover the narrow streets and squares lined with old houses and shops.

For a picnic. Saturday morning market on the Place du Soubeyran.

Sweet snack. This artisan confectioner offers delicious homemade ice-creams in the summer and cakes and chocolates all year round. Among the specialities, try the Gévaudan cake. Pâtisserie Malafosse - 8 r. Sadi-Carnot - ✆ 04 66 32 11 79 - Tues.-Sat. 7 a.m.-12:30 p.m., 2-7:30 p.m., Sun. 7 a.m.-1 p.m.

THE CÉVENNES LINE

Constructed in the mid-19th century, this iconic railway line was built where no roads went. A titanic project, the line follows the turbulent Allier river, crosses its gorges via its many viaducts and takes shortcuts through its many tunnels. The journey promises remarkable and unspoilt views of gorges, deserted causse plateaus, forests and high valleys dotted with historic villages where time seems to have stood still.

⭐ **FROM LANGOGNE TO NIMES - 6 DAYS**

- Non-stop trip: 3h
- Frequency: 4 liO trains/day, 1 extra at w'ends
- Timetables: www.ter.sncf.com/occitanie/se-deplacer/fiches-horaires
- Non-stop trip: €23.70
- Onboard services: free bike transport
- Useful to know: in season, a tourist train runs between Langogne and Langeac (see box insert p. 36)
- Connected lines: Lozère line from La Bastide-St-Laurent; Mediterranean line, Pont du Gard and Rhône line, and Camargue line from Nimes

📷 Where best to sit to admire the landscape? Left-hand side in the direction of travel.

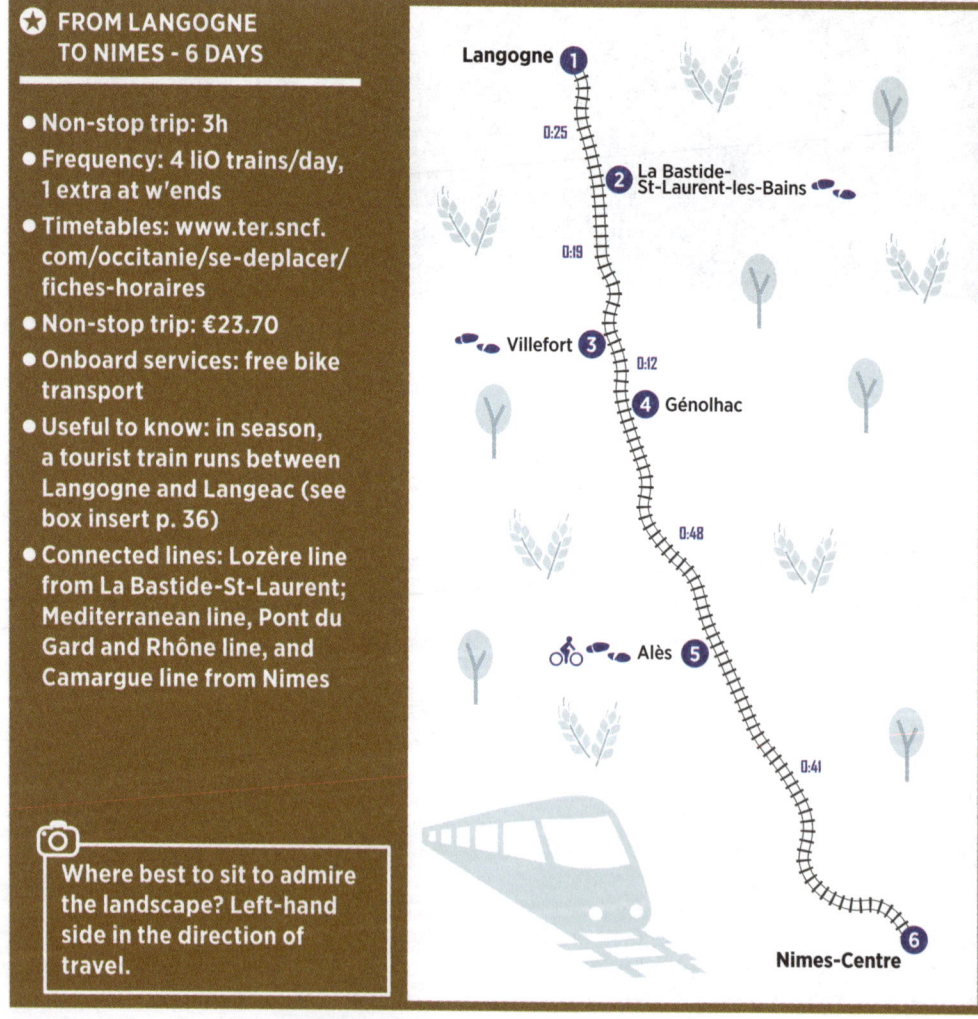

Naussac Lake. M.Dupont/hemis.fr

❶ LANGOGNE

The "Pearl of Gévaudan". Here, different ages coexist. The Middle Ages are revealed in a small church nestled in a maze of alleys and low-ceilinged houses, while the 18th century asserts itself in the high grain halls, with their round pillars and flagstone roofs, which today house the market. Situated at the confluence of the Allier and Langouyrou rivers, Langogne has developed along the water's edge.
Tourist office - 15 bd des Capucins - ☏ 04 66 69 01 38 - www.ot-langogne.com.

Dining and overnighting. A 7-minute walk from the station, this comfortable and friendly establishment has nicely renovated light wood rooms and a brasserie where you can enjoy a coffee, a beer or a dish of the day at any time.
Hôtel-brasserie Le Beausejour - 22 av. Mar.-Foch - ☏ 04 66 69 01 18 - www.lebeausejour48.fr - 10 rms. €49.50/€59.50 - ☕ €8.90 - 🍴 €15/30.

Splashing around on Naussac lake. In order to control the Allier, a dam was built, forever burying the old village of Naussac in the process. Now, a vast 1,080-hectare stretch of water is home to a large watersports centre where you can enjoy a wide range of outdoor activities (hiking, mountain biking, tennis, golf, fishing), take advantage of the heated swimming pool, as well as indulge in water sports on Naussac lake or in white water (rafting, canyoning, kayaking).

The establishment, which overlooks Naussac lake, is also a hotel-restaurant. The rooms, with simple comforts, are impeccable. The restaurant, which serves local cuisine, has a pleasant terrace overlooking the lake.
Les Terrasses du Lac - 35min walk from the station - ☏ 04 66 69 29 62 - www.naussac.com - from mid-Apr. to mid-Oct. - 17 rms. €75/95 - ☕ €11 - 🍴 menu: €17.50 - watersport centre prices: contact for details.

❷ LA BASTIDE-ST-LAURENT-LES-BAINS

See the Lozère line p. 29.

FABULOUS JOURNEYS BY RAIL

A TRIP ON A TOURIST TRAIN!
If you love the gorges of the Allier, take the train! On the same railway line as the regular liO train, this tourist train runs at a leisurely pace and slows right down when approaching exceptional panoramas. You're in for a guaranteed getaway with the magnificent spectacle of a nature in all its unspoiled beauty, from Langeac to Langogne. In 2 hours, it passes through 51 tunnels and negotiates many difficult slopes, twists and turns.
Tourist train of the Allier gorges - 04 71 77 70 17 - www.train-gorges-allier.com - from mid-Jul. to mid-Aug. - dep. from Langeac Wed. (only) at 9:10 a.m. (advance booking required, arrival at station advised for 8 a.m.) - 25min stop at Langogne before return trip - great crossing of the Allier gorges €29 return.

sauna (€15/30min), jacuzzi (€20/30min) - 5 rms. €70/80 - €90/100 in 1/2 board.
Dining. Brasserie menu, on the blackboard, in this eatery decked out all in wood: grilled meats, fisherman's salad, pizzas, burgers. The products are fresh and of good quality.
La Brindille - 10 av. des Cévennes - 09 88 47 62 47 - €10/25.

An afternoon at the waterside. To the north of the village (37min from the centre) is Villefort lake, a vast 27-hectare stretch of water, surrounded by a hiking trail. Behind the dam, 70 m above the level of the river, you will find a watersports centre and a beach, very popular in summer, ideal for swimming (supervised in Jul.-Aug.) and water sports (canoeing, paddle, windsurfing, etc.).
Grandeur Nature - 04 66 46 80 62 (outdoor activities centre) or 04 66 46 87 26 (watersports centre) - www.grandeurnature48.com - office open every day exc. Sat. 10 a.m.-noon; watersports centre open Jul.-Aug: 9 a.m.-6 p.m.

❸ VILLEFORT

➜ The station is a 12-minute walk from the village.

Stop the clocks. In this welcoming village, all schist and granite, time seems to have stood still. Its cobbled streets and alleys shaded by plane trees are nestled in the Cévennes hills and chestnut groves.
Tourist office - 43 pl. du Bosquet - 04 66 46 87 30 - www.en.destination-montlozere.fr.

A bed for the night. Perched on a mountainside above the village of Villefort, the Le Mas de l'Affenadou guest house is a haven of serenity. Just 10 minutes' walk from the station, the rustic charm of the rooms and the homely cuisine featuring local produce, not to mention the small heated swimming pool, sauna and jacuzzi, make this a very pleasant retreat. The owner also offers reiki treatments and massages.
Le Mas de l'Affenadou - 4 r. de l'Affenadou - 04 66 46 97 23 - www.gite-lozere.com -

❹ GÉNOLHAC

A pretty Medieval town. Set against the backdrop of Mount Lozère, the town's Romanesque church with its curious bell gable and its large temple bear witness to the wars of religion that ravaged the region over the centuries. Today the town is a peaceful place, offering shady walks through its winding streets, with its South of France-style squares for soaking up the sun, and the opportunity to cool off by the river. Housed in a beautiful building dating from the end of the 16th century, the Maison du Parc National des Cévennes provides numerous documents on the Park. There are often exhibitions on the ground floor of the reception and information centre.
Tourist office - 15 pl. du Vieux-Colombier - 04 66 61 09 48 - www.cevennes-montlozere.com.
Maison du Parc - Documentation and archives centre - 3 Grand-Rue - 04 66 61 19 97 - www.cevennes-parcnational.fr.

Fabulous Journeys

Turn back the clock on the Régordane Way

➔ The Cévennes line serves several villages through which the Régordane Way passes: Langogne, La Bastide, Villefort and Génolhac.

The Régordane Way is first and foremost a superb hike on the GR 700, running for 240 km from the Auvergne volcanoes to the Camargue. From the Neolithic era to the present day, mankind has left its mark here. It starts at the Château de Luc, located halfway between Langogne and La Bastide: built on a Celtic site, this fortress experienced, among other things, the Hundred Years War, the Wars of Religion and the legend of the Beast of Gévaudan. Efforts to climb the tower are rewarded with a magnificent 360-degree panorama. After an overnight stop, the route continues towards Le Thort, where you will discover the Palet de Gargantua, a Neolithic dolmen, as well as medieval ruts dating from the 11th century. These authentic rails were etched into the rock to facilitate the passage of goods wagons. Then it is on to Mount Lozère and the village of La Garde-Guérin, whose cobbled streets are swathed in gentle tranquillity. After an overnight stay, continue on your way for Villefort and its lake, where you can take a refreshing break *(see opposite)*. At last you arrive in Lozère, upon reaching St-André-Capcèze, which stages a cool jazz festival in July. Needless to say, you can continue on your way into the Gard department, if you feel up to it !

3 days - €150 per pers. - from April to October.
Contact: Langogne tourist office.

Villefort lake.
kodachrome25/Getty Images Plus

FABULOUS JOURNEYS BY RAIL

Chamborigaud viaduct, between Alès and Génolhac.
Patrice Thebault/CRT Occitanie

Dining and overnighting. The Café du Commerce is a rustic and friendly address, with its vaulted dining room and a beautiful terrace around a fountain. Its fare consists of nicely prepared local recipes and generous portions. Do not be surprised if you smell exotic aromas wafting out of the kitchen. The Chalet is a hotel-restaurant run by a friendly family from Réunion who have settled in this part of the Cévennes. On the menu: samossas, sausage rougail, chicken in coconut milk. Simple but comfortable rooms for a colourful stopover.
Café du Commerce - 46 Grand-Rue - ☎ 04 66 25 01 35 - meal deals: €25/29.
Le Chalet - 28 av. de la Gare - ☎ 04 66 61 11 08 - 9 ch. - ☕ €7 - dishes €10.

For a picnic. Proud of its "Boutique paysanne" label, La Lausète offers products from local and organic producers at low prices: bread, cheese, meat, yoghurts, fruit and vegetables, sweets...
La Lausète - 10 r. Pasteur - ☎ 04 66 54 02 38 - closed Sun.

⑤ ALÈS

🚲 **Bike hire.** The "Ales'y à vélo" service offers e-bikes for hire. The 7 km of greenway, separated from the road, allows you to cross Alès from north to south.
Hire locations: **bus station (beside the railway station)** - 15 av. Gén.-de-Gaulle - ☎ 04 66 52 31 31 - Mon.-Fri. 8:45 a.m.-noon, 1:45-5:15 p.m. - €15/day.

The South of France on the threshold of the Cevennes mountains. Although there are still some typical old streets, a large part of the town centre of Alès was rebuilt in the 1960s and offers a somewhat confusing ensemble, between the cathedral and the Gardon d'Alès (the river). In the summer, the Monday market is packed with craft stands, and the festivals offer quality cultural entertainment in this town with its endearing charm, fostered by its museums and its South of France atmosphere.
Tourist office - pl. de l'Hôtel-de-Ville - ☎ 04 66 52 32 15 - www.cevennes-tourisme.fr.

A bed for the night. Located 200 metres from the station, this small hotel run by very friendly owners has spacious and well-appointed rooms (including several family rooms). It also has a bar and a nice sunny terrace.
Hôtel Durand Le Patio - 3 bd Anatole-France - ☎ 04 66 86 28 94 - 17 rms. €50/86 - ☕ €8.90.

Dining. Le Ricochet is a little restaurant offering traditional cuisine with local and seasonal produce (organic vegetables). The dishes are generous and full of flavour. Friendly service. Good value for money.
Le Ricochet - 12 bd Louis-Blanc - ☎ 04 66 24 38 31 - closed Mon.- Sun. - lunch deal:€ 15 - menus: €22/28.

For a picnic. The markets of Alès are replete with fine regional produce, great for a quality picnic!
Food market - Mon.-Sat. morning in the Abbey market halls.
Fairground market - Mon. morning around the cathedral, pl. de la Mairie and pl. de l'Abbaye.
Night market - Wed. in summer.

Take to the heights on the Ermitage walk. From the station, go to the Rochebelle bridge (16min), then climb to the top of the Ermitage hill (290 m - 20min climb), to reach the Notre-Dame des Mines sanctuary. There, you will enjoy a sweeping panorama of the Alès region (orientation table to help you).

⑥ NIMES-CENTRE

➔ Nimes-Pont-du-Gard station, outside the town, is linked to Nimes-Centre station by regular liO train connections (every 9 min).

A multi-faceted town. Imbued with both Catholic and Protestant influences, drawn between the Cévennes on one side and the Camargue on the other, sometimes austere, sometimes unbridled when the ferias bring to life its magnificent amphitheatre and a thousand bodegas invade its streets, this "French Rome" is rightly proud of its prestigious ancient monuments, such as the Arena and the Maison Carrée, as well as the Magne Tower which dominates it like a beacon. Lose yourself in the "Écusson" district, the labyrinth of narrow streets in the medieval centre of the town, squeezed between boulevards shaded by hackberry trees and dotted with beautiful private townhouses.
Tourist office - 6 bd des Arènes - ☎ 04 66 58 38 00 - www.nimes-tourisme.com.

A bed for the night. À A 10-minute walk from the train station, the charm of the Côté Patio hotel lies precisely with its patio, where breakfast is served in the shade of the parasols, as well as with its colourful and personalised rooms. More functional, the Hotel des Tuileries is located in a fairly quiet street, a stone's throw from the old town and a 5-minute walk from the station. Its rooms are renovated and nicely decorated, well-appointed, and each with a small balcony.
Hôtel Côté Patio - 31 r. de Beaucaire - ☎ 04 66 67 60 17 - www.hotel-cote-patio.com - 17 rms. €60/140 - ☕ €10.
Hôtel des Tuileries - 22 r. Roussy - ☎ 04 66 21 31 15 - www.hoteldestuileries.com - 11 rms. €69/120 - ☕ €9.

Roman Nimes. In 31 BCE, the Romans settled in the city, surrounding it with a 16 km long wall, of which the Magne Tower (today in the Fountain Gardens) is the most imposing vestige: from its small platform, the view is superb and an orientation table presents Nimes as it was in Roman times. The city was then filled with splendid buildings of which Nimes has kept remarkably well-preserved vestiges, such as the Maison Carrée (closed for renovation, scheduled to reopen in July 2022), a temple probably dedicated to the imperial cult, beside the forum, and an amphitheatre (the majestic Arena of Nimes). Opposite the Arena, the Roman Museum (Musée de la Romanité) is the key to understanding Nimes and its history. It houses in particular the rich collections of the former Archaeological Museum.
Visiting the Roman monuments - ☎ 04 66 21 82 56 - www.arenes-nimes.com - timetables on the website - Pass for the Arena, Maison Carrée and Magne Tower (purchase in the first monument visited): €13 (under 17s: €6).
Musée de la Romanité - 18 bd des Arènes - ☎ 04 48 21 02 10 - museedelaromanite.fr - €9 (7-17 year-olds: €3).

Dining. A popular address in the city centre, La Marmite offers tasty local cuisine based on seasonal produce. The atmosphere is friendly and the prices are very reasonable. Booking advised.

Arena of Nîmes. bbsferrary/Getty Images Plus

La Marmite - 13 r. de l'Agau - ☏ 04 66 29 98 23 - closed Sun.- Mon., Tues.- Wed. evening - lunch deal: €16 - menu: €25.

For a picnic. In the city centre, two large food markets with regional products will tickle your taste buds!
Covered market halls - 5 r. des Halles - leshallesdenimes.fr - 7 a.m.-7 p.m. (Sat.-Sun. 7 a.m.-2 p.m.).
Farmers' market - bd Jean-Jaurès-Sud - Fri. 7 a.m.-1 p.m.

Sweet snack. On the 3rd floor of the Carré d'Art museum there is a tea room, which can be frequented without visiting the museum. Superb rooftop view of the monuments.
Le Ciel de Nîmes - Carré d'Art (3rd floor) - 16 pl. de la Maison-Carrée - ☏ 04 66 36 71 70 - Tues.-Sun. 10 a.m.-6 p.m. (May-Sept. : Sat. 8 p.m.-1 a.m.).

Aperitif time. This listed brewery, built in 1813, remains a great place to go to take a break or enjoy a little drink. It has to be said that it is the finest cafe in Nîmes!

Le Napoléon - 46 bd Victor-Hugo - ☏ 04 66 05 98 25 - www.le-napo.fr - 8 a.m.-12:30 a.m. - lunch deal: €16.50.

Spotting Ben Hur. In the spring, Nîmes celebrates its Roman history with various events, culminating in the Arena with a full-scale reproduction of equestrian games, chariot races and gladiatorial combats.
The Great Roman Games - www.arenes-nimes.com - Apr.-May

Feast on the effervescence of the Feria. There are two Ferias in the year: the best-known is the Whitsun feria (Wednesday to Monday), with a street "pegoulade" (torchlit procession), "abrivados", "novilladas" and "corridas" (bull-running and bullfights) in the mornings and evenings, as well as concerts and various events around town. The Harvest feria is just as popular, and takes place on the 3rd weekend in Sept. (Thurs.-Sun.).
Rental office - 4 r. de la Violette - ☏ 0 891 701 401 (toll number) - www.arenesdenimes.com

Excursion out of Nimes

The Cévennes steam train

➔ From Nimes station, take the liO 112 coach to Anduze. if you don't want the return trip, it is also possible to return by liO 112 coach from St-Jean-du-Gard.
Info: www.lio-occitanie.fr.

From Anduze to St-Jean-du-Gard, you get to discover the Gardons valley and sumptuous panoramas from an authentic steam train dating from the early 20th century. The 14-kilometre railway line, completed in 1909, required the construction of seven viaducts, a metal bridge, and four tunnels. It carried passengers and goods before being decommissioned in 1960. The line would have been dismantled if an association of enthusiasts had not had the idea of creating a tourist train. The public has turned up in droves, and the line has been saved!

All aboard at Anduze, to travel on an authentic steam train, a Krupp locomotive from 1937. In summer, open carriages allow you to enjoy the fresh air and, above all, a clear view from the bends and viaducts. The route, negotiated at a steady 30 kph, begins with a tunnel that leads to a first breathtaking panorama: the majestic 104 m-high metal bridge over the Gardon river. The line then passes via two shorter viaducts before stopping at La Bambouseraie. In summer, if you leave in the morning, you can get off at La Bambouseraie to explore its park and take the next train. This exotic garden was created in 1855 by Eugène Mazel, a Cévennes native with a passion for botany. He went to the Far East to study the mulberry bushes needed for silkworm farming, and brought back bamboo plants from his trip. The garden's wide, shady paths, lined with trees from all over the world, provide an enchanting setting for a walk (www.bambouseraie.com, tickets from €8.20).

The train next passes over the three viaducts of Mescladou, Corbès and the plain of Thoiras-Lasalle before arriving at St-Jean-du-Gard. Here the train terminates. Depending on your programme, you can go for a walk or grab an ice cream before getting back on the train for the return trip.

📞 04 66 60 59 00 - www.trainavapeur.com - dep. from Anduze : 4 return trips per day from mid-Jul. to end August; - rest of the year: contact for details. closed Nov.-March - €13 single (4-12 year-olds: €9.50), €17 return (4-12 year-olds: €11.50).

Cévennes steam train.
D. Zylberyng/hemis.fr

THE CÉVENNES LINE

FABULOUS JOURNEYS BY RAIL

THE MEDITERRANEAN LINE

Journey from Gard to Pyrénées-Orientales, discovering some of the pearls of Occitanie: Nimes, Montpellier, Sète, Béziers, Narbonne, Perpignan... for the cultural heritage.
For the beaches, choose from Frontignan, Marseillan or Cap d'Agde, depending on whether you're looking for peace and quiet or fun and games. As for the pleasures of the table, the region's delicate vineyards and culinary traditions will guarantee you good fare all along the way, to go with all that sunshine.

⊕ FROM NIMES TO PERPIGNAN - 15 DAYS

- Non-stop trip: 2h30
- Frequency: approx. 15 liO trains/day
- Timetables: www.ter.sncf.com/occitanie/se-deplacer/fiches-horaires
- Non-stop trip: €33.80
- Onboard service: bikes carried free of charge

- Line connections: Cévennes line, Pont du Gard and Rhône line, and Camargue line from Nimes; Catalan country line and Côte Vermeille line from Perpignan

Where best to sit to admire the landscape? On the left of the train, in the direction of travel.

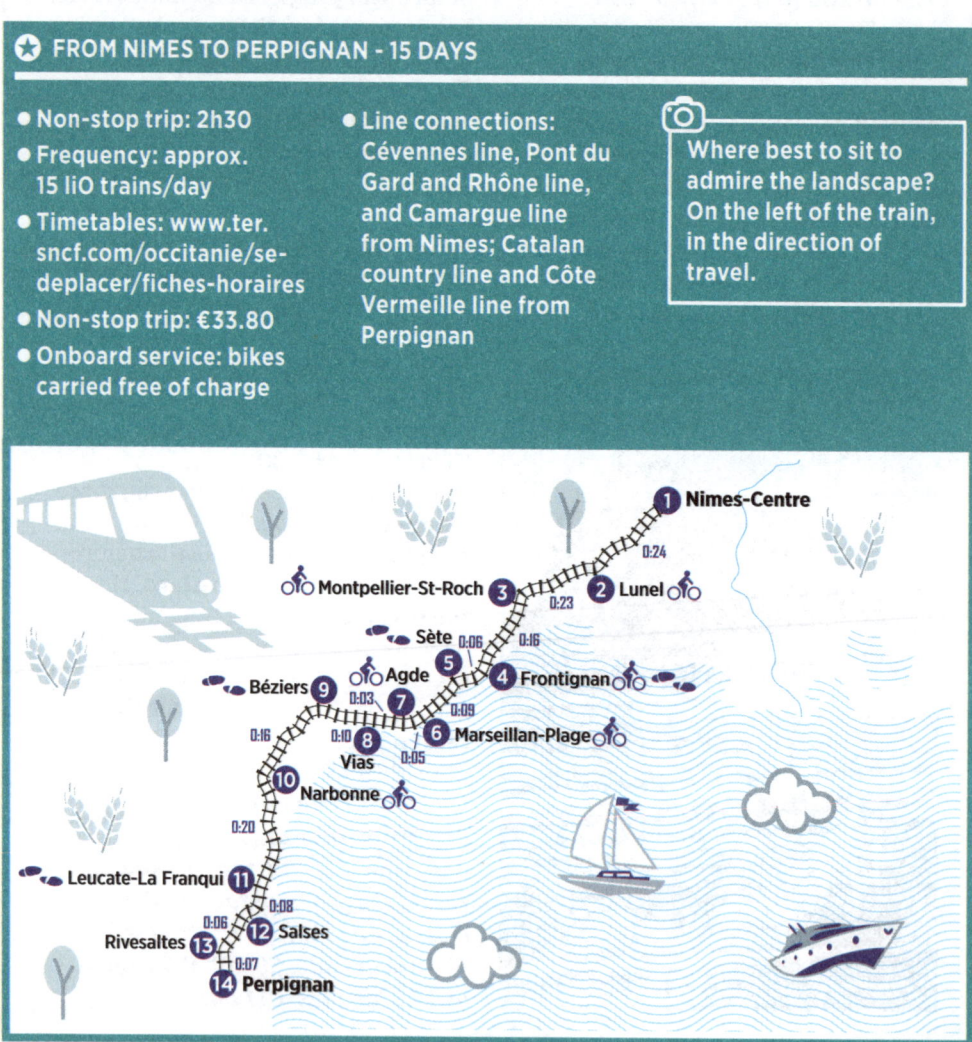

The liO train, between Narbonne and Leucate.
Laurent Boutonnet/Région Occitanie

THE MEDITERRANEAN LINE

① NIMES-CENTRE
See Cévennes line p. 39.

② LUNEL

Bike hire. 7 minutes' walk from the station.
Rêve de vélo - *235 avenue de Lattre-de-Tassigny - 04 67 71 16 09 - www.revedevelo.com - bike/e-bike €21/€40 per 1/2 day.*

At home with the "moon fishers". In the old town centre, signposting has been put in place to point out the main cultural, architectural, and historical heritage sites. Famous for its Muscat wine, this small town is proud of its bullfighting traditions (both Spanish and Camargue), the name of its inhabitants, the Pescalunes (meaning "moon fishers"), and a prestigious past. In the 13th century, its Talmudic school trained renowned rabbis: the remains of the synagogue can be seen at 207 rue Alphonse-Ménard. Discover too, in old Lunel, the vaulted passage of the Caladons (13th century), the church of Notre-Dame-du-Lac (17th century), the Hotel de Bernis (17th century), the Hotel de Brignac (18th century), and the market halls (early 20th century).

Tourist office - 16 cours Gabriel-Péri - 04 67 71 01 37 - www.ot-paysdelunel.fr.

A bed for the night. Just a 15-minute walk from the station, you would not expect to find such a peaceful haven, especially as the neighbouring housing estate is somewhat lacking in character. Once through the door, you discover some lovely rooms that overlook a large swimming pool. A warm welcome assured and a kitchen at your disposal.
Le Relais d'Angélique - *35 r. des Cèpes - 06 24 17 81 15 - www.lerelaisdangelique.com - 5 rms. €90/€110.*

Dining. In its 19th century building or its shady courtyard in the heart of town, this gastronomic stop takes you back to basics, with seasonal dishes and local produce. Every day, its "mystery" menu promises surprising combinations and flavours as well as some delightful discoveries.
Le Bistrot de Caro - *129 cours Gabriel-Péri - www.lebistrotdecaro.fr - closed Sun.-Tues. - lunch deal €35, evening menu €68.*

Mountain biking. Taking in vineyard hillsides and the Petite Camargue, this VTT-FFC (French MTB federation) site proposes 185 km

43

of MTB routes comprising 9 circuits of different levels (from 9 to 34 km).
"Espace VTT-FFC" of the Pays de Lunel - info and brochures for downloading at www.ot-pays delunel.fr.

③ MONTPELLIER-ST-ROCH

→ Setting off from Montpellier-St-Roch station. The "Montpellier-Sud de France" TGV station is 6 km from the city centre. A shuttle links the station with the Place de France, a tram stop on line 1 (the city has 4 tram lines), the line serving St-Roch station.
Info: www.tam-voyages.com.

🚲 Bike hire. The Vélomagg service (2 hours of free hire, then €0.50/hour) allows you to hire a bicycle, 24 hours a day, from any of the 57 automatic stations spread throughout the city, including 4 in the direct vicinity of the railway station.

The capital of Languedoc! This is a dynamic and vibrant metropolis, with a harmonious mix of old and resolutely contemporary districts. Old Montpellier has pedestrian spaces tucked away, where it is nice to have a rest after wandering through its lively streets. Between the Place de la Comédie and the Porte de Peyrou triumphal arch, extending either side of Rue Foch, are the city's old districts, a labyrinth of tortuous and narrow streets characteristic of medieval cities. Take time to pause a while during the day in the charming Place Ste-Anne, with the music of the neighbouring Conservatoire filling the air. In the evening, the lively atmosphere of the Place St-Roch gets our vote.

Tourist office - 30 allée Jean-de-Lattre-de-Tassigny (pl. de la Comédie) - ☏ 04 67 60 60 60 - www.montpellier-tourisme.fr.

A bed for the night. Located in the heart of the city, right next to the station (2 minutes' walk) and not far from the Place de la Comédie, the apartment hotel Les Occitanes has lots going for it. Spacious and modern rooms with kitchenette. Best avoided however are the street-side rooms.

Looking for a historic hotel? Behind the majestic facade of the Métropole, the prestigious lounges, the frescoes, and the solid wood floors have been restored to their former glory. The

Place de la Comédie, Montpellier.
C. Deschamps/CRT Occitanie

rooms are modern, with high ceilings and warm colours. A 3-minute walk from the Place de la Comédie and St-Roch station.
Appart'hôtel Les Occitanes - 20 r. de la République - ☎ 04 67 02 92 50 - www.odalys-vacances.com - 92 rms. €90/€200.
Hôtel Océania Le Métropole - 3 r. Clos-René - ☎ 04 67 12 32 32 - www.oceaniahotels.com - 96 rms. €110/€200 - 🛏 €16.

"Beyond the black". The Pierre Soulages collection at the Musée Fabre is one of the most important collections of the artist after that of the Soulages Museum in Rodez. Bequeathed by the artist himself, it comprises some thirty works, from the first paintings of 1952 to his famous "outrenoir" ("beyond black"). The Musée Fabre is also the most important museum in the South-East, and one of the richest in France. It is organised into three main sections: the ancient period, the modern period, and the decorative arts, which are housed in the Hôtel Cabrières-Sabatier d'Espeyran (rue Montpelliéret).
Musée Fabre - 39 bd Bonne-Nouvelle - ☎ 04 67 14 83 00 - www.museefabre.fr - 10 a.m.-6 p.m. - closed Mon. - €9.

Dining. In the lively St-Roch district, Rosemarie, a cosy little restaurant, offers tasty Mediterranean cuisine. It has a pleasant terrace with its old-fashioned tables and chairs, and with seafood the main focus on the menu. In the evening, all the starters can be served as tapas, for sharing and getting a taste of everything! Just a stone's throw from Place Ste-Anne, chef Pierrick Xueref makes sure the menu in his Abacus restaurant mirrors the seasons, with pride of place given to local produce. The chef likes to play with the senses, juggling with flavours and textures to create very visual and colourful dishes.
Rosemarie - 3 r. des Sœurs-Noires - ☎ 04 67 66 15 95 - rosemarie-montpellier.fr - 9 a.m.-1 a.m. - dishes €4.50/€16.
Abacus - 6 r. Terral - ☎ 04 34 35 32 86 - abacus-restaurant.fr - advance booking required - Tue-Fri. eve. only, Sat. lunch and eve. - lunch menu €27 - eve. menu €38/€43.

For a picnic. Every day there are food markets in the Castellane (r. de la Loge) and Jacques-Cœur (bd d'Antigone) market halls. A farmers' market is held on Sunday mornings in the Antigone district (pl. du Nombre-d'Or).

Time for a nice ice. This craft ice cream parlour makes a wide range of ice creams and sorbets every day, with flavours ranging from classic chocolate-vanilla to more original combinations such as lemon-thyme or ricotta-orange.
La Banquise - 2 r. du Petit-St-Jean - ☎ 04 67 86 45 94 - www.labanquisemontpellier.fr - Mon.-Sat. noon-7 p.m., Sun. 2-7 p.m.

Aperitif time. This is one of the most fashionable cocktail bars in Montpellier. Its refined and minimalist setting serves as a showcase for its exceptional cocktails. To be enjoyed (in moderation) alongside the dishes proposed by the chef, or simply sipped while admiring the stone-vaulted interior.
Aperture - 2 r. des Trésoriers-de-la-Bourse - ☎ 09 87 17 44 33 - aperturemontpellier.com - Tues.-Sat. 6 p.m.-1 a.m. - cocktails €10/€12.

🚴 **Beaches on the Montpellier coast.** A cycle track leads to Palavas-les-Flots, Carnon, and La Grande-Motte from the Place de la Comédie (around 50 minutes' ride). Worth a visit, 4 km from Palavas-les-Flots, is the cathedral-fortress of Maguelone, isolated on a peninsula in the middle of the lagoons. Nestled within a copse of stone pines, cedars and eucalyptus, it offers up an image of unusual beauty.
Domaine de Maguelone - ☎ 04 67 50 63 63 - www.compagnons-de-maguelone.org - 9 a.m.-6 p.m. - free entry - €4.50 audioguide.

Patronal festival. Every year, on 16 August, the Feast of Saint Roch is the occasion for great festivities and a procession through the town leading to 19 bis rue de la Loge, in front of the house where Saint Roch was born.

④ FRONTIGNAN

→ **The station serves the village. Frontignan-Plage beach resort is a 30-minute walk or 10-minute bike ride away.**

🚴 **Bike hire.** There is a hire shop in Frontignan-Plage that delivers bikes to the station on request.

THE MEDITERRANEAN LINE

Galexia Bien-Être - 104 av. Vauban - Frontignan-Plage - ☏ 06 19 98 75 88 - galexiabienetre-deferlantes.fr - bikes/e-bikes €10/€30 per 1/2 day.

Between Med and Muscat! This small town has lent its name to a famous, golden-hued Muscat wine, whose vineyards cover nearly 800 hectares on the banks of the Ingril lagoon. Just over 2 km from the station, the small seaside resort of Frontignan-Plage has over 7 km of unspoilt coastline and protected natural areas. In addition to its marina, it offers a full range of watersports activities and various discovery excursions, along the trails of the Gardiole massif and around the lagoon. In the village, the Church of St. Paul (12th century) was rebuilt in the Southern French Gothic style in the 14th century. Built into the town's original ramparts, it can be identified by its square bell tower (a former keep) with its corner watchtower.

Tourist office - av. des Étangs - ☏ 04 67 18 31 60 - www.frontignan-tourisme.com.

Dining and overnighting. This restaurant-hotel in the centre of Frontignan is just a 5-minute walk from the station. It offers 3 bright and pleasant rooms, as well as quality regional cuisine. You can also order good take-away food for your days out around town.

Le Goût des Hôtes - 18 bd Gambetta - ☏ 06 62 20 30 24 - www.restauranthotel-frontignan-legoutdeshotes.fr - 3 rms. €75/€105 - 🍽 €8/€14 - 🍴 lunch deals €16/€29 - menu €29.

For a picnic. On the Place du Château, in the renovated Baltard de Frontignan (1897) market halls, you will find local produce and regional specialities (closed Mon.).

Aperitif time. Buy your Frontignan Muscat in the town's cooperative cellar. Take it away for aperitif on the beach (in moderation, of course)!

Frontignan Muscat - 14 av. du Muscat - ☏ 04 67 48 93 20 - www.frontignanmuscat.fr - Jul.-Aug.: 9:30 a.m.-1 p.m., 3-7:30 p.m.; rest of the year: 9:30 a.m.-12:30 p.m., 2:30-6:30 p.m.

Muscat festival. This fine dessert wine is celebrated every year in July, with tastings offered by the winegrowers of Frontignan.

🚲 **The lagoons, the old salt pans, and Aresquiers beach.** This nature trail, on the flat, runs around the Ingril lagoon. An ideal circuit to discover the ecosystem of the lagoon, the old salt pans and the Aresquiers wood, all of which now form a Natura 2000 reserve. You can pass some time at the beautiful beach of Aresquiers, away from it all, fringed by lagoons and the canal.

Access via the Plan du Bassin, behind the station - 3h30 on foot, 1h45 by bike - easy loop.

⑤ SÈTE

A land of poets. Sète lies at the foot of the limestone hill of Mount Saint-Clair, between the Thau lagoon and the Mediterranean. A fishing, yachting and trading port, the town owes its reputation to the canals that run through it, but also to the poets and artists who have called it home. Let us start with Paul Valéry, to whom homage can be paid at the "cimetière marin", or graveyard by the sea, his last resting place and the name of his eponymous poem, and at the Paul-Valéry Museum, on the flanks of Mount Saint-Clair. Continue your pilgrimage by heading to the Espace Georges-Brassens, dedicated to this native son of Sète, great chansonnier and lover of his native town (his song "*Supplique pour être enterré à la plage de Sète*" is a plea to be buried on the beach at Sète!). Finally, stroll along the Pointe Courte in the footsteps of Agnès Varda, before continuing on to the Cadre Royal and the quays of the old port, where all kinds of boats are docked.

Tourist office - 60 Grand'Rue-Mario-Roustan - ☏ 04 99 04 71 71 - www.tourisme-sete.com.

Musée Paul-Valéry - rue François-Desnoyer - ☏ 04 99 04 76 16 - museepaulvalery-sete.fr - Apr.-Oct.: 9:30 a.m.-7 p.m.; Nov.-Mar.: 10 a.m.-6 p.m. - €6.20 (€9.90 with exhibition) - closed Mon.

Espace Georges-Brassens - 67 bd Camille-Blanc - ☏ 04 99 04 76 26 - www.espace-brassens.fr - Jun.-Sept.: 10 a.m.-6 p.m.; Oct.-May: daily except Mon. 9 a.m.-noon, 2-6 p.m. - €6 (children €2.50).

A bed for the night. Located in a quiet area, next to the Molière Theatre and a 6-minute walk from the station, this family hotel has

The Jousts of Sète during the Fêtes de la Saint-Louis festival.
A. Spani/hemis.fr

been tastefully renovated. Pleasant rooms and a very warm welcome. Good value for money.
<u>Hôtel Le National</u> - 2 r. Pons-de-l'Hérault - ☏ 04 67 74 67 85 - www.hotellenational.fr - 22 rms. €69/€119 - ☕ €9.50 (buffet).

Around the Old Port. With its canals lined with colourful facades, its bridges, its pleasure boats, its trawlers, and its old sailing craft, the old port is the beating heart of town. Restaurants and terraces abound along the Canal de la Marine, as far as the southern tip sheltered by the Môle St-Louis: constructed in 1666, this pier offers a beautiful promenade in the brisk sea breeze. From Quai Aspirant-Herber, you can enjoy a fine view of the town with Mount St-Clair rising up behind it. The Quartier Haut ("high district"), now a fishermen's and artists' quarter, is more peaceful, but no less picturesque.

Dining. Just a stone's throw from the Halles de Sète market, chef Jordan Yuste proposes creative and inspired cuisine. He puts a new spin on Sète classics and makes everything himself, right down to the charcuterie which he matures in his cellar! The short menu changes daily. With a small dining room and just a few tables on the terrace, it's better to book ahead.
<u>L'Arrivage</u> - 13-15 r. André-Portes - www.restaurant-larrivage.com - Thu.-Sat. lunch and Tue.-Sat. eve. - menus €32/€45 (lunch)/€89 (evening).

For a picnic. Could Adrienne Verducci have imagined that the tielle, a kind of savoury turnover garnished with octopus and tomato that she created in 1937, would become one of the town's culinary specialities? Her descendants continue to maintain the tradition of this tasty creation.
<u>Paradiso</u> - 11 quai de la Résistance - ☏ 04 67 74 26 48 - daily except Tues. 8:30 a.m.-7 p.m.

If you've got your sea legs. In Sète, two nautical centres offer sailing dinghy, windsurfing, kayaking, and paddleboard lessons.
<u>Base nautique Françoise-Pascal</u> - port des Quilles - Corniche de Neuburg (on the sea side) - ☏ 04 67 18 96 10 - www.nautisme-sete.fr.
<u>Base nautique Miaille et Munoz</u> - 41 r. des Fauvettes (on the Thau lagoon side) - ☏ 04 99 04 76 60 - www.nautisme-sete.fr.

Sweet snack. Nestled beneath the arcades of a building, this biscuit factory has been making "navettes cettoises" by hand since 1913, the delicious biscuits flavoured with aniseed, lemon, vanilla, cinnamon or orange blossom. <u>Biscuiterie Pouget</u> - 47 quai de Bosc and in the Halls (No. 52) - ☎ 04 67 74 72 38 - Wed. and Fri. 9 a.m.-12:30 p.m., 3-6 p.m., Sat. 9 a.m.-12:30 p.m.

Patronal festival. Every year around 20 August, the Saint Louis festival lasts for a week, in honour of the town's patron saint. This is when the final tournament of the famous nautical Jousts of Sète is organised, a maritime tradition that dates back to 1666, the year of the town's creation. On the waters of the Cadre Royal, the jousting schools rely on their agility and balance to compete for victory in the most prestigious of the tourneys on the Monday of Saint-Louis, the last day of the festival. Fireworks and the Sète open water swim race complete the programme.

Beaches and Mount St-Clair. Lazaret beach, the closest beach to the town centre, takes its name from the point that marks the limit of its small harbour. At the Canal des Quilles, the Corniche beach, located 2 km from the town centre, has children's playgrounds, bars and restaurants. If you'd like a longer walk, continuing along you will reach Villeroy beach, with its 12 km of golden sands stretching all the way to Marseillan in a protected nature area. If you prefer the heights to the beach, you can climb the magnificent Mount St-Clair on foot, taking Rue Louis-Ramond, at the end of Rue Paul-Valéry, then Rue de Belfort and Chemin de Biscan Pas (30-45 minutes one-way). This hill, once covered with pine and oak forests, rises 183 m above the sea and offers a choice viewpoint.

❻ MARSEILLAN-PLAGE

➔From the station, allow for 20 minutes to walk to Marseillan-Plage. From here, there is a bus link with Marseillan-Ville all year round. In season (Apr.-Sept.), the Sète-Marseillan line 9 passes via the SNCF railway station.
<u>Info</u>: www.mobilite.agglopole.fr

Oyster farm on Thau lagoon
visualllook/Getty Images Plus

Bike hire. A large network of cycle paths is in place for reaching Marseillan-Ville from Marseillan-Plage, where you'll find this rental compagny:
Vélos et rosalies - 39 av. de la Méditerranée - 04 67 31 69 19 - Apr.-Sept. - min. hire 3 days.

The land of shellfish farming. Marseillan-Plage beach extends for miles, while 6 km away Marseillan-Ville remains a fishing village that retains the charm of its fishermens' huts hidden in the reeds on the banks of the Thau lagoon. It is in this lagoon, separated from the sea by the Onglous isthmus, that oyster and mussel farming has been practised since Antiquity. In this lagoon setting, let yourself be tempted by a shellfish tasting session accompanied by a fresh local white wine... a Picpoul-de-Pinet, for example - in moderation, of course! Marseillan is also the birthplace of Noilly Prat, the dry vermouth whose cellars can be visited in the village.
Tourist office - av. de la Méditerranée - Marseillan-Plage - 04 67 21 82 43 - www.marseillan.com.

A bed for the night. A 20-minute walk from the station, this 5-star campsite (pitches for tents and cabins to rent) offers all the water fun you could want, with direct access to the beach, an outdoor water park, and an indoor balneo-therapy area. The facilities combine style and comfort in a shady location. Free access to the facilities and services of the two neighbouring campsites (also 5-star).
Camping Les Méditerranées Beach Garden - av. des Campings - 04 67 21 92 83 - www.lesmediterranees.com - Apr.-Sept. - bungalow for 4-6 people. €70/€170 per night.

Dining. In Marseillan-Ville, enjoy a relaxing fireside atmosphere with a view of the Thau lagoon. On the menu: oysters fresh from the water or "brasucade" of mussels cooked on the barbecue in front of you.
La Cabane - 1 chemin de l'Étang - 06 11 17 23 50 - closed Sun. eve. and Mon. - €6/€10.

For a picnic. This delicatessen with a strong focus on charcuterie is packed with local produce. And you get service with a smile!

Le Cochon Gourmand - 22 bd Lamartine - Marseillan-Ville - 04 67 00 73 30 - 9 a.m.-8 p.m. except Mon. and Sun. eve.

Discover the Thau lagoon. Climb aboard for a one-hour boat trip in amongst the oyster beds to discover the fascinating trades of shellfish farming and fishing.
L'Étoile de Thau IV - Marseillan-Ville marina - 06 03 23 73 65 - promenade-bateau-marseillan.com - all year by prior request - 1h: €13.50 (under 12s: €9).

Sweet snack. This archetypal English tea room offers a shady terrace, in the heart of the city centre, where you can enjoy scones, pancakes, cookies, lemon cake... all home-made. Special mention for the iced coffee with a hint of bitter almond, a real treat!
La Fabrique à Goût-Thé - 1 r. Achille-Maffre-de-Baugé - Marseillan-Ville - 8 a.m.-6 p.m. - closed Wed.

⑦ AGDE

→ Agde station is 5 km from the seaside resort of Cap d'Agde. It is easy to get around thanks to the bus network, or by bicycle (a map of "soft mobility routes" can be downloaded from the tourist office website).
Info: www.capbus.fr.

Bike hire. Bicycles delivered free of charge to Agde station, on request.
Thau Cycles - 07 82 37 03 31 - www.thaucycles.com - 9 a.m.-7 p.m. - from €13 per day.

The Mediterranean town and its seventies offshoot. Established at the crossroads of the Hérault and the Canal du Midi, close to the volcanic hill of Mount St-Loup, ancient Agde retains a picturesque town centre, with beautiful relics of its rich past. An entirely different atmosphere awaits at the seaside resort of Cap d'Agde, where festive fun and modernity have been its hallmarks since its creation in the 1970s, and which has become a major tourist destination on the Mediterranean coast.
Tourist office - pl. de la Belle-Agathoise - Îlot Molière - 04 67 31 87 50 - www.capdagde.com.

A bed for the night. Located less than a 10-minute walk from the station and 100 metres from the cathedral, this renovated hotel offers modern and comfortable accommodation in the heart of Agde.
Logis Hôtel Yseria - 2 pl. Jean-Jaurès - ☏ 04 67 11 40 90 - www.yseria.fr - 16 rms. €60/€130 - 🍽 €10.

The treasures of Agathe. Founded around 535 BCE, the town has bequeathed a host of archaeological treasures that illustrate the history of navigation in the Hérault delta since Antiquity. The museum is best known for its antique bronzes, including the magnificent late-Hellenistic Youth of Agde (l'Éphèbe d'Agde), thought to represent Alexander the Great.
Musée de l'Éphèbe et d'Archéologie sous-marine - av. des Hallebardes - ☏ 04 67 94 69 60 - www.museecapdagde.com - Jul.-Sept. : 10 a.m.-6.30 p.m.; rest of the year: 10 a.m.-5.30 p.m., w'end 10:30 a.m.-5 p.m. - €6 (under 16s free).

Dining. A modern setting is the backdrop for delicious contemporary cuisine. Nibbles galore in the tapas bar. When the weather's good, soak up the sun on the terrace.
Le Bistro d'Hervé - 47 r. Brescou - ☏ 04 67 62 30 69 - www.lebistrodherve.com - closed Sun.-Mon. - lunch deal: €19.

Watersports activities at Cap d'Agde. Catamaran, canoe, windsurf, and paddleboard rental for making the most of the Med.
Cap d'Agde Nautical Centre - av. du Passeur-Challies (Richelieu-East beach) - ☏ 04 67 01 46 46 - www.centrenautique-capdagde.com - Mon.-Fri. 9 a.m.-12.30 p.m., 2-6 p.m., Sat. 2-5:30 p.m.

Sea jousting. From June to September, the sea jousting at Agde, like its equivalent in Sète, makes for exciting competition.

VIAS

→ The station is a 10-minute walk from the town centre, which can be reached via the Avenue d'Agde to the west.

Pray come. A former fortified town, Vias is now a place of pilgrimage. People still come to pray to the ancient and miraculous Virgin of Vias, brought back from Syria by sailors. A Gothic-style edifice (late 14th-early 15th century), the St-Jean-Baptiste Church is built of black stone of volcanic origin. On the west facade, a beautiful rose window was once framed by two polygonal crenellated turrets, only one of which remains. Inside, in the Chapel of the Blessed Sacrament (to the right of the main altar), there is the Miraculous Virgin, a beautiful carved wooden statue covered with gilded plaster.
Tourist office - av. de la Méditerranée - ☏ 04 67 21 76 25 - www.ot-vias.com.

A bed for the night. Just a 12-minute walk from the station and close to the town centre is this small family hotel with a sunny terrace and jacuzzi. Breakfast is served as a mini-brunch with homemade pancakes, crepes, scrambled eggs, and lots more.
Le Gambetta - 36 bd Gambetta - ☏ 04 67 21 60 94 - www.hotel-legambetta.fr - 18 rms. €119 - 🍽 €13.90.

Dining. A traditional restaurant on a listed historic site, promising fresh, seasonal produce and 100% home-made food. What more could you ask for?
Le Vieux Logis - 25 r. de la République - ☏ 04 67 21 77 56 - www.restaurant-levieuxlogis.com - closed Mon., Tues. lunch and Sat. lunch - menu €34.

Sample the legend. Every year, a medieval festival by the sea allows you to discover the legend of the ancient and miraculous Virgin, with dances, a procession, and fireworks.
Festival of Stella Maris and Sant Joan de la Mar - Late Jun-early Jul.

⑨ BÉZIERS

Between the Mediterranean and the mountains of the the Haut-Languedoc. Perched on a spur overlooking the Orb river, crowned by a fortified cathedral whose outline is an emblematic sight of the city, Béziers is also the capital of the Languedoc vineyards, for those who like nice, full-bodied wines. A repository of Occitan culture, the town, which comes ablaze in August for the Feria and which keeps alive the memory of the golden days of its legendary

The nine locks at Fonséranes.
A. Spani/hemis.fr

rugby team, is also turned toward the future: proof of this is the "Latin quarter", which sprang up around the media library designed by Jean-Michel Wilmotte.
Tourist office - pl. du Forum - ☏ 04 99 41 36 36 - www.beziers-mediterranee.com.

A bed for the night. Neat, contemporary rooms in this small, comfortable hotel in the centre (8 minutes from the station). The breakfast room, warmed in winter by a fireplace, opens onto the Poets' Park.
Hôtel des Poètes - 80 allées Paul-Riquet - ☏ 04 67 76 38 66 - www.hoteldespoetes.fr - 14 rms. €63/€81 - ☕ €8.

Perched cathedral. Built on a terrace above the river Orb, the cathedral was the symbol of the power of the bishops of the diocese of Béziers from 760 to 1789. The Romanesque edifice, almost completely destroyed in 1209, underwent reconstructive work from 1215 to the 15th century. The western facade, flanked by two fortified towers (late 14th century), has a beautiful rose window. At the apse, the fortifications are a decorative element: the arches between the buttresses form machicolations. Don't miss the view from the top of the central bell tower and the unfinished cloister, which gives access to the Bishops' Garden. From here, there is a beautiful panorama of the church of St. Jude and of the Orb river, which is crossed by the old 13th century bridge.
Béziers Cathedral - pl. de la Révolution - Jun.-Aug.: 9 a.m.-7 p.m.; rest of the year: 9 a.m.-noon, 2:30-5:30 p.m..

Dining. A great address near the Place des Trois-Six. Such a tempting menu, you are spoilt for choice! Lightly snacked salmon with wasabi cream, creamy tagliatelle with shellfish, grilled sausage cooked in Alaryk de Béziers dark beer, meat cooked on the hot stone...
L'Attablé(e) - 23 r. des Anciens-Combattants - ☏ 04 30 41 59 28 - l-attablee-beziers.eatbu.com - closed Sun.-Mon. - wk. lunch deals €15/€18 - eve. deal/menu €29/€35.

For a picnic. Producers' and traders' market in Baltard-style market halls (1891).

Saturday mornings, organic market on Place Pablo-Neruda.
Market halls - *pl. Pierre-Sémard - daily except Mon. 7 a.m.-1:30 p.m.*

Sweet snack. Menodiciotto's artisanal ice creams and sorbets come straight from Italy, in a range of delicious flavours such as gianduja (with Piedmont hazelnuts) and pink grapefruit.
Glacier XIX - *20 pl. Jean-Jaurès* - 📞 *04 67 48 04 00 - 2-11 p.m.*

Feat of engineering on the Canal du Midi. Fonseranes Locks (👣 1 km west of the centre along the banks of the canal) are among the most impressive engineering structures on the Canal du Midi, and are listed as a UNESCO World Heritage Site. Originally made up of nine locks (only seven are still in service), this rare series of eight interlinked lock levels resembles a 312 m-long staircase through which boats can be raised or lowered 21.5 m. You can visit them on foot or by barge.
Fonseranes Locks - *Maison du Coche d'eau* - 📞 *04 99 41 36 36 - Jun.-Sept. : 10 a.m.-7 p.m.* (8 p.m. from mid-July to mid-August); *from mid-March to end of May and Oct-Nov. : 10 a.m.-6 p.m.; rest of the year: daily except Mon.-Tues. 10 a.m.-12:30 p.m., 1:30-5 p.m.*
Les Bateaux du Soleil - *Maison du Coche d'eau* - 📞 *04 67 94 08 79 - www.bateaux-du-soleil.fr - Jul.-Aug.: 9:30 a.m.-6 p.m. - €15/€30 (children €9/€15).*

Aperitif time. Handsome light wood decoration for this wine and tapas bar. On the terrace, in the shade of palm and plane trees, you can try all kinds of local wines and wines from further afield, selected with great care, accompanied by delicious platters of charcuterie or cheeses.
Le Chameau Ivre - *15 bd Jean-Jaurès* - 📞 *04 67 80 20 20 - 10 a.m.-2:30 p.m., 6 p.m.-midnight - closed Sun.-Mon. - tapas €6/€7.*

Feria. Around 15 August, the Feria sets Béziers alight with musical and bull-related events in the town, and bullfights in the bullring.
Info: www.feriabeziers.fr.

Place de l'Hôtel-de-Ville, Narbonne.
BrianScantlebury/Getty Images Plus

⑩ NARBONNE

🚲 **Bike hire.** 3 minutes' walk from the station, for the rental of bicycles, tandems, and e-bikes, with accessories.
Paulette bike rental - 11 bd Condorcet - ☏ 04 68 42 43 92 - paulette.bike/fr - daily except Sun. 8 a.m.-noon, 2-6:30 p.m. - Hybrid/mountain bikes from €18/day, e-bike €30/day - book online.

A thousand-year heritage. Capital of Roman Gallia Narbonensis, residence of the Visigoth kings, archiepiscopal city, lively trading port: discover old Narbonne by setting off on foot from Place de l'Hôtel-de-Ville, towered over by the Archbishops' Palace *(see opposite)*. Continue your stroll to the Place du Forum (site of the forum and the ancient capitole) and to Saint Sebastian's Church. The Horreum, a nicely restored Roman warehouse, is well worth a visit. Continue on to the St-Paul-Serge Basilica (early Christian crypt), the Chapel of the Pénitents-Bleus (18th century), and the old gunpowder magazine (17th century). If you still have time, take a stroll along the Promenade des Barques (Cours de la République) and over the footbridge that links it to the Cours Mirabeau on the right bank. A little further on is the Pont des Marchands, a Roman bridge incorporating a double row of colourful houses, and the Halles, a Baltard-style covered market dating from 1901.
Tourist office - 31 r. Jean-Jaurès - ☏ 04 68 65 15 60 - www.narbonne-tourisme.com.

A bed for the night. An intimate and modern hotel with cosy rooms and trendy decor, in a very quiet street just around the corner from the historic centre and a 12-minute walk from the railway station. With a sun terrace for sunbathing during the day or stargazing at night! Very friendly welcome.
The C Boutique Hôtel - 15 r. Suffren - ☏ 09 67 17 56 54 - www.cboutiquehotel.fr - 10 rms. €105/€175 - ☕ €12.

A trip to the palace. Together with the cathedral, the Archbishops' Palace forms a remarkable architectural ensemble, combining the religious, the military and the civil, where the centuries have left their mark, from the 12th (Old Palace) to the 19th (Town Hall). Its facade has three square towers: the Gilles-Aycelin keep, the St-Martial tower, and the Madeleine tower (the oldest). Between the first two, Viollet-le-Duc built the town hall in a neo-Gothic style. The foundation stone of Narbonne Cathedral was laid on 3 April 1272, sent from Rome by Pope Clement IV, former archbishop of the city.
Palais-musée des Archevêques - pl. de l'Hôtel-de-Ville - ☏ 04 68 90 26 38 - www.musees-narbonne.fr - Jun.-Sept. : 10 a.m.-6 p.m.; rest of the year: daily except Tues. 10 a.m.-12:45 p.m., 2-5 p.m. - €6 (ages 10-18: €4).

Dining. A bistro with a 1930's feel where fine produce (charcuterie and fish in particular) and bistro-style cuisine are celebrated. The well-stocked cellar and wine bar (complete with a fine tapas menu for aperitif time) will delight wine connoisseurs!
Le Petit Comptoir - 4 bd du Maréchal-Joffre - ☏ 04 68 42 30 35 - www.petitcomptoir.com - closed Sun. - €35/€50.

For a picnic. There is hustle and bustle aplenty in the wide aisles of the market halls, where colourful stalls full of fresh produce are manned by around 70 traders.
Market halls - cours Mirabeau - ☏ 04 68 32 63 99 - www.narbonne.halles.fr - daily 7 a.m.-2 p.m.

Gabare ahoy! A different way of seeing Narbonne is onboard a "gabare" (a traditional barge for transporting goods) on the Canal de la Robine, a UNESCO World Heritage site.
Le Solal - boat ride departures - ☏ 07 69 98 95 15 - www.petittrain-narbonne.fr - duration 1h - Apr.-May: 2:30 & 4 p.m.; Jun.: 2, 3:30 & 4:45 p.m.; Jul.-Aug.: 12:30, 2, 3:30, 4:45 & 6 p.m.; Sept. : 2, 3:30 & 4:45 p.m. - closed Thur. - €10 (ages 4-11: €6).

Barques en Scène Festival. Last weekend of August: bodegas, concerts and street arts.

🚲 **The Catalan coast.** *See p. 144.*

⑪ LEUCATE-LA FRANQUI

➜ Leucate-La Franqui station is located 2 km from Leucate-Village and 15 km from Port-

Kite surf in Port-Leucate.
Office de Tourisme de Leucate

Leucate. A shuttle (line 15) serves the different entities that make up Leucate.
Info: timetable on the tourist office website (see opposite).

Lagoon and beaches. On the coastline that separates the Étang de Leucate (Leucate lagoon) from the Mediterranean, miles of beaches and lots of tourist facilities attract summer holidaymakers in their thousands. Although shellfish farming and fishing have historically been the main activities on and around the lagoon, they now share its waters with nautical pastimes such as windsurfing, kite-surfing, and pleasure boating, which began to be developed in the 1970s. There's something for everyone!
Tourist office - Espace Henry de Monfreid - 185 r. du Veyret - Port-Leucate - 📞 04 68 40 91 31 - www.tourisme-leucate.fr.

A bed for the night. In the pretty fishing village of La Franqui, a 30-minute walk from the station or 5 minutes by shuttle bus, this pleasant guest house has several colourful rooms with sea or garden views. It also has a fine bar-restaurant, and bikes are for hire (on reservation).
La Stregheria - 18 av. de la Méditerranée - La Franqui - 📞 09 81 93 93 25 - www.la-stregheria.com - 4 rms. €100/€150.

Dining. It might look like a simple beach hut, but it has actually become something of institution and a place where art and inspiration reign. Biquet is a larger-than-life personality offering seafood cuisine based on the day's catch, shellfish dishes, and tellinas fried in garlic and parsley, often with the chef's own exotic touches.
Biquet-Plage - Chemin du Mouret - 📞 07 69 60 83 63 - biquet.kards.fr - 10 a.m.-1:30 a.m. - tapas €7/€18 - menu €30/€50.

Port-Leucate: take a dip. At Cap Leucate, make the most of the immense beaches, and if you have the time, why not hire a paddleboard, a pirogue or a canoe? Dinghy sailing, catamaran, windsurfing, and sand yachting hire and lessons available.
Cercle de voile du cap Leucate - base de la Marina - av. de la Pinède - 📞 04 68 40 72 66 - www.cercledevoile.com - Summer: 10 a.m.-6 p.m.; rest of the year: 10 a.m.-5 p.m.

Aperitif time. Enjoy a plate of oysters and a glass of local white wine in one of the typical oyster huts run by the producers at the Port-Leucate oyster centre. Why not try the famous "Caramoun" oyster, raised in "suspension", which gives these oysters more "bite".
Oyster hut - Port-Leucate - huitres-leucate.com - 📞 06 16 94 39 10 depending on the size of the oyster: €6/€10 the half-dozen.

◦ Panoramas and cliffs at Cap Leucate. From the viewpoint near the lighthouse at Cap Leucate, you see all along the coast from the Languedoc to the Albera Massif. Follow the cliffside path (take care, and be wary of causing rock falls), with the cliffs on your right, from which you can enjoy the splendid views out to sea over the Gulf of Lion. You finally reach La Franqui, a small seaside resort. Coussoules beach, a vast and still wild area, is an inviting place to take a dip in the sea after a nice hike.
Sentier du guetteur - starting from the Leucate-Plage lighthouse - 2h30 circuit - map can be downloaded from the tourist office website.

⑫ SALSES

A bed for the night. This charming bed and breakfast, located 5 minutes' walk from the station, offers an intimate haven set in 1,200 square metres of gardens. The villa's owners are antique dealers who have harmoniously combined period pieces with contemporary art to ensure you enjoy a comfortable and elegant stay.
Casa Montes - 1 clos des Abricotiers - ☎ 06 11 10 90 28 - www.casa-montes.com - 3 rms. €80/€110 *.*

Guardian of the Corbières. Emerging from the vineyards, the Fortress of Salses is poised between the Leucate lagoon and the mountains beyond. The aesthetic effect of the pink sandstone and red brick softens the severity of the monument, whose dimensions are impressive. Built in the 15th century, this star-shaped fort is a unique example of Spanish medieval military architecture in France, which Vauban later adapted to the requirements of modern artillery. You can still walk along the tops of the walls, affording a close-up view of the rounded crest of the curtain walls. The vaulted basement around the central courtyard served as stables, which could accommodate around 100 horses and 1500 men. The keep, divided into seven levels, housed the governor's residence and was used as a powder magazine in the 19th century.
Forteresse de Salses - 15 minutes' walk from the station - ☎ 04 68 38 60 13 - www.forteresse-salses.fr - 10 a.m.-6 p.m. - €8 (free entry to under 18s).

Dining. "The establishment is not suited to people in a hurry or merely seeking a simple snack": you have been warned! But this traditional restaurant (20 place settings only) will delight gourmets keen to discover Catalan gastronomy.
La Loge - 38 av. Xavier-Lloberes - ☎ 04 68 38 62 86 - www.lalogesalses.com - open for lunch and on Fri. and Sat. evenings for bookings. - lunch deal €26.50, single menu in the evenings at €28.50.

For a picnic. There is a market at Salses every Wednesday morning in the Place de la République.

⑬ RIVESALTES

➔ To get to the Rivesaltes camp memorial, located 7 km from the station, take an A2R taxi (☎ 04 68 64 08 00) or bus line 16 (www.sankeo.com); from the Rivesaltes terminus, direction Cap Roussillon, alight at the Espace Entreprises stop (15 min bus and 20 min walk).

Rivesaltes Memories. On the right bank of the Agly, Rivesaltes is one of the wine capitals of Roussillon. It was the birthplace of Marshal Joffre (1852-1931), whose equestrian statue stands on the central esplanade of the town. The house where Joffre was born is now a museum dedicated to his life and career. Yet the memories of Rivesaltes also contain the painful memory of the Rivesaltes camp *(see below)*.
Tourist office - 9 av. Ledru-Rollin - ☎ 04 68 64 73 23 - www.tourisme-rivesaltes.fr.
Marshall Joffre Museum - early Jul. to mid-Sept.: Tues.-Sat. 10:30 a.m.-noon, 3:30-6:30 p.m. - €3.

A bed for the night. 200 m from the train station, this late 19th century manor house now offers three superb guest rooms (one of which is a master suite) that have retained the character of the old bourgeois residences of yesteryear. The leafy courtyard with its garden furniture under a pergola is the ideal spot for relaxation. Set menu (on reservation), featuring regional specialties done in the house style.
La Maison d'Antoine - 19 av. Gambetta - ☎ 06 86 17 53 33 - lamaisondantoine.fr - 3 rms. €105 ⌑ - ✕ €25.

A page of history. The Rivesaltes camp recalls an inglorious page of national history: the site of one of the most important internment camps in Western Europe. Spanish Republicans, Jews, gypsies, prisoners of war, harkis, Guinean riflemen... More than 60,000 "undesirables" were interned here in 1941-1942, 1945-1948, and 1962-1966 in abominable living conditions. Created in 2015, the visit to the memorial includes an outdoor tour, with the remains of the barracks, and an underground museum designed by Rudy Ricciotti, designed to resemble a long subterranean corridor gradually opening up to the light.

Rivesaltes Camp Museum-Memorial - av. Christian-Bourquin - ✆ 04 68 08 39 70 - www.memorialcamprivesaltes.eu - Apr.-Oct.: 10 a.m.-6 p.m.; rest of the year: daily except Mon. 10 a.m.-6 p.m. - €9.50 (free entry for under 18s).

Dining. This restaurant in the heart of the Domaine Cazes offers food and wine pairings combining the estate's wines with Catalan and Mediterranean-inspired cuisine.

La Table d'Aimé - 4 r. Francisco-Ferrer - ✆ 04 68 34 35 77 - www.latabledaime.com - closed Sun. eve.-Mon. - menus €30/€40.

Apricot and Muscat festival. In July, the apricot takes centre stage for festivities including an apricot eating competition, in celebration of this emblematic fruit of Roussillon and Rivesaltes! Muscat-tasting sessions, "abricotade" cocktails, and a Catalan ball are also on the agenda.

14 PERPIGNAN

→ The new station opens on to the town centre on one side and the St-Assiscle district on the other. Take the town centre exit.

Catalan pride. Counts of Roussillon, kings of Majorca, Catalans and Aragonese have fought over the town down the centuries and have left many a mark. Le Castillet *(see opposite)* marks the medieval heart of the town, with its Catalan influences and streets paved with pink Villefranche-de-Conflent marble. The very lively Place de la Loge, with its pretty statue of *Venus* by Aristide Maillol (a sculptor born in Banyuls-sur-Mer), owes its name to the former maritime trade court, which adjoins the town hall. Built in 1397, it was remodelled and enlarged in the 16th century. To the north is Perpignan Cathedral, with its archetypal Catalan "cayroux" (brick and pebble) walls. It is flanked on the right by a square clock tower topped by a beautiful wrought iron cage (18th century) housing two 15th century bells. Finally, to the south of the city centre, your stroll takes you to the enormous Palace of the Kings of Majorca (1276-1344), with its Romanesque and Gothic architecture, and which occupies the entire hill of Puig del Rei. From the ramparts of its Spanish citadel there is a beautiful view of the coast.

Tourist office - pl. de la Loge - ✆ 04 68 66 30 30 - www.perpignantourisme.com.

A bed for the night. The Hotel de France is a historic establishment that first opened in 1833 and which has hosted many celebrities, including Salvador Dalí. It has a prime, central location, and is less than 20 minutes' walk from the station.

Less prestigious but ideally located between the town centre and the station (a 6-minute walk), the Nyx Hotel is a small, tastefully decorated family-run hotel. The rooms are not to be faulted, and some have a terrace and balcony.

Hôtel de France - 28 quai Sadi-Carnot - ✆ 04 68 84 80 35 - www.hoteldefrance-perpignan.fr - 24 rms. €59/€90 - ☕ €10.

Nyx Hotel - 62 bis av. du Gén.-de-Gaulle - ✆ 04 68 34 87 48 - nyxhotel.fr - 17 rms. €88/€160 - ☕ €12.

From the top of the Castillet. The Perpignan banner atop the Castillet bears the "blood and gold" colours of Catalonia. The edifice dominates the Place de la Victoire, its two large towers crowned with exceptionally high battlements and machicolations. Inside, the Casa Pairal Museum displays collections of archaeology, arts, and popular traditions, and details the monument's history. From the top of the tower (142 steps), you are treated to a view of the town's monuments, the Canigou, the Albera Massif to the south, and the Corbières Massif to the north.

Castillet - pl. de Verdun - ✆ 04 68 35 42 05 - Jun.-Sept.: 10:30 a.m.-6:30 p.m.; Oct.-May:

Perpignan Cathedral.
JackF/Getty Images Plus

daily except Mon. 11 a.m.-5:30 p.m. - €2 (aged under 26: free entry).

Dining. Right next-door to the cathedral, Le 17 attracts an in-the-know clientele. The chef is a real enthusiast who focuses on extra-fresh local produce to concoct refined dishes full of flavour, and where fish has pride of place. A delight for the eyes and the taste buds! Fine selection of wines to enjoy on the terrace. Booking recommended. Other possibility: La Galinette. To compose his beautiful menus, Christophe Comes has two aces up his sleeve: his talent, of course, but also his love of fine produce. The fish is caught locally and the vegetables come from the vegetable garden. The result? Honest, fine, fresh cuisine: a real treat!
Le 17 - 1 r. Cité-Bartissol - 04 68 38 56 82 - closed Sun.-Mon. (May-Sept.); Sun. and Mon.-Thurs. eve. (Oct.-Apr.) - lunch deals: €28, menu €27/€65.
La Galinette - 23 r. Jean-Payra - 04 68 35 00 90 - www.restaurant-galinette.com - closed Sun.-Mon. - lunch deal: 33 € - menus 70/78 €.

For a picnic. The Sala family has been running this grocery store since 1913. It owes its reputation to two specialities in particular: Collioure anchovies (in brine or boquerone tapas), and wild cod. You can also find what you need for a "cargolade" (a dish of snails cooked in their shells). The store front abounds with all kinds of dried fruit and vegetables, olives, and spices.
Maison Sala - 1 r. René-Paratilla - 04 68 51 03 75 - 8:30 a.m.-7 p.m. - closed Sun.-Mon.

Aperitif time. The indoor market halls house more than twenty craft eateries and street-food stalls where you can meet up at aperitif time to drink a glass of wine accompanied by some high-quality nibbles.
Les halles Vauban - quai Vauban - Tues.-Sat. 8 a.m.-8 p.m., Sun. 8 a.m.-3 p.m. The Bar des Halles closes at 2 in the morning on Fri. and Sat.

Festa Major. In late June, for one week, Catalan traditions are showcased. Big show on 23 June for the Fête de la St-Jean festivities.

Fabulous Journeys

A timeless journey on the Train Rouge (Red Train) of the Cathar Country and Fenouillèdes

From the Aude gorges to the Agly valley, from the Cathar country to the Fenouillèdes vineyards, we invite you to a real offbeat adventure by rail. On board the Train Rouge, the famous Red Train tourist railway, you will ride along a railway line that is more than a hundred years old, linking Axat (Aude) to Rivesaltes (Pyrénées-Orientales). You're in for a memorable day out, whatever the season or the stretch chosen to travel. And we're off! 2 hours' travel (not counting the stops) at 30 kph, across breathtaking scenery.

Immediate boarding

Having booked in advance and with tickets in hand, you'll be eager to get on your way as you wait inside the small country station of Axat, starting point of your Fabulous Journey through the mountains, between the Pyrenees and the Corbières Massif. And finally the train, with its old-fashioned charm, pulls up at the platform! With everyone so keen to get onboard, there is already a cheery atmosphere. In the space of a few minutes, you will no doubt get to know your fellow passengers. The adventure can begin.

Climbing to the heights through pine and fir

The locomotive glides slowly along the rails for a contemplative ride to the rhythm of the driver's whistle. From the comfort of your seat, you can enjoy the magic of this heritage railway, with a real sense of freedom in the great outdoors. The line climbs gently through a dense forest of hundred-year-old conifers where you can expect to come across roe deer, stags, wild boars... and even (who knows?) the odd

The red train crosses the Fenouillèdes.
P. Benoist/TPCF/CRT Occitanie

ALL IN THE SAME TRAIN!

Few tourist trains can boast the precious Tourism & Handicap label, especially when the route is off the beaten track. The stations and platforms of the Red Train have been made accessible and modernised by railway enthusiasts with the aim of allowing anyone and everyone to enjoy this extraordinary rail journey. The carriages have been specially adapted with lifts and suitable toilet facilities.

Pyrenean bear! You then get to the Col Campérié (511 m altitude) before starting the descent to Puilaurens.

Dropping down to Fenouillèdes

As soon as the Col has been crossed, the landscape changes dramatically. The atmosphere takes a Mediterranean turn, with the valley opening towards the east and the quality of the light already heralding the first vineyards and olive groves of Catalan country. As it passes over the Lapradelle-Puilaurens viaduct, the train gets almost within touching distance of the tiled village rooftops and the tops of the fir trees. If you look up, you will see why the impregnable Cathar castle of Puilaurens is known as one of the "citadelles du vertige" ("citadelles of the dizzying heights"). Bolder adventurers may seek to climb up to it. For the others, the ride continues, accompanied by the commentary of railway enthusiasts who will share with you their anecdotes and their passion for a rail infrastructure dating from the 1960s.

From the Galamus gorges to the Maury vineyards

On your left, the first vineyards and the garrigue share the slopes of the mountains up to the limestone crests of the Corbières Massif. Suddenly, a vast breach seems to split the impassable wall: the Gorges de Galamus, overlooked by the fascinating hermitage of Saint-Antoine de Galamus, built in a natural cavity in the cliff. You can get to the gorges and the hermitage from Saint-Paul-de-Fenouillet by shuttle bus (€1/trip). Otherwise, stay on the train for Maury, 19 minutes further along the line.

Vineyards and wine-tasting

The train passes through several appellation vineyards: Maury, Rivesaltes, Côtes du Roussillon Villages, Latour de France, Lesquerde and Tautavel... and the good news is that wine tastings are proposed at the halts along the line during the summer. And if you have a little time, why not visit the cellars, such as the one at Mas Amiel, to sample a chocolate and Maury wine pairing! On the skyline, Quéribus castle seems to watch over the entire valley.

Halt!

The Red Train continues on its way to Rivesaltes, but it is at Cases-de-Pène that you get off (to spend the night or make the return trip). Walk up the path (a 45-min walk from the station) which leads to the hermitage of Notre-Dame de Pène, where its caretaker awaits (in high season) in a most unusual western-like setting.

1 day (return trip) without stops (which are optional) - Apr.-May: Tue., Thu. and Sun. dep. from Rivesaltes; Jun.: Tue., Thu., Fri. and Sun. dep. from Rivesaltes and Axat; Jul.-Aug.: Tue., Fri. and Sun. dep. from Rivesaltes and Axat; - €26 return - www.letrainrouge.fr.

THE MEDITERRANEAN LINE

THE CATALAN COUNTRY LINE

Departing from Perpignan, this line offers up some gorgeous landscapes. First stop at Ille-sur-Têt, in the heart of the Roussillon, where the majestic mineral columns, or "orgues" with their organ pipe-like shapes, await your discovery. The route then winds its way between the foothills of Mount Canigou and the river Têt, to finally arrive at the edge of the Catalan Pyrenees Regional Natural Park, with its magnificent natural and architectural heritage.

★ PERPIGNAN TO VILLEFRANCHE-DE-CONFLENT - 5 DAYS

- Non-stop trip: 47min
- Frequency : 8 liO trains/day
- Timetables: www.ter.sncf.com/occitanie/se-deplacer/fiches-horaires
- Non-stop trip: €1
- Onboard services: bike transport authorised in the liO trains
- Connected lines: Train Jaune (Yellow Train) line from Villefranche-de-Conflen; Mediterranean and Côte Vermeille lines from Perpignan

Where best to sit to admire the landscape? On the left of the train in the direction of travel for the best view of the Canigou.

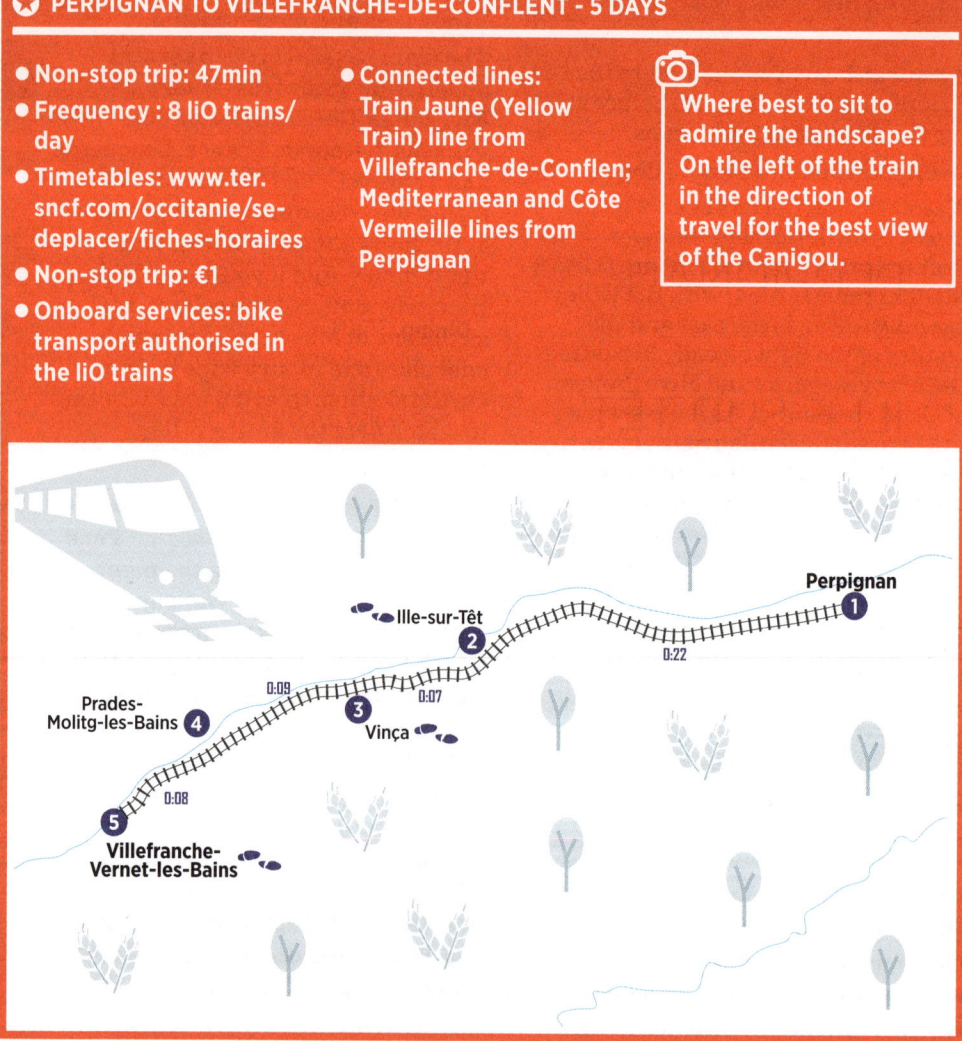

The majestic mineral columns of Ille-sur-Têt.
Ocean Prod/Getty Images Plus

❶ PERPIGNAN

See the Mediterranean line p. 56.

❷ ILLE-SUR-TÊT

Têt on high. In the heart of the plain, above the ramparts, the red-tiled roofs of Ille-sur-Têt mark the landscape. This small town on the plain, whose name, "Ille", is pronounced as "ee" and not as " eel»", is situated in the heart of an immense orchard of apricot, peach and cherry trees, irrigated by the Têt and the Boulès, its tributary. Hardly surprising, then, that the fruit and veg market is such a lively place!
<u>Tourist office</u> - pl. Henri-Demay - ☎ 04 68 57 99 00 - www.tourisme-roussillon-conflent.fr.

A bed for the night. A 4-minute walk from the station, in a vast, skilfully restored 19th century manor house, there are four spacious and refined guest rooms with the flavour of yesteryear. The lounge and library are also fitted out with period furniture. In fine weather, breakfast is served on the large terrace overlooking the flower garden.
<u>Les Buis</u> – 37 r. Carnot - ☎ 04 68 57 67 43 - www.lesbuis.com - 🛏 -4 rms. €95/€145 ☕.

Dining. The dining room makes up for its small size with its warm character. In season, the eponymous little square furnishes welcome shade. There is also a comprehensive menu, with very good and generously-portioned Mediterranean dishes.
<u>Le Square</u> - 55 av. Pasteur - ☎ 04 68 61 48 40 - closed Sun.-Mon. - €15/€25.

Ille the mysterious. A 30-minute walk north of Ille-sur-Têt along the D2 road, the water here has worn its way into the soft rock, causing columns to emerge from the ground, topped by harder, less easily eroded stone. Mysterious forms, lacy stone patterns, fairy chimneys... The ochre hues gleam in the sunlight. Follow the guided trail that leads you to this mineral amphitheatre, sculpted by the river Têt. It was when the Pyrenees collapsed more than five million years ago that the ancient hill was transformed into a sandy cirque.
<u>Orgues d'Ille</u> - chemin de Regleilles - ☎ 04 68 84 13 13 - orgues.netinfo.pro - mid-Jun. to mid-Sept. : 9:15 a.m.-8 p.m.; rest of the year : contact for details. - €5 (ages 10-13: €3.50).

Hiking excursion in the Canigou

➔ **Setting off from Prades station.**

Whether you are on the summits of the Corbières, the Conflent, or the Cerdanya, in the Perpignan plain, or even on the beaches of the Roussillon, you can see it from everywhere: with its altitude of 2,784 m, the Canigou rises high above the orchards. You can get there from Prades provided that you are dropped off at the Cortalets refuge by an approved guide. From there, you need to cover an altitude difference of 650 m (2h hike) to reach the Canigou summit. To the west of the chalet, walk along the GR10 hiking trail that runs alongside a pond and then up the eastern slope of the Joffre Peak. Leave this path at the Perdrix fountain, at the point where it descends towards Vernet, and continue climbing to the left under the ridge. A winding path among the rocks takes you up to the summit (3.5 hours there and back; suitable for all walkers).

A cross and the remains of a stone hut used in the 18th and 19th centuries for scientific observations crown the summit. At the top, the panorama is immense, to the north-east, east and south-east, towards the plain of Roussillon and the Mediterranean coast. Sometimes you can see far into Catalonia, all the way to the Costa Brava. To the northwest and west, the crystalline basement ranges of the eastern Pyrenees succeed one another on several levels, contrasting with the more rugged limestone ridges of the Corbières Massif. Magical!

Approved carriers from Prades: Castellane (le-canigou.fr - ☏ 04 68 05 27 08), Le Canigou en 4x4 (canigou-en-4x4.com - ☏ 04 68 05 99 89) or Passcanigo (www.passcanigo.com - ☏ 06 82 04 17 81). Departure at 8/8:30 a.m. and return at 3/3:30 p.m., or at 11 a.m. and return at 6 p.m. Between €25 & €30 return.

Mount Canigou
A.and_D/Getty Images Plus

③ VINÇA

Life size. This fortified town has an 18th-century church built in the Southern French Gothic style, whose interior is surprisingly richly decorated: nine Baroque altarpieces, including that of Our Lady of the Rosary by Josep Sunyer; a Pietà; a 15th-century Entombment scene; and an imposing high altar dedicated to the Virgin of the Assumption. It is also a nature destination thanks to its lake, which is the starting point for many hikes in the region.
Tourist office - Winegrowers' cooperative - 6 av. de la Gare - 04 68 05 49 86 - www.tourisme-canigou.com.

A bed for the night. A 13-minute walk from the station, this shady campsite on the waterfront also offers mobile homes by the night or by the week. Its private beach promises a pleasant stay with swimming, canoeing, fishing, mountain biking, and hiking.
Camping Lac de Vinça (Escoumes campsite) - r. des Escoumes - 04 68 05 84 78 - www.camping-lac-de-vinca.com - closed from mid-Oct. to mid-April - 114 places, mobile homes from €80/night.

Dining. As there are few restaurants in the vicinity, you will be only too happy to take advantage of the restaurant/tapas bar at this water park by the lake in Vinça. You can enjoy grills, salads and dishes of the day, or just a sweet snack, on one of its two shaded terraces.
AquaGliss 66 - lac des Escoumes - www.aquagliss.fr - closed from mid-Sept. to end of Apr.

To the North Balconies of Canigou. Among the many possible walks, an easy 5.5 km loop (2h10) takes you to various panoramas of the Roc del Moro and the Canigou massif.
PR76: Vinça - The Balconies of Canigou, Marcevol Loop - download map from www.tourisme-canigou.com.

④ PRADES-MOLITG-LES-BAINS

➔ The station serves Prades, a stopover point described below.

Town in pink. Ensconced amidst opulent orchards, Prades nestles between the foothills of Mount Canigou and the alluvial plain of the Têt. Its buildings adorned with the pink marble of Conflent, the centre is a maze of narrow streets and alleys revealing decorated porches and facades, along with fountains and old washhouses. Rebuilt in the 17th century, the Church of St. Peter has nevertheless kept its typical Southern Romanesque bell tower. In the choir, the spectacular altarpiece (1696-1699) by the Catalan sculptor Josep Sunyer features more than a hundred sculpted figures and tells the story, in six tableaus, of the life of the Apostle Peter, whose statue is enthroned in the centre. The town is the starting point of many hikes. Every summer it also becomes a meeting place for music lovers, with the Pablo Casals Festival.
Tourist office - 10 pl. de la République - 04 68 05 41 02 - www.tourisme-canigou.com.

A bed for the night. A 4-minute walk from the station, this is a beautiful guest house with cosy rooms and a family atmosphere. The front of the building looks on to the main street, but at the back it conceals a pleasant little garden where you can enjoy breakfast or dinner when the weather is fine.
Maison Prades - 51 av. du Gén.-de-Gaulle - 06 89 17 91 31 - www.maisonprades.com - 5 rms. €82/€92 - set menu: €28.

Dining. Here, there is no point hanging around on the ground floor: head upstairs to discover a modern and comfortable dining room, where a friendly young couple lay on some fine cuisine with market produce that is very much in keeping with the times. The chef's speciality? Lobster fricassee in lobster sauce and rice vermicelli…
Le Galie - 3 av. du Gén.-de-Gaulle - 04 68 05 53 76 - www.restaurantlegalie.com - closed Sun.-Mon. and Tue.-Thurs. eve. - lunch deal: €20, menus: €32/€73.

Chapels festival. In the summer, some thirty concerts take place in St-Michel-de-Cuxa, St-Pierre de Prades, and in some of the region's most beautiful churches.
Festival Pablo Casals - www.prades-festival-casals.com - late Jul. to mid-Aug.

⑤ VILLEFRANCHE-VERNET-LES-BAINS

→ The station serves Villefranche-de-Conflent, the stopover described here.

The strategic bulwark of the Pyrenees. Villefranche-de-Conflent served for a long time as an outpost for the kingdom of Aragon: fortified from the outset, completed in the 17th century by Vauban with Fort Liberia overlooking it, the town is listed as a UNESCO World Heritage Site as one of the Major Sites of Vauban. Enter the fortified town through the Porte de France, opened under Louis XVI, or through the Porte d'Espagne, redesigned as a monumental entrance in 1791, and where the machinery of the old drawbridge remains. What a pleasure it is to stroll along the Rue St-Jacques and Rue St-Jean, whose 13th and 14th century houses, coloured with the pink marble of Villefranche-de-Conflent, have often retained their porches and beautiful wrought-iron guild signs.

Tourist office - 33 r. St-Jacques - 04 68 05 41 02 - www.tourisme-canigou.com.

A bed for the night. What a joy to take refuge in the fortified town at nightfall! Occupying the former post office building, the establishment offers four guest rooms, within a less than 10-minute walk from the station. Bathroom with hot tub. Sauna and kitchen access. Generous breakfast and a very warm welcome.

Chambres d'hôtes de l'Ancienne Poste - 31 r. St-Jacques - 04 68 30 97 35 - www.ancienne postedelacite.com - 3 rms. €130/€150.

Double-tour of the ramparts. The circuit of the ramparts allows you to discover their two levels of galleries: a vaulted walkway, built into the thickness of the wall in the 11th century, and a sheltered upper gallery (17th century), pierced by loopholes opening on to the outside. In the 13th and 14th centuries, the curtain walls were flanked by round towers, and in the 17th century by six bastions (clockwise from the Porte de France: Corneilla, la Montagne, la Reine, le Roi, la Boucherie and le Dauphin). Between them, an open-air walkway, punctuated with arches, allows you to discover the northern front, along the Têt.

The Ramparts - 2 r. St-Jean (near the Porte d'Espagne) - 04 68 05 87 05 - www.villefranchedeconflent.fr - Jul.-Aug.: 10 a.m.-8 p.m.; Jun. and Sept.: 10 a.m-7 p.m.; Apr.-May and Oct.: 11 a.m.-6 p.m.; Nov.-Mar.: 1-5 p.m. - closed Jan. - €5 (under 10s: €2).

Dining. Julian Blaya is the chef who presides over the kitchen of this fine restaurant in the walled city. Expect creative cuisine, prepared with good local produce, and beautifully presented. The menu changes regularly.

La Senyera - 81 r. St-Jean - 04 68 96 17 65 - la-senyera-restaurant.eatbu.com - closed Wed., Tues. and Sun. eve. - menus €20/€39.

For a picnic. On the very lively Rue St-Jean, you will find grocery stores and delicatessens for purchasing both the savoury (charcuterie, cheese, mushrooms) and the sweet (such as rousquille biscuits and honey). Many craft stores and shops selling Catalan products (including the famous "vigatane" sandals) also ply their trade here.

Taking to the heights. From the small fortified St-Pierre bridge (1263) crossing over the Têt, start your ascent to Fort Libéria via the "thousand steps" staircase, or by the path (20min - warning: a demanding climb). Built on Belloc mountain under the direction of Vauban, the fort follows the contours by means of its three enclosures constructed one above the other. Restructured in the 19th century, it was at this time that the famous staircase (which in reality has 734 steps) was added, all in pink marble. From the fort you are treated to impressive views of the valleys and the Canigou.

Fort Libéria - 04 68 96 34 01 - www.fort-liberia.com - Jul.-Aug.: 9 a.m.-8 p.m.; May-Jun. and Sept.: 10 a.m.-7 p.m.; rest of the year: 10 a.m.-6 p.m. - €7 (ages 5-10: €4.20).

→ This is where you take the connection to the famous Yellow Train (Train Jaune - see p. 66).

The Train Jaune (Yellow Train) line starts from Villefranche-de-Conflent.
Guillaume Payen/CRT Occitanie

THE CATALAN COUNTRY LINE

THE YELLOW TRAIN LINE

Starting out from Villefranche-de-Conflent, the "Canary", i.e.: the famous Train Jaune (Yellow Train), takes off for the heights of Cerdanya, via the highest station in France, at an altitude of 1593 m. Taking in historic strongholds, peaceful villages, and resorts with many outdoor activities, the Yellow Train and its stops promise a breathtaking journey.

FROM VILLEFRANCHE-DE-CONFLENT TO LATOUR-DE-CAROL - 9 DAYS

- Non-stop trip: 3h05
- Frequency : 3 liO trains/day
- Timetables: www.ter.sncf.com/occitanie/se-deplacer/fiches-horaires
- Non-stop trip: €22.50 - tickets on sale only at Villefranche, Mont-Louis, Font-Romeu and Bourg-Madame stations, depending on availability; for other stations, tickets are sold directly by the ticket inspectors on board the train
- Useful to know: In summer, availability is limited, but as it is not possible to make a reservation, make sure you arrive about 30 min before the train departure time
- Line connections: Catalan country line from Perpignan to Villefranche-de-Conflent; Pyrenees line from Latour-de-Carol

Where best to sit to admire the landscape? Wherever you sit, you've a clear view of the country all around!

FABULOUS JOURNEYS BY RAIL

The «Canary», hanging in the air.
Office de Tourisme de Font-Romeu/CRT Occitanie

① VILLEFRANCHE-VERNET-LES-BAINS

See the Catalan country line p. 64.

② THUÈS-CARANÇA

→ **No accommodation near the station: this is a visit to be done in the day from Villefranche. Remember to take a picnic!**

→ **As the stop is optional on the Yellow Train line, you must signal to the driver that you want to get on or off here.**

Carança gorges. The gorges offer a wide choice of waymarked walks, lasting from 1 hour to several days. What with rocks, suspension bridges, footbridges and vertiginous ledges, there is something to appeal to all levels of hiker. A short loop (approx. 1.5 hours) follows the gorge, passing via a waterfall and a footbridge. The path climbs steeply up from the other bank of the river to a crossroads where you turn right (signposted "parc auto par chambre d'eau" - Chambre d'Eau car park). After a narrow cliff-edge passage, the path descends along a penstock to the car park. A long loop (3h) is reserved for good hikers, who need to come well-equipped and with a head for heights: here too, follow the river up to the first footbridge, but instead of crossing it, continue straight on along a path that keeps climbing. The main difficulty is the return to the other bank: via a monkey bridge and a fairly vertiginous ledge equipped with handrails.

Access via the car park, a 5-minute walk from the station.

③ MONT-LOUIS-LA CABANASSE

→ **The station is about a 20-minute walk from the village of Mont-Louis.**

🚲 **Bike hire. Mountain bikes, hybrid bikes and e-bikes can be rented throughout the Cerdanya-Capcir region. Various pick-up points to collect your equipment, including one at the Yellow Train station in Mont-Louis/La Cabanasse.**

Lac des Bouillouses, Circuit of the 9 lakes of the Carlit hike.
F. Guiziou/hemis.fr

<u>Eco Bike</u> *- 2 r. des Fontêtes - ☎ 07 87 71 64 72 - www.ecobike.fr - from €35/4h or €55/day - advance booking required.*

Solar fortress. The Louis in whose honour the fortified city, built by Vauban, is named is obviously Louis XIV. A fine homage to the so-called Sun-King, the town is also known today for its solar furnace, installed in 1953. Its structure, made up of nearly 1,400 mirrors, concentrates the sun's rays on to a focal point, enabling temperatures of 3,000 to 3,500°C to be obtained. Representing a promising step forward towards the exploitation of new energies, this solar furnace has been used, since July 1993, for the production of ceramic art, among other things. You will discover its concrete applications and, depending on the weather conditions, you will be able to witness live firing of ceramics or bronze casting.
<u>Tourist office</u> *- 6 bd Vauban - ☎ 04 68 04 21 97 - www.mont-louis.net.*
<u>Solar furnace</u> *- bd Vauban - ☎ 04 68 04 14 89 - guided tour only (1h) - 5-7 guided tours daily - 10:30 a.m.-6 p.m. - closed Nov. to mid-Apr. - €7.50 (ages 6-16: €5.90).*

A bed for the night. Less than 15 minutes' walk from the station, before entering the walled city, this massive stone building houses a hotel complex and a balneotherapy centre with a great view of the valley. The rooms, which are perfectly decent, come with a considerable asset: free entry to the Aquaforme facilities (heated swimming pool, jacuzzi, steam room, sauna, etc.). Various care packages are optionally available.
<u>Le Clos Cerdan</u> *- RN 116 - ☎ 04 68 04 23 29 - www.lecloscerdan.com - ⌇ - 60 rms. €89/€146 - ⌇ €13 - half board or full board available.*

La Citadelle. Built in 1679, this citadel has always had a military purpose and was able to accommodate up to 2,500 soldiers. Since 1964 it has been home to the National Commando Training Centre-1st Shock regiment (CNEC). It has a square floor plan with bastions at the corners. Three ravelins protect the curtain walls. Note the Puits des Forçats, literally "Slaves' Well", a wooden 18th century structure, which was used to supply the citadelle with water.
<u>Guided tours</u> *(1h) organised by the tourist office - Jul.-Aug.: at 10 a.m., 11 a.m., 2 p.m. and*

3 p.m., Sun. at 10 a.m. and 2 p.m.; rest of the year : daily exc. Sun. at 11 a.m and 2 p.m. - €6.50 (ages 11-17: €4.50) - proof of ID required.

For a picnic. In preparing for your hikes, you can buy fresh and local produce (cheese, charcuterie) at the Mont-Louis market on Thursday mornings, in the Place de l'Église.

Great mountain bike country. At the crossroads of Capcir and Cerdanya, Mont-Louis is the ideal starting point for exploring these majestic mountains by bike. In Cerdanya, you can breathe it all in! Here the air here is pure and, to top it all, you get the best of the sunshine. On the Capcir side, where the slopes are more or less rugged, the wooded massifs with their mountain pines, Scots pines and firs are served by forest roads offering multiple excursion routes.

Hiking around the Lac des Bouillouses. At an altitude of 2,017 m, in the heart of a listed site with 27 natural lakes, the Lac des Bouillouses lies in a beautiful setting. A dam has transformed it into an impressive 180-hectare reservoir that supplies the irrigation canals and hydroelectric plants of the Têt valley. There are a number of hiking options, with several waymarked routes ranging from 6.5 km to 9.7 km (allow 2h20 to 3h30 - free information sheet available at the Info Point), including the Circuit of the 9 lakes of the Carlit (from the Bones Hores refuge car park).
In Jul.-Aug. and the w'ends of Jun. and Sept., access is by liO 564 coach up to Pla de Barrès, then on foot or by shuttle bus (every 15 min from 7 a.m.-7 p.m., then every 30 min from 7 p.m.-9 p.m. - €5, ages 5-12: €2). Access also possible by the chairlift of Font-Romeu.

Dining at the Lac des Bouillouses. This vast panoramic terrace overlooking the lake is in a lovely setting. This large mountain restaurant offers simple but wholesome food, with all kinds of grilled dishes. Ideal for lunch before or after a hike. Possibility of spending the night in a refuge.
Hôtel-restaurant Les Bones Hores - ☏ 04 68 04 24 22 - www.boneshores.com - closed Nov.-Apr. - menus €24.

➜ The route to Thuès-Carança is particularly spectacular and breathtaking. Pont Gisclard bridge, suspended 80 m above the river, is at a dizzying height. Further on, to the right, amidst the terraced crops, are the hamlets of St-Thomas-les-Bains and Prats-Balaguer. The line then takes you over the elegant Séjourné viaduct, 2.5 km before Thuès.

④ BOLQUÈRE-EYNE

➜ The station is a 15-minute walk from the village of Bolquère. This is an optional stop on the Yellow Train line: signal to the driver if you want to alight or board here.

The highest station in France... but that's not all! Perched at 1,592 m, Bolquère holds the national altitude record for a railway station! The pretty mountain village is a pleasant place to be all year round: in winter you can ski at the Pyrénées 2000 resort, and in summer you can take the time to discover the region's fine local fare. Bolquère is a place that remains very attached to the traditions of pastoralism, typical of the region, and to the high quality of its produce: you can find this out for yourself, by frequenting the restaurants, hoteliers, and local producers. With its outdoor sports and its gastronomic delights, Bolquère is far more than just the highest railway station in France!
Tourist office - av. du Serrat-de-l'Ours - ☏ 04 68 30 12 42 - www.pyrenees2000.com.

A bed for the night. A 25-minute walk from the station but just 5 minutes from the town centre, former mountain pasture granaries grouped in a hamlet have been transformed into elegant chalets. Refined decor and meticulous service. Plus point: everyone gets to share a chalet-spa (sauna, hammam, jacuzzi), where it is great to unwind after a day's exertions in the great outdoors. Ideal for an authentic mountain break!
Les Chalets Secrets - 2 bis chemin de Font-Romeu - ☏ 06 13 03 86 61 - www.leschalets-secrets.com - 10 chalets (2/13 pers.) from €160 per night (2 nights min. in high season).

Dining. This restaurant, with its focus on local cuisine, has been awarded the Bistrot de Pays label: you will find all the region's typical dishes, perfectly prepared and served up using quality local products. Veal is the great speciality here: the last remaining breeder in Bolquère provides meat from calves raised on their mother's milk, giving it an exceptional flavour. To keep things fresh, the menu changes daily according to the produce available. A gastronomic stop not to be missed!
Le Lassus - 14 pl. Pierre-Patau - 09 74 56 14 70 - www.restaurant-lassus.fr - closed Sat. lunch and Sun. - menus €17.50/€35.

For a picnic. In both winter and summer, there is a market every Monday morning at the foot of the Pyrénées 2000 slopes.

An adventure holiday. In addition to the Pyrénées 2000 ski area, Bolquère offers plenty to do for mountain thrill-seekers, both in summer and winter, such as canyoning, snowshoeing, horse riding, riverboarding and rafting.
Bureau Montagne Nature - av. du Serrat-de-l'Ours - 06 16 23 38 01 - www.aventurine-rando.com - site office open 6:15-7:15 p.m.

What a magnificent mountain! Serge Rossell, a mountain guide and ski instructor based in Bolquère, can serve as your guide on all the region's hiking trails, according to your wishes and physical abilities. A keen advocate of pastoralism and the agricultural heritage of Bolquère, he can organise outings to visit the farms and meet the shepherds of the region. And in winter, ski excursions are available.
Serge Rossell - pl. de la Mairie - 06 08 33 78 72.

⑤ FONT-ROMEU-ODEILLO-VIA

→ The Font-Romeu-Odeillo-Via station is a 45-minute walk from Font-Romeu and serves these three eponymous villages. In season (Dec.-Mar. and Jul.-Aug.), there are free shuttles between the station and the tourist office. Otherwise, take a taxi.
Altitude Taxis - 06 22 86 85 40.

Bike hire. Bikes for hire in the station or from www.ouibike.net (with bike delivery and pick-up service).

The outdoor activities capital. Bordered by a lush pine forest and sheltered from the north winds, Font-Romeu occupies a prime spot in the region of Cerdanya. Its altitude, its sunshine, and its exceptional air quality all played a part in a ski resort being set up here. Its sports facilities enable athletes from the world over to train here. And the casual outdoor sports enthusiast will not feel left out either, as there is a wide range of mountain activities for all levels: climbing, mountaineering, caving, rafting, hydrospeed (riverboarding), etc. In winter, there is snowshoeing and warm water canyoning.
Tourist office - 82 av. Emmanuel-Brousse - 04 68 30 68 30 - font-romeu.fr.
Aventure Pyrénéenne - Maison de la Montagne - 41 av. Emmanuel-Brousse - 04 68 30 58 54 - aventure-pyreneenne.com. Team of guides proposing lots of outdoor activities.

A bed for the night. In the heart of the resort, this family-run hotel has rooms decorated in a contemporary style with a mountain feel, some with a balcony and view of the Pyrenees. Jacuzzi, sauna and covered pool on the roof.
Le Grand Tétras - 14 av. Emmanuel-Brousse - 04 68 30 01 20 - www.hotelgrandtetras.fr - 36 rms. €114/€160 - €12.

Dining. Put your skis or hiking boots to one side! At the entrance to the resort, you are sure to fall for the charm of this inviting cottage-style restaurant with its predominantly wooden decor. On the menu: a fine selection of Catalan dishes and regional wines. The owner is a great fan of fine produce (choice meats, local vegetables) and has even created his own ham cellar.
La Chaumière - 96 av. Emmanuel-Brousse - 04 68 30 04 40 - www.restaurantlachaumiere.fr - closed Mon, May-Jun. and Oct.-Nov. - lunch deal: €19.50 - menus: €35.

For a picnic. Four addresses in one: cheese shop, delicatessen (organic vegetables and fruit), wine cellar, and restaurant. Here you will find a wide selection of delicious cheeses, quality charcuterie, and other regional products. All

There are lots of things to do in Font-Romeu.
toos/Getty Images Plus

THE YELLOW TRAIN LINE

🚵 **Mountain bike rides.** With forty waymarked circuits for all levels on 500 km of cycling trails, mountain bike enthusiasts are in for a treat. The chairlifts from La Calme take downhill mountain bikers to the top of the slopes.
"Espace VTT-FFC" of the Catalan Pyrenees - sitesvtt.ffc.fr/sites/pyrenees-catalanes/ - trails map on sale from the tourist office.

6 SAILLAGOUSE

Delicious ham! The village of Saillagouse is nestled in the heart of Cerdanya, in a peaceful and bucolic setting. It is above all a centre of production for the famous Cerdan sausages. *"Butifarre"*, *"foet"* and *"llonganisse"*: once tasted, never forgotten! If you really have a taste for it, don't miss a visit to the natural drying room with 1,500 hams in the Cerdan Charcuterie Museum. Find out all about this traditional culinary craft.
Tourist office - 1 pl. du Roser - ☎ 04 68 04 15 47 - pyrenees-cerdagne.com.
Musée de la Charcuterie cerdane - rte d'Estavar - ☎ 04 68 30 14 27 - Jun.-Sept. : Tues.-Sat. 10 a.m.-noon, 3-7 p.m. - free entry.

Dining and overnighting. The Planes hotel-restaurant is a former coaching inn with renovated rooms, a 10-minute walk from the station. Its annex, the Planotel, dates from the 1970s. You have access to a swimming pool with sliding roof and a 1,400 m² park. The restaurant offers typical mountain cuisine in a rustic setting. The game, hunted and cooked by the establishment, is particularly famous in the region.
Hôtel Planes et Planotel - 6 pl. de Cerdagne - ☎ 04 68 04 72 08 - www.chezplanes.com - 🛏 - 18 rms. €90/€120 - 🍽 12 € - 🍴 lunch deal €19 - menus €36/€50.

For a picnic. Here, in the heart of one of the centres of Catalan sausage production, is a shop where you can fill your knapsack with hams, cured sausages, *Boles de Picolat*, *foets*, pâtés... On site you can try platters of charcuterie and cheese, accompanied by a glass of wine (booking required).
Charcuterie Bonzom - rte Nationale - ☎ 04 68 30 14 27 - www.charcuterie-catalane-bonzom.

these good foods can be found on the restaurant's menu, where you can enjoy cheese specialities such as fondue or raclette.
La Ferme des Lloses - 3 av. du Mar.-Joffre - ☎ 04 68 04 79 51 - Jul.-Aug., Christmas and February hols. : 10 a.m.-2 p.m., 5-10 p.m.; rest of the year: contact for details

Open-air museum. The municipal forest of Font-Romeu is the setting for an outdoor museum bringing together some twenty contemporary works by artists from the region. This pleasant cultural trail, lined with sculptures of all sizes, in wood, stone, resin, bronze or metal, also offers a breathtaking view of the valley. Along the way, rest a while on the unique benches, made from old skis or snowboards.
Museum without walls - museesansmurs.e-monsite.com - dep. from beside the Casino - leaflet from the tourist office - free access.

Jazz Altitude Festival. In summer, the town comes alive with a series of jazz concerts. You will find an easygoing atmosphere, with cocktails in the company of the musicians after the concerts.

com - 8 a.m.-12:30 p.m., 3-7:30 p.m. - closed Sun. afternoon and Mon.

Potters' market. At the start of August, the "potters' market" ("marché des potiers") is held, and has been for more than 30 years: introduction to pottery, demonstrations in the gardens of the town hall, and exhibitions of Saillagouse craftspersons.

On the red soil of Saillagouse. An easy hiking trail (loop from the town hall - blue signposting - 1h30) on land composed of reddish silt, clay, schist debris, granite and sand, which give the region around Saillagouse its distinctive colour, long appreciated by the potters of the village. With a change in altitude of less than 250 m, this walk is pleasant and accessible to all.

7 STE-LÉOCADIE

→ As there is no hotel near the station, this is a stop to be done as a day trip from Saillagouse or Bourg-Madame. Take a picnic.

→ As the stop is optional on the Yellow Train line, you must signal to the driver that you want to get on or off here.

Getting to know Cerdanya. The Cal Mateu farmhouse, which houses the Cerdanya Museum, traces the history of the Cerdanya's attachment to France. This handsome 17th-18th century building is the setting for various permanent and temporary exhibitions on shepherds, ploughmen, haymaking, and the manufacturing of gourds made from animal skins. All these exhibitions recount the local history, that of a border area, and the life of this former agricultural estate that was a working farm until 1952. The orchard and the vegetable garden abound in ancient local varieties, fodder plants, and cereals, which allowed the people here to live in self-sufficiency and feed their livestock.

Musée de Cerdagne - next to the town hall - 04 68 04 08 05 - www.museedecerdagne.com - Jul.-Aug.: 10 a.m.-1:30 p.m., 2:30-6:30 p.m.; Oct.-March.: Mon.-Fri. 2-5 p.m.; rest of the year: 10 a.m.-12:30 p.m., 2-5:30 p.m.; €6 (child: €3/€4).

The Yellow Train in winter.
imelenchon/Getty Images Plus

8 BOURG-MADAME

From Hix to Madame Royale. At the crossroads of France, Spain and Andorra, Bourg-Madame is the last French village before the border: the Spanish town of Puigcerdà is only a few minutes walk away! Formerly the residence of the Counts of Cerdanya and the region's commercial capital until the 12th century, Hix was downgraded to the status of a simple hamlet in 1177, when King Alfonso II of Aragon had the capital (and its inhabitants) transferred to the less vulnerable site of "Mount Cerdan" (Puigcerdà). Bourg-Madame, which developed just west of the hamlet, on the site of Les Guinguettes d'Hix, only took its present name in 1815, in honour of Madame Royale, daughter of Louis XVI. Today, visitors stop here to enjoy the peace and quiet, and to see the lovely Romanesque church of St Martin d'Hix in the hamlet. It has two very fine statues: a wooden Christ from the 13th century and a Virgin from the 12th century, as well as an altarpiece from the 16th century that is characteristic of Cerdan art.

Church of St-Martin d'Hix - visit by booking 48 hours in advance at the Bourg-Madame town hall - ✆ 04 68 04 52 41 - Mon.-Fri. 9 a.m.-noon, 1:30-5 p.m.

A bed for the night. Located a 5-minute walk from the station, this quiet family-run hotel offers simple rooms with old-fashioned charm. Unobstructed view of the park and the mountains.
Hôtel Celisol - 1 av. des Guinguettes - ✆ 04 68 04 53 70 - www.hotelcelisolcerdagne.fr - 13 rms. €62/€74 - 🍽 €8.

Sweet snack. This boutique-tea room full of sweet delights offers delicate homemade rousquilles (a traditional Catalan biscuit made from aniseed), accompanied by a selection of organic teas, rooibos and herbal teas. Time for a little indulgent break.
Les Rousquilles du Palais - 20 av. Porte-de-France - ✆ 06 48 55 28 60 - lesrousquillesdupalais.fr - Tues.-Sat. 10 a.m.-noon, 3-7 p.m.

The second capital of Cerdanya. On the other side of the border (👣 a 20-25min walk from Bourg-Madame), perched on a terrace overlooking the Segre river, Puigcerdà is the capital of Cerdanya and one of the main tourist centres in the Catalan Pyrenees. Its streets, lined with old buildings and traditional shops, converge on Plaça Santa Maria, which is pedestrianised and with a lively atmosphere all day long. An imposing symbol of the town and the last vestige of the Gothic church destroyed in 1936, the bell tower of Santa Maria dominates the square: from the top, you can enjoy a 360° view of the entire Cerdanya plain. A few minutes walk away, the artificial lake of Puigcerdà is lined with charming villas, most of which date from the early 20th century. Enjoy strolling along its banks, home to swans and shaded by weeping willows and conifers. In summer, boats are available for hire.
Campanar de Santa Maria - pl. Santa Maria, 46 - Puigcerdà - Mon.-Fri. 9:30 a.m.-1 p.m. (last ascent), 4:30-6.30 p.m., Sat. 10 a.m.-1 p.m., 5-7.30 p.m., Sun. 10 a.m.-1 p.m. - €1.50 (under-12s free).

Dining. What better than to pop over to the Spanish side (👣 20-25min walk from Bourg-Madame) to enjoy a tapas lunch or dinner in Santa Maria square? For a full meal, the pretty Taverna del Call brasserie, set in a pedestrian square, offers grilled specialities in a warm, modern setting. Jump at the chance if the daily menu features typical dishes such as *tiró amb naps* (goose with Cerdanya turnips) and rabbit with the famous Puigcerdà pears.
Taverna del Call - pl. del Call s/n - Puigcerdà - ✆ (+34) 972 14 10 36 - closed Mon. - lunch deals: €15/€19.50 - menu: €25/€35.

👣 **The Cami de Caldegues.** This easy loop (2h duration) starting from the placette d'Hix offers breathtaking 360° panoramic views of the Cerdan plateau and the surrounding mountains, and will lead you to the beautiful Romanesque chapel of St-Romain de Caldégas (11th century), with its delicate wall paintings (13th century).

⑨ LATOUR-DE-CAROL-ENVEITG

The train terminates here! The village of Latour-de-Carol is the final destination of the Yellow Train line (but also of the night train from Paris-Austerlitz)! Apart from that, the church too is worth a visit for the altarpiece on the high altar (1717), probably sculpted by the great Catalan sculptor, Josep Sunyer. All that remains of the medieval castle, however, are the two towers. The village, which overlooks the Carol valley, is also a good starting point for hiking.

Dining and overnighting. Located a 12-minute walk from the station, this small hotel residence offers a "home from home" experience, only better! In its mountain setting, the residence has two nicely decorated apartments (for 2 or 5 people), with a view of the mountains and a wellness area (jacuzzi, sauna and hammam) to boot. The restaurant offers Catalan cuisine with a twist, prepared using seasonal produce.
Le Mirasol - 11 av. du Belvédère-de-Cerdagne - Enveitg - ✆ 04 68 04 29 25 - www.vacances-balneo-cerdagne.com - appart. €85 (2 pers.) per night - 🍴 meal deal: €21.50, menu: €25.50.

THE PYRENEES LINE

From Latour-de-Carol onwards, the train fringes the peaks and makes its way due north between the Catalan Pyrenees Regional Nature Park and the Principality of Andorra. It follows the path of the Ariège, which still looks more like a mountain stream at this altitude. After Tarascon-sur-Ariège, the Regional Nature Park of the Ariège Pyrenees hoves into view, stretching to Pamiers. For the last third of the journey, the train follows the river before crossing its confluence, the Garonne, harbinger of Toulouse, the "pink city".

⭐ **FROM LATOUR-DE-CAROL TO TOULOUSE - 11 DAYS**

- Non-stop trip: 2h43
- Frequency : 4 liO trains/day
- Timetables: www.ter.sncf.com/occitanie/se-deplacer/fiches-horaires
- Non-stop trip: €28.10
- Onboard services: bicycle transport authorised
- Line connections: Yellow Train line from Latour-de-Carol; Lot and Dordogne line, Bastides and most beautiful villages line, Cathedrals line, Canal du Midi line, Piémont line and Gers line from Toulouse

📷 Where best to sit to admire the landscape? Left-hand side in the direction of travel.

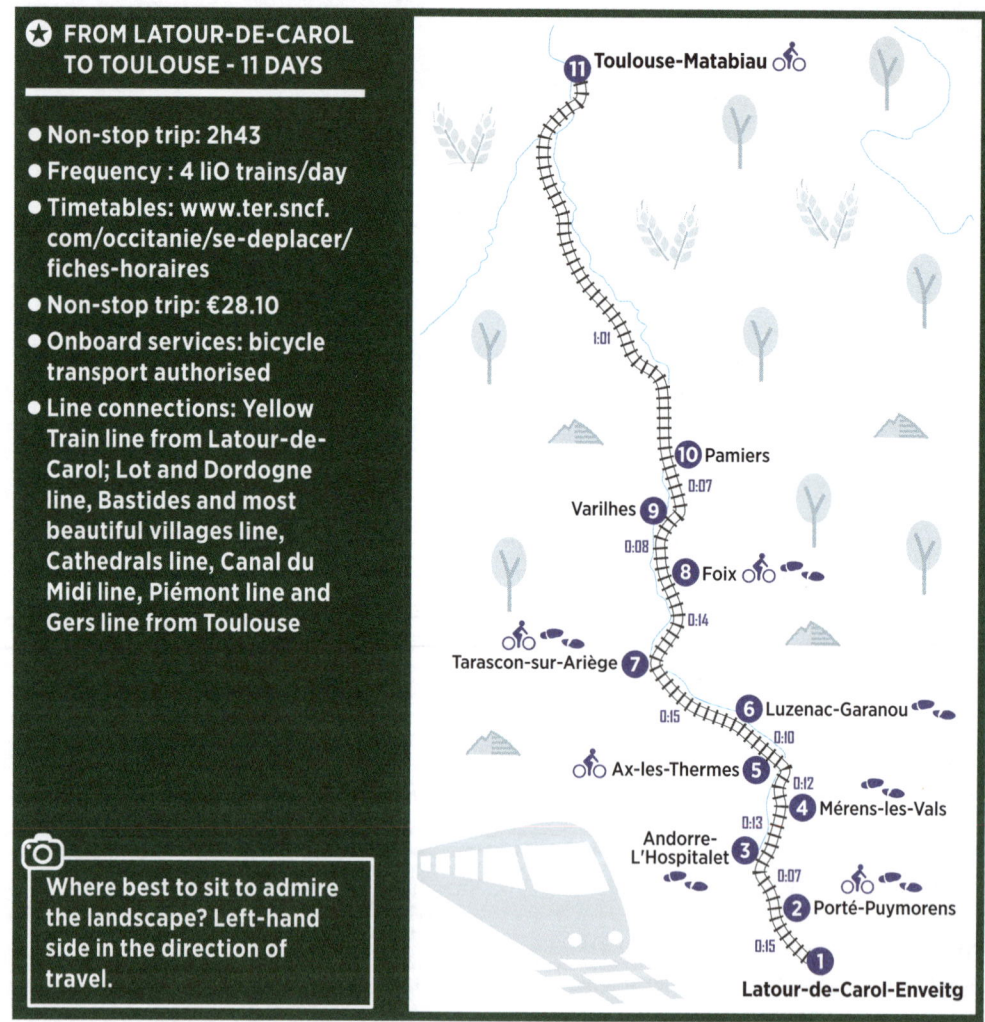

Street in Toulouse, with the St-Sernin bell tower in the background.
agafapaperiapunta/Getty Images Plus

❶ LATOUR-DE-CAROL-ENVEITG

See the Yellow Train line p. 73.

❷ PORTÉ-PUYMORENS

➜ **The station is an 18-minute walk from the village entrance and the chairlift to the resort. There are shuttle buses from the station in the winter.**

🚲 **Bike hire.** Bikes for hire from www.ouibike.net (with bike delivery and pick-up service).

Kissing the peaks. This village is perched at 1 600 m altitude, at the gateway to the Catalan Pyrenees Regional Nature Park, and on the crossroads to Andorra (10 km away) and Spain (20 km away). Surrounded by forests and mountains, this is an ideal place for hiking, either on foot in summer or by snowshoe in winter. The area is north-north-east facing, with skiing up to an altitude of 2 500 m. It is home to the small ski resort of Porté-Puymorens, also known as the "three nations" on account of its geographical location between Spain, France and Andorra. It has 10 lifts, 35 ski runs and an 8 km cross-country circuit.

Tourist office - at Saillagouse - ☎ 04 68 04 15 47 - www.pyrenees-cerdagne.com.

A bed for the night. There are no hotels in Porté-Puymorens, only accommodation listed by the town hall. The nearest place to stay from the station, an 18-minute walk away, is above the Le Castel Isard restaurant, at the foot of the chairlift to the resort. Here you will find traditional cuisine and take-away food.

Le Castel Isard - 11 av. du Puymorens - ☎ 06 24 49 61 46 - le-castel-isard.amenitiz.io - 🍴 dishes €15/€26 - closed Mon. evening and Tue. eve. in Jan. - 3 studios and 5 apts from €200 for two nights.

Dining. At the foot of the slopes, at an altitude of 2,056 m, this mountain restaurant is well worth the diversion – even for a simple return trip, without necessarily skiing – to the Porté-Puymorens ski resort.

La Tramontane - in the ski resort - ☎ 04 68 04 89 70 - 9 a.m.-5 p.m. - dish of the day €16, menu €30.

🚶 🚴 **In the great outdoors.** The tourist office has identified 7 more or less easy routes (including 4 accessible by bike) centred on the village. The two easiest, "La Tour Cerdane" (4.1 km) and "Le Lac du Passet" (9.2 km) are accessible to everyone.
Info: www.pyrenees-cerdagne.com/planifier/activites/itineraires-activites-de-pleine-nature.

❸ ANDORRA-L'HOSPITALET

On the border. L'Hospitalet-près-l'Andorre is the last village before the big climb to Andorra or the Col de Puymorens. You reach this first town in the Ariège valley, at an altitude of 1,436 m, after crossing a landscape that becomes increasingly harsh the higher you climb, with scattered herds of horses running free.
Tourist office - pl. Soulé (in the town hall) - ☎ 05 61 05 20 04 - www.mairie-hospitalet.fr.

Dining and overnighting. A 3-minute walk from the station, this hotel is a small establishment with an excellent restaurant. Its simple rooms are ideally located at the foot of the hiking trails.
Hôtel du Puymorens - ☎ 05 61 05 20 03 - www.hoteldupuymorens.fr - 11 rms. €60 - ☕ €8 - 🍴 1/2 board €60/pers.

🚶 **The path to bonhomie.** The village is on the Chemin des Bonshommes border trail (224 km), between Montgailhard (near Foix) and Berga, in Spain. The trail can be taken to get to the next stopover at Mérens-les-Vals.
Info: www.ariegepyrenees.com/preparer/randonner/itinerance-plusieurs-jours/chemin-des-bonshommes.

Excursion into Andorra. The border with the small principality is only 3 km away and the Pas de la Casa resort only a little further after that. To get there, there is a regular taxi service between L'Hospitalet and Andorra. Situated on the left bank of the Ariège – which is still only a mountain stream at this altitude, the "Pas de la Casa" ("pass of the house" in Catalan) still a simple border post at the start of the 20th century, underwent massive development over the course of the last century. This small town, the highest in Europe apart from a few hamlets in the Alps, has a year-round population of 3 000 and is the second largest commercial centre in Andorra after Andorra la Vella.
Pas de la Casa - ☎ (+376) 755 100 - www.encamp.ad - L'Hospitalet Taxi: ☎ 06 87 90 20 76; Pas de la Casa Taxi: ☎ (+376) 856 255.

❹ MÉRENS-LES-VALS

Stop when it turns green. The village was rebuilt along the roadside after the fire of Mérens-d'en-Haut, lit by Miquelets – feared Spanish mercenaries operating since the 16th century – in 1811, during the Napoleonic War in Spain. After Mérens and their eponymous gorges, the route heads up into the high valley of the Ariège, in the midst of beautiful forests. On the left can be seen the Dent d'Orlu peak.
Info: www.merenslesvals.fr.

Dining and overnighting. An 18-minute walk from the station, this farm hostel is particularly recommended for hikers making a stopover. Overnighting possibilities in a dormitory or guest room. From the kitchen you can enjoy produce from the farm.
Auberge du Nabre - 1105 rte de Vives - ☎ 05 61 01 89 36 - www.aubergedunabre.com - 🍴 Jul.-Aug.: lunch and evening; rest of the year: Fri. and Sat. evenings by booking in advance. - menu €21, picnic €8 - 90 dormitory beds €23 ☕ - 5 guest rooms €54/€60 - ☕ €7.

🚶 **To the source!** Mérens-les-Vals is the only village in the Ax valley crossed by the famous GR 10 footpath. From Jouliane, near the station, a walking trail takes you to its sulphurous waters with panoramic views of the surrounding mountains.
"The sulphurous sources of Mérens" walk - www.pyrenees-ariegeoises.com/a-voir-a-faire/balades-et-randonnees/balades-a-pied.

⑤ AX-LES-THERMES

🚴 **Bike hire.** Road bikes, trail MTBs, enduro bikes and e-bikes are for hire a 2-minute walk from the station.
Ax Sports Loisirs - 29 av. Delcassé - ☎ 05 61 64 21 77 - ax-sports-loisirs-velo.notresphere.com - bike €40/day, e-MTB €65 /day.

Its history naturally springs to mind. A summer holiday resort, Ax-les-Thermes is also a renowned spa town and the gateway to a popular winter sports destination. It is a very attractive little town, with its colourful, cheerful facades and pedestrianised streets. It makes for an ideal base for exploring the rich surrounding valleys, the dense Pyrenean forests and the caves of Tarascon, or for an excursion into Andorra or Spain. Its 80 hot springs, with temperatures varying from 18 to 78°C, supply three establishments: Le Couloubret, Le Modèle and Le Teich. The waters are used mainly to treat rheumatism, respiratory ailments and some skin diseases. The centre of the resort is crossed by the Couloubret walk.
Tourist office - 6 av. Théophile-Delcassé - ☎ 05 61 64 60 60 - www.pyrenees-ariegeoises.com.

Dining and overnighting. A 13-minute walk from the station, you will find rooms that are very pleasant and modern, right next to the gondolas that will take you up to the slopes during the season. This is a also a great place to eat: dishes that are elegantly presented with subtle flavours, all prepared by the chef, Frédéric Debèves, who adds his own talented touch to regional specialities. Lovely terrace over the river.
Le Chalet Hotel-restaurant - 4 av. Durandeau - ☎ 05 61 64 24 31 - www.le-chalet.fr - closed Sun. eve., Tue. lunch and Mon. - menus €33/€60 - 19 rms. €70/€100 - ☕ €10.

Strolling around the old town. It is thanks to Gaston, Count of Foix, that the city of Ax, in the 14th century, became a free city and was enclosed within a wall (now destroyed)

Ax-les-Thermes.
Leonid Andronov/Getty Images Plus

defended by eight towers. Setting off from the casino, built in 1903, walk to the Church of St-Vincent, in its extended composite style (12th-19th centuries). On the Place du Breilh, which marks the entrance to the historic old town, a plume of steam indicates the Bassin des Ladres footbath (1250), filled with natural hot water. It is said to have been established by St. Louis, for treating soldiers with leprosy on their return from the Crusades. It has since been used for various purposes, such as washing wool or boiling pig carcasses. Founded in 1260, the St-Louis hospital was enlarged in 1846. Its bell tower bears witness to the "spa" style in vogue in the 19th century. The adjoining Breilh thermal baths (1813) are now closed. In the maze of small streets of Coustou, Constant-Alibert, Escaliers, Moulinas and Boucarie, you will come across fountains, half-timbered houses from the Middle Ages, and the old St-Jérôme chapel.

For a picnic. The produce in this friendly, rustic shop comes exclusively from the farm: meat, foie gras, preserves, local charcuterie, Ariège honeys, cheese, wine, liqueurs, and some typical mountain souvenirs. Walks and guided transhumance tours are organised in the summer. Guided tours of the farm in the winter.
La Boutique de la Ferme - pl. du Breilh - 05 61 01 54 63 - www.laboutiquedelaferme.com - 9:30 a.m.-12:30 p.m. and 3-7 p.m. - closed Mon.

Take a bath. On the site of an ancient spa, the baths, situated on two floors, offer the pleasures of the old Roman baths (cold, hot and steam baths), a Nordic area (sauna), a Carthaginian area (hammam), as well as relaxation and well-being treatments. There are two outdoor pools with water play facilities.
Les Bains du Couloubret - prom. Paul-Salette - 05 61 02 64 41 - www.bains-couloubret.com - open all year - from €19/2h (children: €15.50) to €33/5h (children: €27) ; care treatments €55/€117.

Spectacles de Grands Chemins festival. This street theatre festival celebrates circus and dance in the canton of Haute-Ariège.
Info: www.ax-animation.com - Jul.- early Aug.

❻ LUZENAC-GARANOU

➔ The station is located in the commune of Garanou, near Luzenac, with the town centre a 10-minute walk away.

A fine quarry. Dominated by the ruins of the Cathar castle of Lordat, Luzenac has built its reputation since the end of the 19th century on its talc mining. The talc is extracted in its raw state from the Trimouns quarry, located in the heart of the St-Barthélemy mountains, at an altitude of between 1,700 and 1,850 m. It is brought down in trailers to the factory in the valley where it is dried, crushed and packaged.
Tourist office - 6 r. de la Mairie - 05 61 64 68 05 - Jul.-Aug. - www.pyrenees-ariegeoises.com.

Dining and overnighting. Just a 3-minute walk from the station, this family-run hotel offers inexpensive, simple, and functional rooms. The restaurant serves up traditional cuisine and fresh produce.
Hôtel La Pierre Blanche - 6 av. de la Gare - 05 61 03 26 30 - www.lapierreblanche.fr - 10 rms. €56/€64 - €9 - closed Sun. - menu €15/€30.

From one station to the other. From Luzenac-Garanou station, an easy circuit (15.9 km, 5h) follows the railway and reaches the village of Les Cabannes where there is a small station on the same line. The walk passes through villages in the upper Ariège valley, such as Vernaux, Lordat, Axiat, Caychax, and Senconac.
Hikes & Train Circuit "The Corniche from Luzenac" - www.pyrenees-ariegeoises.com/a-voir-a-faire/balades-et-randonnees/balades-a-pied.

❼ TARASCON-SUR-ARIÈGE

➔ The station is in the town centre, but quite a way from any sites of interest. However, shuttles are laid on from the station to the

Prehistoric Park, Tarascon-sur-Ariège. A. Spani/hemis.fr

following 4 sites: Prehistoric Park, Bédeilhac cave, Lombrives cave and Ussat-les-Bains spa. Weekends only. *Info: lio-occitanie.fr*

🚲 **Bike hire.** A 10-minute walk from the station, a comprehensive service is offered with city bikes, road bikes, mountain bikes and electric bikes. Multiple-day packages available.
Point glisse - 7 av. St-Roch - ☎ 05 61 05 75 08 - www.location-point-glisse.com - leisure bike €9 per 1/2 day, e-bike €30 per 1/2 day.

Into the depths. Tarascon is THE place to go in the Pyrenees for scientific and tourist caving. Situated at the confluence of the Ariège and Vicdessos rivers, the little town backs onto a foothill of the Pyrenees, whose rocky faces are dotted with some fifty natural caves, including a dozen containing wall paintings, such as the famous Cave of Niaux. The limestone cliffs carved and shaped by the river provide an attractive backdrop for the town, and the magnificent forests all around offer unforgettable walks. A dozen or so painted prehistoric caves make the Tarascon region a veritable capital of prehistory, a must for enthusiasts interested in how our distant ancestors lived.

Tourist office - av. Paul-Joucla - ☎ 05 61 05 94 94 - www.pyrenees-ariegeoises.com.

A bed for the night. An 11-minute walk from the station, the former Château Piquemal now houses 15 spacious rooms with contemporary decor. The Saveurs du Manoir restaurant serves fine regional fare with a twist.
Hôtel-restaurant Le Manoir d'Agnès - 2 r. St-Roch - ☎ 05 61 02 32 81 - www.manoiragnes.com - 15 rms. €135/€245 - ☕ €12 - 🍴 menu €24/€58.

In the steps of Cro-Magnon. In its beautiful mountain setting, the Prehistoric Park is devoted to cave art and the life of the Magdalenians, by way of a theme trail and immersive outdoor workshops (allow for 4 or 5 hours on site). In addition to the restaurant-cafeteria and the shop, a contemporary building houses the Grand Atelier, full of fascinating things to see. The first rooms present The Giants of the Ice Age (Megaloceros deer, steppe bison, woolly mammoth, and cave lion). The visit continues with the incredible "dune des Pas" sand dune (part of the Clastres de Niaux network) which contains the footprints of two adults and three children, more than

5,000 years old (castings), and the representation, unique in the world, of a weasel. The "In the steps of Cro-Magnon" immersive space reconstitutes a shelter under a rock. The visit ends with the superb facsimile of the Black Hall in Niaux, created by Renaud Sanson, who produced Lascaux 2 in Montignac.

Parc de la Préhistoire - rte de Banat - lieu-dit Lacombe - 05 61 05 10 10 - www.sites-touristiques-ariege.fr/parc-de-la-prehistoire - 10 a.m.-6 p.m. - closed Nov.-Apr. - €11.50 (ages 5-17 €8), family ticket (2 adults + 2 children) €36.

Dining. In the town centre, 8 minutes' walk from the station, the Le Vieux Carré restaurant offers excellent value for money. A friendly, centrally located establishment with a varied menu. Otherwise, in the grounds of the Prehistoric Park itself, the Restaurant du Parc offers a dining experience with great views through the picture windows. Here you can enjoy local cuisine with a twist: burger with pan-fried foie gras, duck ravioli with morels, etc.

Restaurant Le Vieux Carré - pl. Ste-Quitterie - 05 61 05 08 30 - www.levieuxcarre.fr - closed from mid-Dec. to 1st Jan. and Sun. - menu €20/€35.

Restaurant du Parc - rte de Banat, Prehistoric Park - 05 61 05 10 10 - www.sites-touristiques-ariege.fr - daily from Apr. to early Nov. - menus €13/€26.

Walking underground. The third most visited site in Ariège, after Montségur and the Prehistoric Park, the Lombrives cave is one of the wonders of the department. A "guided hike" offers visitors a marvellous experience: you pass through ten or so rooms, all different, some hewn into the limestone, others lined with red sandstone or marble of various colours, until you reach the underground lake and the Tomb of Pyrene. It is this legend that led King Henri IV – who considered himself a descendant of Hercules – to visit the cave in 1578. He left an inscription there that you will find 400 m from the entrance. Many other traces bear witness to human passage here, from a vast Neolithic cemetery to inscriptions from the Middle Ages. Some of these are the marks of the last of the Cathars, who took refuge here after the fall of Montségur.

Lombrives Cave.
B. Gardel/hemis.fr

Lombrives Cave - at Ussat (accessible by shuttle from the station - see p. 78) - ☏ 06 49 44 45 00 - www.grottedelombrives.com - guided tours (2h) - open all year, bookings strongly advised via *Internet or tel. - Apr.-Sept. and school hols.*: daily; rest of the year, contact for details. - €12 (ages 13-17: €10). Come equipped with stout footwear and a warm top, even in summer (13 °C in the cave). If coming with a baby, make sure to have a front carrier (back carriers prohibited) - a little train (€2) takes you to the cave located 1 km from the ticket office.

⑧ FOIX

 **Bike hire. There is a hire shop 3 minutes' walk from the station.**
Foix Mobilités - 17 cours Irénée-Cros - ☏ 07 69 71 03 20 - www.foixmobilites.org - hybrid bike €18 per 1/2 day, e-bike €35 per 1/2 day.

Foix and its sights. The town of Foix, one of the least populated prefectures in France, is peaceful and welcoming. For a small town, it has a particularly rich and fascinating history. At the mouth of the ancient glacial valley of the Ariège, Foix suddenly appears against a majestically wild landscape of sheer peaks. The three towers of its castle seem to survey, from atop their austere rock, the last defile of the river as it winds through the Plantaurel range. The town is quite small and can be got round quickly. The old part of town, with its narrow streets, has, as its centre, on the corner of Rue de Labistour and Rue des Marchands, the crossroads where the small bronze Goose Fountain stands. The old town contrasts with the administrative district, built in the 19th century around vast esplanades, the Allées de la Villote, and the Champ-de-Mars.
Tourist office - 29 r. Delcassé - ☏ 05 61 65 12 12 - www.foix-tourisme.com.

A bed for the night. A 9-minute walk from the station, easily identifiable by its wooden corner tower, this simple, renovated hotel is conveniently located for visiting the town.
Hotel Eychenne - 11 r. Peyrevidal - ☏ 05 61 65 00 04 - www.hotel-eychenne.com - 18 rms. from €65.

Courtly pursuits... A fun, interactive tour offers an immersive discovery of the castle and the lineage of the Counts of Foix. The castle, whose first foundations date back to the 10th century, is a solid stronghold that Simon de Montfort besieged in vain in 1211 and 1212, during the Albigensian Crusade. But in 1272, when the Count of Foix refused to recognise the sovereignty of the King of France, Philip the Bold personally led an expedition against the town. Having run out of food and faced with the attack on the rocky edifice, the Count capitulated. Following the Council of Béarn and the County of Foix in 1290, the town was all but abandoned by the Counts. Gaston Fébus (14th century) was the last person to live in the castle, which became the seat of the governor of the Pays de Foix, the headquarters of a garrison until the Revolution, and finally a prison until 1862.
Castle - pl. du Palais-de-Justice - ☏ 05 61 05 10 10 - www.sites-touristiques-ariege.fr - *April to mid-Nov.*: 10 a.m.-6 p.m. (7 p.m. Jul.-Aug.); rest of the year: contact for details. - €11.50 (under-17s: €8, family pass, 2 adults + 2 children: €36).

Dining. Le Phoebus is the place to go to enjoy traditional cuisine in a room overlooking the Ariège and the castle of Fébus. Warm welcome assured. Au Grilladou is a small, friendly restaurant at the foot of the castle, offering pizzas, grills, salads and fresh homemade pasta at very reasonable prices. Efficient service with a smile. Summer terrace in the pedestrianised street.
Le Phoebus - 3 cours Irénée-Cros - ☏ 05 61 65 10 42 - closed Sat. lunch, Sun. evening and Mon. - menus €29/€59.
Au Grilladou - 7 r. Lafaurie - ☏ 05 61 64 00 74 - www.restaurant-foix-augrilladou.fr - closed Sat. lunch and Sun. except Jul.-Aug. - menus €15/€30.

Biking on the greenway. The old railway line between Foix and St-Girons has been converted into a hiking trail. Discover: old structures, tunnels, viaducts, guard posts, and the possibility of meeting local producers along the way.

Fabulous Journeys

First time in Foix

The imposing castle of the town of Foix, the ancient earldom that will serve as a base for this Fabulous Journey, immediately sets the tone, with its ubiquitous sense of history and its monuments.

You will see this for yourself when, after catching your breath after a short climb, you stand in front of the ruins of the spectacular castle of Montségur, perched on its "pog", or rock. Experience a poignant souvenir of the drama that unfolded in 1244, and a 360-degree panorama of the Pyrenean peaks. The perfect spot for a memorable picnic. Continue your voyage back in time to the prehistoric age, with a visit to the Cave of Niaux and its superb wall paintings.

The Pyrenees also provide a fantastic natural backdrop for outward-bound activities, whether on foot (for a short or long hike, maybe before chilling in the Ax-les-Thermes baths), by bike, by canyoning in the Argensou gorges, or by way of an offbeat visit to the Labouiche river, 60 m underground.

Consider yourself a food lover? You will be bowled over by the fine places to eat, and by the covered market of Foix, which is brimming with local specialities (don't forget to try the "mounjetado", or Ariège cassoulet, and the "garbure", a kind of thick stew). Lastly, if you're the romantic or contemplative type, or if you just like stargazing, simply look up after nightfall to appreciate the incredibly clear, starry skies.

4 days, 3 nights - accommodation in Foix, from €64 per night for 2 people. - visit in spring and summer. Contact: Foix tourist office.

Foix, the fortress at nightfall. A. Spani/hemis.fr

The Foix-Saint-Girons greenway - www.foix-tourisme.com/accueil/bouger/circuit-velo.

Cathar Trail. From Foix, you can head first for Roquefixade (15 km), the initial stage of the Cathar Trail which connects Foix to the Mediterranean in 12 stages, from mountain to sea, through a variety of landscapes (forests of L'Escale and Picaussel, Quillan and the canyon of Agly, Port-la-Nouvelle).
The Cathar Trail (GR 367) - download the trail guide from www.audetourisme.com/fr/a-voir-a-faire/incontournables/sentier-cathare.

⑨ VARILHES

→ **The trains to and from Foix are regular and rapid (10-minute journey), making for an easy day trip.**

Varilhes for a change. Once dominated by an imposing medieval castle, this small town has a centre dedicated to the history of resistance and deportation. The collections it has on show are original and very moving, supported by educational information panels, and allow visitors to discover the history of the Ariège during the Second World War. The exhibition is organised in three parts (resistance, deportation, memory), with a particular focus on the specifics of this mountain territory, on the border with Spain.
Resistance and deportation history centre - 18 av. des Pyrénées - 05 61 69 02 60 - www.resistance-ariege.fr - Tues.-Sat. 10 a.m.-noon, 1:30-5.30 p.m. - free admission.

Dining. This inn is a very friendly place which wins over visitors as much through its decor, with its large open fireplace, as its menu.
Auberge du Lapin blanc - 13 av. de Foix - 09 73 25 74 73 - closed Mon., Tue. eve., Wed. eve., Thu. eve., Sun. eve. - menu €15/€25.

⑩ PAMIERS

Along the canals. The largest town in the Ariège department, with some 15 000 inhabitants, Pamiers is surrounded by canals Its name derives from Apamea (Asia Minor), in memory of the participation in the first crusade of Roger II, Count of Foix. The great composer, Gabriel Fauré (1845-1924), "the most musical musician, along with Mozart", according to Arthur Honegger, was born here. His bust was erected on the Castella promenade, created on the site of the old castle, the foundations of which can still be seen when leaving through the Nerviau gate and heading towards the Pont Neuf. There is a lot to see in Pamiers: from the Pamiers Cathedral to the Church of Notre-Dame-du-Camp, by way of the Carmel and the Tour de la Monnaie tower, there is plenty to fill your day!
Tourist office - 27 r. Charles-de-Gaulle - 05 61 67 52 52 - www.pap-tourisme.fr.

A bed for the night. Just a 12-minute walk from the train station, the Hôtel de la Paix, a former coaching inn, features colourful, well-renovated rooms. The dining room, with its remarkable moulded ceilings, has a warm, olde-worlde atmosphere. The Hôtel de France, in the city centre, has undergone a beneficial facelift and now offers rooms with a new look and contemporary furnishings.
Hôtel de la Paix - 05 61 67 12 71 - www.hoteldelapaix-pamiers.com - closed 24 Dec.-3 Jan. - 14 rms. €70/€75 - €8 - daily except Sun. noon-1:30 p.m., 7:30-9:30 p.m. - menu €25/€35.
Hôtel de France - 5 cours Joseph-Rambaud - 05 61 60 20 88 - www.hotel-de-france-pamiers.com closed Fri-Sun. - 31 rms. €110/€115 - lunch menu €25.

5-star canvasses. In Pamiers Cathedral (pl. du Mercadal), only the portal bears witness to the original church built in the 12th century. The beautiful bell tower, in the Toulouse style, rests on a fortified foundation. Note also the chimeras that crown this edifice. In the choir, with its beautiful polychrome marble floor, you will see five large canvasses by the Toulouse artist, Bénézet, representing the life of Saint Anthoninus. The church of Notre-Dame-du-Camp has a monumental crenellated brick facade surmounted by two towers. The unique nave dates from the 17th century.

Dining. A traditional restaurant, with home-made cuisine and fresh produce. You wait for your meal at the water's edge, in a peaceful and pleasant setting, with a terrace open from spring to mid-October.
Le Moulin - 1 r. d'Emparis - ☏ 05 61 68 22 41 - page Facebook - closed Mon. - menus €25/€35.

⑪ TOULOUSE-MATABIAU

→ Toulouse station is located in the city centre, a 15-minute walk from the Place du Capitole via the new Rue Bayard link or the Allées Jean-Jaurès, which have been redeveloped into ramblas. Otherwise, take tram line A (9 min).

🚲 **Bike hire.** More than 280 self-service bicycle rental stations in the city.
VélÔToulouse - www.velo.toulouse.fr - €1.20 /24h.

Tickled pink. Former capital of old Occitanie and the prosperous "pays de Cocagne", the "pink city" has established itself in the 21st century as a major urban centre, always on the move. Yet it retains a timeless charm with its streets and squares, the refinement of its churches, the beauty of its heritage and the wealth of its museums. As the sun goes down, admire the colours of the Romanesque bell towers and neoclassical facades along the riverside, from the footbridge and Port Viguerie, on the left bank of the Garonne.
Tourist office - sq. Charles-de-Gaulle - ☏ 05 17 42 31 31 - www.toulouse-tourisme.com.

A bed for the night. 10 minutes on foot from the station, a friendly welcome awaits at the Castellane hotel, built around a courtyard. Simple, renovated rooms, some with terraces; some are perfectly suited to families. Nestled between Place Wilson and the station (8 minutes' walk), the small Saint-Claire hotel offers quiet and nicely renovated rooms, with works of art in each room.
Hôtel Castellane - 17 r. Castellane - ☏ 05 61 62 18 82 - www.hotelcastellane.com - 53 rms. €88/€100 - ☕ €8.90.
Urban Style Hôtel Saint-Claire - 29 pl. Nicolas-Bachelier - ☏ 05 34 40 58 88 - www.stclairehotel.fr - 16 rms. €84/€134 - ☕ €13.

Remarkable churches. Listed by Unesco, the St-Sernin basilica (11th-15th century) is the most famous Romanesque church in the south of France and the richest in the country in terms of relics. The brick and stone edifice forms a magnificent ensemble with its stepped roofs, dominated by the octagonal bell tower. St-Sernin is the epitome of the great pilgrimage church, designed to facilitate congregational worship. Pilgrims would flock to touch the sculpted feet of St Christopher, their patron saint, to ensure protection on their way to Santiago de Compostela. Be sure to take in the recently revealed and restored Romanesque wall paintings in the north semitransept. Another marvellous monument, the Church of the Jacobins (13th-14th century), built entirely in brick, is a masterpiece of the Southern French Gothic school. With its large arches and octagonal tower, the exterior contrasts with the elegance and lightness of its interior architecture, dominated by polychrome decor and its fabulous "palm tree" column that supports the 22-ribbed vault of the apse. Don't fail to take in the cloister with its 160 columns, the chapterhouse, or the murals in the Saint Anthoninus chapel.
Basilica of Saint-Sernin - pl. St-Sernin - www.basilique-saint-sernin.fr.
Church of the Jacobins - pl. des Jacobins - www.jacobins.toulouse.fr - convent: every day except Mon. 10 a.m.-6 p.m. - €5.

Consider yourself a collector. The Hôtel d'Assézat, undoubtedly the most beautiful Renaissance grand townhouse in Toulouse, houses the Bemberg Foundation. It is a real joy to visit. The collections, assembled by the art connoisseur, Georges Bemberg, include paintings, sculptures, furniture and objets d'art from the Renaissance to the 20th century. Ancient art (16th-18th century, 1st floor) is presented as if in a private home around which you can stroll, from the elegant Louis XVI French room to the Portrait Gallery, where elegant 18th century Venetian furniture and 16th century objets d'art sit alongside Renaissance paintings by the likes of Cranach,

*Place du Capitole, Toulouse.
saiko3p/Getty Images Plus*

François Clouet, Veronese and Titian. Change of decor on the 2nd floor, dedicated to modern art. The collection, which includes a magnificent group of paintings by Bonnard, brings together practically all the great names of the French school of the 19th and early 20th century (Gauguin, Matisse, Monet, Dufy, etc.).
Fondation Bemberg - pl. d'Assézat - ☎ 05 61 12 06 89 - www.fondation-bemberg.fr - closed Mon. - €10.

Dining. Opposite the station, Le Vélo Sentimental is the perfect spot for lunch between trains. With a garden and a nice upstairs dining room, it has a colourful, second-hand bike shop feel. People come here for its handy location, its philosophy (work-opportunities restaurant), and its great food! Vegetarian dishes served. Just waiting to be discovered!
Au Petit Bonheur offers an excellent welcome in a simple and colourful setting. Traditional cuisine gets the house treatment to great effect. An address to be recommended!
Le Vélo Sentimental - 12 bd Bonrepos - ☎ 05 34 42 92 51 - www.maisonduvelotoulouse.com - open daily Mon.-Tues. 9 a.m.-4:30 p.m., Wed.-Fri. 9 a.m.-10:30 p.m., Sat. 9 a.m-4 p.m., closed Sun. - €10/€20.
Au Petit Bonheur - 20 r. des Filatiers - ☎ 05 61 14 07 06 - closed Tues. and Thu. lunch and Wed. - meal deal €27 - menu €40.

For a picnic. To find gastronomic delights of Toulouse for your picnic hamper, go to the covered market, on Place Victor-Hugo (closed Mon.). On Sunday mornings, the farmers' market is held around the Church of St-Aubin, where small producers bring their fare for sale. An organic market is held on Tuesday and Saturday mornings at the foot of the Donjon du Capitole (www.marchebiotoulouse.org).

Sweet snack. Charming café in the small garden of the Musée St-Raymond (entrance to the museum is not necessary to access the café). A verdant haven of peace, in the shadow of the Basilica of St-Sernin. Good coffee for just €1!
Café du Musée St-Raymond - pl. St-Sernin - ☎ 05 61 22 31 44 - saintraymond.toulouse.fr - 10:30 a.m.-6 p.m. - closed Sun. and Mon.

Aperitif time. On the Place de la Daurade, this beautiful half-timbered building with its large terrace overlooking the river is worthy of special mention. It's the perfect spot for a break after strolling along the banks of the Garonne.
Le Café des Artistes - 13 pl. de la Daurade - ☎ 05 61 12 06 00 - 11 a.m.-2 p.m.

FABULOUS JOURNEYS BY RAIL

THE LOT AND DORDOGNE LINE

Setting out from Haute-Garonne, our train leaves Toulouse and heads north towards Brive-la-Gaillarde, in Corrèze. From Caussade, the line runs alongside the Causses du Quercy Regional Nature Park, at the foot of escarpments covered in chestnut groves and perched villages. At Cahors, it follows the meandering Lot river, before reaching Souillac, at the gateway to the Périgord Noir (literally "Black Périgord"). So many travel temptations, and so many fine places to dine!

⭐ **TOULOUSE TO BRIVE-LA-GAILLARDE - 7 DAYS**

- Non-stop trip: 2h40
- Frequency : 3 liO trains/day
- Timetables: www.ter.sncf.com/occitanie/se-deplacer/fiches-horaires
- Non-stop trip: €34.30
- Onboard services: bicycle transport authorised
- Connected lines: Pyrenees, Bastides and most beautiful villages, Cathedrals, Canal du Midi, Piémont, and Gers lines from Toulouse; Causses of Quercy line from Brive-la-Gaillarde

📷 Where best to sit to admire the landscape? On the right-hand side, in the direction of travel.

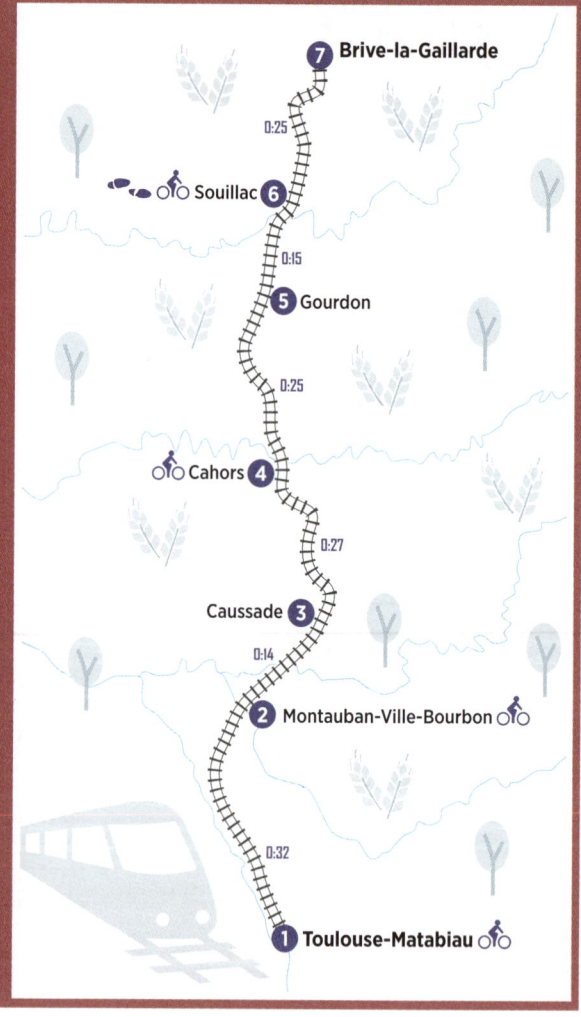

*Montauban.
Lauriane Donzelli/CRT Occitanie*

1 TOULOUSE-MATABIAU

See the Pyrenees line p. 84.

2 MONTAUBAN-VILLE-BOURBON

→ **The station is located on the other side of the Tarn, after the Pont Vieux (Old Bridge). It is a 10-15 minute walk to the old town of Montauban or you can take bus number 1 or 4.**
Info: www.montm.com.

Bike hire. The Maison du Vélo has both traditional and electric bikes for hire.
Maison du Vélo - see p. 95.

Pink brick. Fringed by the hills of lower Quercy and the rich alluvial plains of the Garonne and the Tarn, Montauban is a lively city all year round. The Old Bridge (Pont-Vieux) (14th century) with its seven arches, all in pink-orange brick, spans the Tarn and marks the entrance to old Montauban. Make your way to the Place Nationale, the hub and focal point of the town. Its brick arcades (17th century), with ribbed vaults, comprise a double gallery, while the surrounding houses are connected at each corner by a portico.
Tourist office - 1 pl. Pénélope - 05 63 63 60 60 - www.montauban-tourisme.com.

A bed for the night. This 3-star hotel with character is located in an 18th century house facing the cathedral and 15 minutes from the station. The ancient and the modern combine harmoniously to create a cocoon of pure comfort. Attractive rooms.
Hôtel du Commerce - 9 pl. F.-Roosevelt - 05 63 66 31 32 - www.hotel-commerce-montauban.com - 27 rms. €62/€85 - €9.

Two superstars in one museum. In the former bishop's palace (1664), the Ingres-Bourdelle museum honours two of the town's native sons: the painter Jean-Auguste-Dominique Ingres (1780-1867), who bequeathed his collections of ancient paintings to the city, and Antoine Bourdelle (1861-1929), a sculptor who owes a great deal to his master, Auguste Rodin (1840-1917).
Musée Ingres-Bourdelle - 19 r. de l'Hôtel-de-Ville - 05 63 22 12 91 - museeingresbourdelle.com - closed Mon. - €10 (under 8s free).

Dining. On the pleasant terrace or in the beautiful, well-lit dining room decorated with old wood furnishings, you will get to enjoy traditional, precise and masterful cuisine, based on produce of excellence.
Les Terrasses de l'Empereur - 2 r. de la République - ℘ 05 63 20 41 59 - closed Tue. eve. and Sun. eve., Mon. - €25/€50.

For a picnic. Head for the indoor market, just the place to fill your basket with some of the region's fine victuals.
Indoor market (Marché couvert) - 11 pl. Nationale - daily exc. Mon. 7 a.m.-1 p.m.

Sweet snack. A pâtisserie renowned for its Absolu (almond biscuit, praline crunch, chocolate, and vanilla crème brûlée) and its Baccarat (crunchy pistachio macaroon with fresh raspberries), not forgetting its mille-feuille. Convivial tea room.
Alexandres - 117 fbg Lacapelle - ℘ 05 63 91 25 53 - www.patisserie-alexandres.fr - Mon.-Sat. 9:30 a.m.-7:30 p.m., Sun. 8:30 a.m.-12:30 p.m.

Montech getaway. From the Canal Port in Montauban, the Montech Canal, a 10 km greenway, makes for a pleasant excursion on foot to Montech (pronounced *"Montesh"*) along the water's edge (2h there and back). In addition to a few half-timbered houses, you will discover the Notre-Dame-de-la-Visitation church and its remarkable 46 m-high Toulousian bell tower, but above all, you will be able to appreciate one of the engineering structures built to modernise the Garonne canal, as ingenious as it is spectacular: the Montech water slope. This boat lift variant (inaugurated in 1974) replaces five successive locks, saving valuable navigation time.

③ CAUSSADE

Hats off! There are the Umbrellas of Cherbourg, the Lace of Calais, and the Straw Hats of… Caussade. Were you aware that you were arriving in the straw hats capital of France, responsible for almost two-thirds of national production? Hats have been made for over 200 years in this small village in the Tarn-et-Garonne. L'Épopée chapelière ("The Hatmaker Epic"), an exhibition installed in the tourist office, retraces the great adventure of the Caussade hat industry. A little further on in the village, Willy's Paris milliner's shop has been keeping the hatmaking tradition alive since 1864. You

Montech water slope.
F. Guiziou/hemis.fr

can go behind the scenes of Willy's workshop on a guided tour.
Tourist office - carré des Chapeliers - Les Récollets - ☏ 05 63 26 04 04 - www.tourisme-quercy-caussadais.fr.
Chapellerie Willy's Paris - 63 av. du Gén.-Leclerc - ☏ 05 63 93 09 96 - www.willys-paris.com - Mon.-Fri. 9:30 a.m.-12:30 p.m., 1:30-6 p.m. - guided tour (1h, €3) Thurs. at 10:30 a.m. from Jun. to Sept.

A bed for the night. Coinciding with the arrival of the railway in Caussade, a new hotel was built between 1883 and 1885, opposite the station. And here you are. The residence, which has since been renovated, offers both elegant rooms and apartments. Not to mention a swimming pool.
Hôtel Résidence Laroque - 18 r. du 8-Mai-1945 - ☏ 05 63 65 11 77 - www.hotellarroque.fr - 🏊 - 18 rms. €60/€81 - 🍽 €8.

Dining. Alice's broad smile whets your appetite, and the dishes then served up live up to their promise. In the bright dining room or on the terrace, you get to enjoy the produce of local arable and livestock farmers. Simple, home-made, and convivial.
La Table d'Alice - 24 r. Moissagaise - ☏ 09 86 26 57 79 - www.latabledalice.com - closed Wed. - menu €28/€38.

Extraordinary festival. This event combines a competition and an exhibition of hat designs from around the world. There are also lots of concerts and a night market.
Estivales du Chapeau - www.chapeau-caussade.fashion - Wk. of 14 July.

❹ CAHORS

 **Bike hire.** An efficient and accommodating service just 9-minutes' walk from the station, as well as advice on visits to make around Cahors or further afield.
V-Lot - pont Valentré - ☏ 07 50 59 21 57 - www.v-lot.fr - e-bikes and MTBs €20/€39 per day.

Medieval, and more. Established on a peninsula enclosed in a meander of the Lot, this ancient capital of the Cadurci tribe has taken as its emblem the famous Valentré Bridge, which spans the river with its three imposing fortified towers. As you stroll through its secret gardens, embark on a discovery of the narrow streets and tall houses that bear witness to the medieval history of Cahors. The town has an exceptional protected area around the cathedral, whose grand portal is on a par with any of the finest Romanesque structures in the southwest of France. Also not to be missed: the interesting museum dedicated to the Toulouse-born painter Henri Martin (1860-1943), which reopened in 2022 after six years of renovation work.
Tourist office - pl. François-Mitterrand - ☏ 05 65 53 20 65 - www.cahorsvalleedulot.com.
Henri-Martin Museum, Cahors - 792 r. Émile-Zola - ☏ 05 65 20 88 88 - www.museehenrimartin.fr - 11 a.m.-6 p.m. - closed Mon.-Tue. - €8 (children: €5).

A bed for the night. Everyone off at the Terminus! Facing the station, this 1911 hotel has retained its Art Deco style. The rooms are not brand spanking new, but they are spacious, comfortable and have retained their retro charm. The nicest rooms are those with stained glass windows and antique furniture. Moreover, its restaurant, Le Bistro 1911, has lots going for it. A little further on, 11 minutes' walk from the station, the aptly named Hotel Jean XXII is a

TRUFFLE HUNTING IN LALBENQUE

If you travel between December and early March, why not make a slight detour to the truffle market in Lalbenque, where the "black gold of Quercy" is sold every Tuesday, from 3 p.m., in the town hall concourse. The village is served by our line, between Caussade and Cahors, but the station of Lalbenque-Fontanes is 4 km from the village. The train option can be worthwhile if you have a bicycle, in order to combine the outing with the "Truffle country route" ("Route des paysages trufficole") circuit (23 km, 4h). Otherwise, it is more convenient to take liO 881 coach from Cahors (37min).

convenient and quiet stopover at the foot of the Jean XXII (Pope John XXII) tower. The walls of this ancient palace (13th century), built by the pontiff's family, house comfortable and functional rooms.

Hôtel Terminus - 5 av. Charles-de-Freycinet - ☎ 05 65 53 32 00 - www.terminus-1911.fr - 20 rms. €60/€125 - ☕ €10 - 🍴 €10.

Hôtel Jean XXII - 2 r. Edmond-Albe - ☎ 09 87 75 77 48 - www.hotel-jeanxxii.com - 9 rms. €75/€85 - ☕ €9.

Beneath the cathedral's gilt. Built in the Romanesque-Byzantine style, and crowned by its two exceptional domes, Cahors Cathedral celebrated its 900th anniversary in 2019. On the site of a church dating back to St. Didier (7th century), a Romanesque building was constructed at the beginning of the 12th century, whose high altar was consecrated in 1119 by Pope Callistus II. Modifications made in the 13th and 14th centuries were completed from 1493 onwards with the reconstruction of the cloister in the flamboyant Gothic style and the creation of the chapel of St. Gausbert. The cathedral thus has a composite appearance, consisting of a Romanesque nave with domes, with an apse adjoined at one end and a fortress-like western end. It expresses the power of the bishops, counts and barons of Cahors, who were responsible for overseeing both the religious devotions and the peace of their vassals.

Cahors Cathedral and its cloister - pl. Chapou - ☎ 05 65 35 27 80 - www.paroissedecahors.fr - 9 a.m.-noon, 2-7 p.m., Sun. 2-7 p.m.

On the Valentré bridge. This work is a remarkable example of the military art of the Middle Ages. Its three towers, two of which are fortified, its crenellated parapets and its sharp-edged starlings punctuate the succession of seven arches, thus creating an impression of great harmony. The initial appearance of the bridge, begun in 1308, was significantly modified during the restoration work undertaken in 1879 by Paul Gout, after the style of Viollet-le-Duc : of the two gatehouses that completed the defences, one was destroyed, and the other was modified to acquire its current appearance. As it stood at the time, it formed a sort of isolated fortress determining who got across the river. While the central tower served as an observation post, the end towers were secured with doors and portcullises. The towers rise 40 m above the river. According to legend, the architect of the Valentré Bridge sold his soul to the Devil in exchange for his help. But the architect did not keep his word and, in revenge, Satan is said to have made the same stone from the north-east corner of the central tower fall on to the bridge every day. This is the very place where the 19th century renovators carved the effigy of a devil!

Dining. Le Courson is the product of superb alchemy between one couple: she, the inspired cook, and he, the passionate sommelier. The result is a bistro-bar with an inventive menu that won't cost you a fortune. The cuisine, needless to say, is based on fresh local produce. The Bistrot des Étaliers awaits you in the Halle de Cahors, which was refurbished in 2019. Quick and efficient service and tasty fare. Small dishes (soups, tapas, ravioli) or more copious ones (roast lamb, duck brochettes). Perfect for a quick lunch.

Le Courson - 28 allée Fénelon - ☎ 05 65 35 10 74 - closed Sun.-Mon. - dishes €15/€25.

Le Bistrot des Étaliers - 50 pl. Galdemar (in the Halle) - ☎ 06 47 63 01 74 - 8:30 a.m.-7 p.m., Sun. 9:30 a.m.-2 p.m. - closed Mon. - dishes €10/€22.

Immediate boarding. Treat yourself to a guided cruise (1h15) on the river meander around the city of Cahors, with passage through the Coty lock.

Bateau Le Valentré - quai Valentré - ☎ 05 65 30 16 55 - www.bateau-cahors.com - May-Sept. : 11 a.m., 3 p.m. and 4:30 p.m.; rest of the year: contact for details. - closed Nov.-March - €12.50 (ages 5-13: €6).

Sweet snack. Colour and freshness in one of the prettiest streets in Cahors: for a smoothie or a tart, and based on organic and local products. Delicious!

Lily Bowl - 12 r. Daurade - ☎ 06 30 03 73 89 - 10h-15h - closed Sat.-Mon.

Aperitif time. These small producers offer plenty to eat and drink, and it's all mighty good! Just behind the cathedral, you will find a shop,

Cahors. ZX-6R/Getty Images Plus

a wine bar, and a small restaurant where you can enjoy fresh and local products (salads, foie gras, pasta, etc.).
Les Petits Producteurs - 4 pl. Champollion - ℘ 05 65 31 26 24 or 06 81 04 35 67 - www.lespetitsproducteurs.fr - 9:30 a.m.-7 p.m., Sun. 10 a.m.-3 p.m.

Music! The Cahors Blues Festival inspires a week of concerts by artistes of renown on the Place Bessières. Also in the summer, ClassiCahors lays on a programme of quality classical concerts, played in beautiful venues.
Cahors Blues Festival - www.cahorsbluesfestival.com - mid-Jul.
ClassiCahors - www.classicahors.com - late Jul.

⑤ GOURDON

➔ **The station is a 10-minute walk from the tourist office, on the way to the town centre.**

On its mound. Between the Périgord and Quercy, Gourdon is situated on the side of a rocky mound once topped by a castle. Its remarkably well-preserved medieval architecture is sheltered from traffic, which is confined to the lower boulevards. Away from all the noise, you climb the sloping streets to the esplanade overlooking the valleys of the Bouriane.

Tourist office - 20 bd des Martyrs - ℘ 05 65 27 52 50 - www.tourisme-gourdon.com.

A bed for the night. A 12-minute walk from the station, the establishment has been offering its hospitality since 1898. A handsome location, comfortable rooms, and pleasant service: an establishment in the time-honoured French tradition. Settle in for a nice rest in the well-maintained, rustic rooms. And in the summer, you can enjoy the pleasant tranquillity of the garden.
Hostellerie de la Bouriane - pl. du Foirail - ℘ 05 65 41 16 37 - www.hotellabouriane.fr - closed from early Jan. to mid-Mar. - 20 rms. €113/€149 - ☕ €16 - 🍴 menu €39/€62.

Dining. On a shady terrace, you can tuck into tasty pizzas, grills, salads and local specialities.
Pizzeria La Notté - 30 r. du Corps-Franc-Pommies - ℘ 05 65 41 27 70 - 9 a.m.-2:30 p.m., 5-10:30 p.m. - closed Oct.-May - pizzas €12/€15 - dishes €16/€20.

The Medievals. Tourneys, camps, storytellers, blacksmiths... and medieval feasting in the streets of Gourdon.
Info: www.medievalesdegourdon.jimdofree.com - 1st w'end in Aug.

Fabulous Journeys

From Cahors to Figeac, in the footsteps of the pilgrims to Santiago de Compostela (the Way of Saint James)

The GR® 65, which pilgrims have for centuries called the Via Podiensis, or Chemin du Puy, is a reasonable way to set out on the Way of Saint James that leads all the way to Santiago de Compostela, with beautiful scenery in store: the Haut-Quercy and causses, with their oak trees, rocks and lavender. If you then want to carry on further along the pilgrimage trail, it's entirely up to you!
But before setting off on this Fabulous Journey, take the time to visit Cahors. Make sure to see Cahors Cathedral and the Valentré Bridge, both listed as UNESCO World Heritage sites, and to stroll through the narrow streets of the old town. Notice to food lovers: the market held on Wednesday and Saturday mornings in the Place de la Cathédrale simply is a must, ranked as it is among the twenty-five most beautiful markets in France. As for the wines of Cahors, their reputation precedes them. Drop into one of the town's many wine shops for a wee tasting to see you on your way. Now you're all set to discover some lovely sections of the GR® 65: Varaire, Cajarc and Béduer are the main stops on your way. Finish off with a visit to the town of Figeac. Its medieval streets will lead you to its gothic palaces or to Champollion's birthplace, which houses the Musée des Écritures du Monde (Museum of the world's writing systems). The journey is far from over!

5 days, 4 nights - around €20 per night per person - to be done in spring and autumn.
Contacts: Cahors and Figeac tourist offices.

Way of St. James. Bepsimage/Getty Images Plus

6 SOUILLAC

→ The station is an 18-minute walk from the town centre.

🚲 **Bike hire.** There is a bike hire service an 18-minute walk from the station.
La Bicicleta Ravito - 25 av. de Sarlat - ☎ 06 83 73 12 96/06 08 65 80 91 - www.labicicletaravito.com - hybrid bikes €30/day, e-bikes €45/day.

At the gateway to the Périgord Noir. Souillac has preserved an exceptional architectural heritage, starting with its domed church. You'll enjoy discovering its pretty streets and its gentle hustle and bustle, before heading off to explore Quercy and the Périgord Noir. Road traffic is quickly forgotten as you make your way through the narrow, medieval streets punctuated by small squares where cafe and restaurant terraces are set up on sunny days. They all converge on the pleasant Place du Puits. Pass via the Rue de la Halle until you reach the belfry, and then carry on to Souillac Abbey. A masterpiece of Romanesque-Byzantine art in Haut-Quercy, the Church of St Mary dates back to the 12th century and is similar to the domed buildings in Périgueux and Cahors. Its Musée de l'Automate (Automaton Museum) will also be worth a visit on reopening, after its closure for renovation in 2023.
Tourist office - bd Louis-Jean-Malvy - ☎ 05 65 33 22 00 - www.vallee-dordogne.com.

A bed for the night. A 15-minute walk from the station, Le Quercy promises a family welcome in a comfortable hotel away from the centre. Most of the well-kept rooms have a balcony overlooking the flowered terrace or the pool.
A further 5 minutes' walk will take you to the Grand Hotel, a century-old building with contemporary rooms suited to every customer profile. A patio, pleasantly bathed in natural daylight, illuminates the breakfast room.
Le Quercy - 1 r. de la Recège - ☎ 05 65 37 83 56 - www.le-quercy.fr - closed Dec.-Feb. - 🍴 - 23 rms. €74/€82 - ☕ €12.
Grand Hôtel - 1 allée Verninac - ☎ 05 65 27 76 21 - www.legrandhotel.net - closed from early Nov. to mid.Feb. - 28 rms. €61/€131 - ☕ €12 - 🍴 meal deal: €23/€25, menu €28.

Dining. At La Bicicleta Ravito, in a large house and hangar decked out with second-hand objects and trinkets, people come to rent a bike but also to enjoy lunch, have a drink, and to meet up and chat over a plancha, a fresh juice or a dish made with local produce.
La Bicicleta Ravito - 25 av. de Sarlat - ☎ 06 83 73 12 96 - www.labicicletaravito.com - closed Mon. - dishes €10/€25.

Let yourself get whisked away. A 15-minute walk to the south of the town centre, you can take the plunge. There are canoes and kayaks for paddling on the Dordogne, a water park, and a treetop challenge.
Quercyland - Les Ondines - ☎ 05 65 32 72 61 - www.copeyre.com - 11 a.m.-8 p.m. - closed from mid-Sept. to 1st May - rental €20 pp. with access to park, otherwise €10.

Aperitif time. Regional liqueurs and aperitifs are made here in keeping with a tradition that stretches back almost a century. You can try its Vieille Prune, the eau-de-vie that made the distillery's reputation. Free visit to the cellars, with tasting.
Louis Roque Distillery - 41 av. Jean-Jaurès - ☎ 05 65 32 78 16 - www.lavieilleprune.com - 8:30 a.m.-noon, 2-5:30 p.m. - closed Sat.-Sun.

Jazz in town. The 7-day Sim Copans (Souillac en Jazz) festival is open to all different styles of jazz.
Souillac en jazz - www.souillacenjazz.fr - mid-Jul.

On the heights of Souillac. The Visorando website proposes a walk of medium difficulty (13 km, 4h20) starting from the station. This tour will take you to the heights of Souillac, to the Marjaudes and Présignac viaducts, amidst the diverse and varied flora.
Circuit on the heights above Souillac and its environs - www.visorando.com/randonnee-circuit-sur-les-hauteurs-de-souillac-et-/.

7 BRIVE-LA-GAILLARDE

See the Causses of Quercy line p. 17.

A biking tour

The Aveyron Gorges

85 km in 3 stages, from Montauban to Laguépie.

Higher and higher it goes! But what a beautiful view! From Montauban, to enjoy cycling along the valley and gorges of the Aveyron, the magnificent villages and perched castles, the river beaches and shady banks, there are two solutions: either calves of steel or an e-bike.

Montauban to Montricoux: 33 km

Reserved for strong cyclists (or e-bike users), this circuit starts off gently, for a little over 2 hours in the saddle, with 65 m of ascending gradient. It is a warm-up for what is to come. Take your time and make the most of it. Start with a little ride around bike-friendly Montauban. Starting from the Rue du Fort, near the tourist office, the cycle route is signposted. After a first hill, the route joins the "Promenade des Montalbanais" (3rd km) and remains in its own segregated lane until you get out of town. It then winds its way along quiet roads. At Nègrepelisse (22nd km), you finally meet up with the Aveyron, whose course you follow until Montricoux, the evening stopover. On the way, admire at your leisure - or better still, visit - the castles of Nègrepelisse and Montricoux.

Montricoux to St-Antonin-Noble-Val: 28 km

Be warned: things start getting tougher now! The stage is short but it climbs, with 520 m of ascents (and almost as many descents)! That said: what a view! A causse at the bottom of which flows the Aveyron, with its gorges dotted with villages and castles perched on high, such as that at Bruniquel. These are panoramas that are well worth all that exertion! Using mainly small roads, the route joins the busy D115 twice, with no reserved bicycle lanes, so take particular care between Bruniquel (5th km) and Penne (13th km), then on the 2 km stretch

PRACTICAL INFO

- **Hiring a bike at Montauban**
Maison du Vélo – 16 allée de l'Empereur (15 min. walk from the station) - ☎ 06 17 13 90 72 - www.montm.com/tm-velo - daily exc. Sun. 12:30-7 p.m. Standard bikes (€6/wk.) and e-bikes (€10/day, €25/wk.). Basket included, but not the helmet. Please note that bicycles must be returned during shop opening hours.

- **Where to stay?**
At Montricoux: Le Chat qui dort B&B – 26 Grand'Rue - Montricoux - ☎ 05 63 27 62 81 - 2 rms. €60 ☕. In the heart of the village, this establishment, with its beautiful combination of terracotta tiles, beams and contemporary touches, offers two comfortable rooms. In fine weather, breakfast (with homemade jams) is served in the patio adjacent to the church.
At St-Antonin-Noble-Val: La Résidence B&B - 37 r. Droite - ☎ 05 63 67 37 56 - www.laresidence-france.com - 4 rms. €118/€164 ☕.
At Laguépie: Gîte de Lez - hameau de Lez - ☎ 06 33 89 02 40 - www.gitesdelez.com - Apr.-Nov., rest of the year: on request - 🛏 - 2 rms. €70, chalet €520/€800/wk.

- **And for the return trip?**
Allow at least 2 hours to reach Montauban from Laguépie by train, changing at Toulouse.

- **Useful to know**
Please be aware that this route runs too infrequently along segregated cycle paths to be recommended for children.

---

from Vayrevignes (20th km). Just after that, at the 22nd km, you reach the longest hill on the route (100 m elevation gain)! Well done! You've at last reached the medieval village of St-Antonin-Noble-Val, the day's stopover destination.

St-Antonin-Noble-Val to Laguépie: 24 km

Another uphill stage, but far less than the day before (234 m of hill climbs). You'll need to spend a little over 1h30 in the saddle. The route starts on the left bank of the river, on the quiet D958. At the 7th km, it crosses the river and then the D115 a few hundred metres further on. Take care at the junction! The route runs alongside Lexos railway station. And what a station! It is huge, monumental: incongruous for such a small village! It needs to be remembered that Lexos was an important railway hub from 1864 to 1955. Today, only trains on the Toulouse-Figeac line stop here (see p. 96). A curiosity not to be missed! After Lexos and the 500 m of shared roadway on the rather busy D958, you can take it easy on the last stretch, which is just as spectacular as the previous one, consisting mainly of small, quiet roads at the bottom of the valley, running alongside the Aveyron. This will take you all the way to Laguépie, the end of a beautiful cycle trip, where you can relax on the beach on the banks of the Viaur. Take a dip, or just take it easy. Whatever you choose, it's a great way to finish your excursion!

THE BASTIDES AND MOST BEAUTIFUL VILLAGES LINE

This line makes a clear link between nature and heritage. After the pink roofs of the beautiful city of Toulouse, you next see passing by the window the wooded hills and green valleys of the Tarn and Aveyron, traversed by meandering streams and the Tarn river itself, watched over by ancient bastides, perched castles and Albigensian towns. The age of chivalry!

⭐ **TOULOUSE TO VILLEFRANCHE-DE-ROUERGUE - 9 DAYS**

- Non-stop trip: 1h40
- Frequency : 6 liO trains/day
- Timetables: www.ter.sncf.com/occitanie/se-deplacer/fiches-horaires
- Non-stop trip: €22.20
- Onboard service: bikes carried free of charge
- Useful to know: from Villefranche, you can continue on to Figeac (return to Toulouse from Figeac in 2h30, changing at Capdenac)
- Connected lines: Pyrenees, Lot and Dordogne, Canal du Midi, Piémont and Gers lines from Toulouse; Tarn line from St-Sulpice; the Cathedrals line shares the same route start.

📷 Where best to sit to admire the landscape? On the left, in the direction of travel.

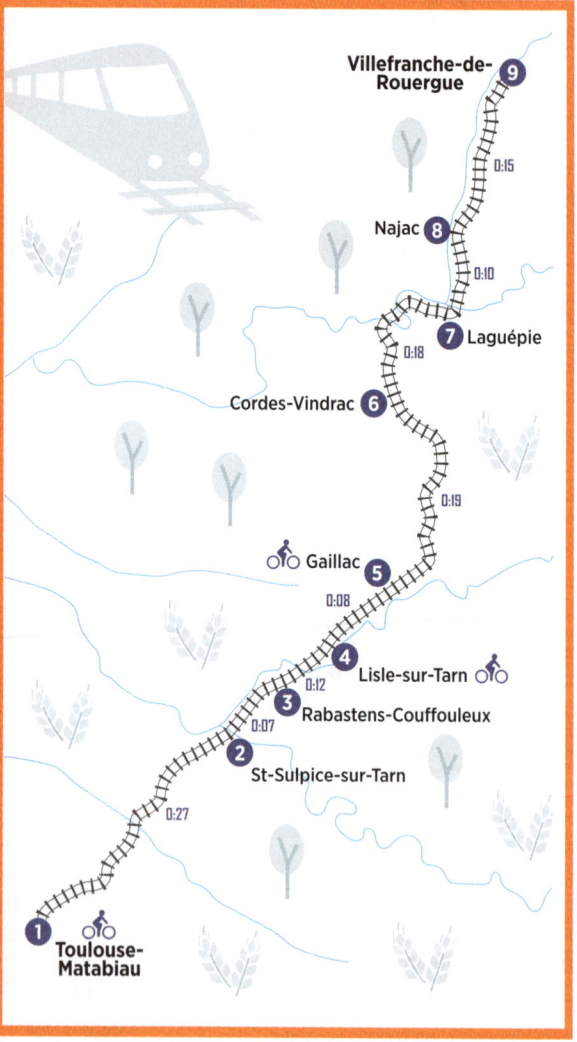

*The Tarn valley.
clodio/Getty Images Plus*

① TOULOUSE-MATABIAU

See the Pyrenees line p. 84.

② ST-SULPICE-SUR-TARN

Making a point. At the confluence of the Tarn and the Agout, St-Sulpice-la-Pointe took its name from the "pointed" shape of its territory. The 14th century brick church has the highest bell tower (40 m) on the Tarn and a graceful suspension bridge which has spanned the Tarn since 1931. This bastide is dominated by the ruins of Castela castle. Beneath these remains, you can visit the 142 m of galleries and its four rooms and retrace the history of those who used it over the centuries, such as counterfeiters or wool spinners.
Tourist office - r. du 3-Mars-1930 - ☏ 05 63 41 89 50 - www.tourisme-tarnagout.com.
Castela Underground - rue du 3-Mars-1930 - guided tour only - from Easter to 1st Nov. - €7.50 (under 15s: €5) - info. from the tourist office.

A bed for the night. Close to the station (5 minutes' walk), this hotel offers spacious rooms with individual terraces. The rather old-fashioned decoration does not detract from the establishment's friendly welcome.
Hôtel Le Cocagne - 1 av. Rhin-et-Danube - ☏ 05 63 41 10 90 - www.hotel-cocagne.fr - 16 rms. €68/€78 - 🍽 €10.

Dining. With its large terrace, this brasserie is the place to be! Warm welcome, fine meats and homemade French fries. Concerts on some nights.
Ô St Sulp - 71 r. de la Loubatière - ☏ 05 63 40 41 67 - closed Sun.-Mon. - €10/€20.

③ RABASTENS-COUFFOULEUX

→ The station serves Rabastens. You have to cross the Tarn to reach the centre.

Do the walls. On the right bank of the Tarn, covered with cereal crops, vines, vegetable plots and orchards, this red brick town dominates the river with its powerful ramparts. Although the town of Rabastens was a strong supporter of the heretics, it did not put up any resistance to the Catholic troops during the Albigensian Crusade, but was forced to destroy its fortifications. All that remains of the old castle is the Place du Plô des Chevaliers. The church of Notre-Dame-du-Bourg resembles a fortress, whose imposing facade is pierced by a portal with beautiful Romanesque capitals. Founded in the 12th century by the Benedictines of Moissac in the lower town, it is listed as a World Heritage Site by UNESCO as part of the Way of St. James (Santiago de Compostela) pilgrimage route.

Tourist office - 2 r. Amédée-Clausade - 0 805 40 08 28 - www.la-toscane-occitane.com.

Dining and overnighting. An 11-minute walk from the station, this intimate, family-run hotel offers spacious rooms and room service on request. You can also dine in the restaurant, whose menu changes with the seasons.

Le 9 en Cuisine - 9 pl. St-Michel - 05 63 33 57 17 - www.9-en-cuisine.fr - 4 rms. €110/€120 - restaurant open Thurs.-Sat. evenings and Sat. lunch - dishes €24.50/€35.

A pleasant dip. The village has one of the few natural beaches in the department, set up each summer on a bank of the Tarn after the winter spates.

Rabastens-Plage beach - walk down to the beach via the stairs at the end of Rue du Fossé-Moulinal or via the Promenade de Constance - Jul.-Aug. - 2:30-6 p.m.

fountain. A stroll through the historic centre reveals some old brick and wood houses from the 16th, 17th and 18th centuries. Some of them are linked to their outbuildings by *"pountets"* (small covered footbridges) spanning the streets overhead. The church of Notre-Dame-de-la-Jonquière has a Romanesque portal and a Toulouse-style bell tower. From the bridge there is a pleasant view of the town and its terraced gardens.

Tourist office - pl. Paul-Saissac - 0 805 40 08 28 - www.la-toscane-occitane.com.

A bed for the night. A 10-minute walk from the station, on a 3-hectare property with century-old cedars, this attractive house with blue shutters offers superb rooms that are comfortable and elegant, some with a private lounge. With spa, jacuzzi, pool, and billiard room.

Domaine Christanna - 1325 rte de Toulouse - 06 49 71 51 31 - domaine-christanna.com - 4 rms. €95/€115 - set menu: €30.

Dining. In the rustic dining room, the ceiling beams and beautiful fireplace with its crackling fire in the winter offer a perfect complement to the traditional and regional cuisine based on fresh produce. The delightful terrace proves very pleasant in fine weather.

Le Romuald - 6 r. du Port - 05 63 33 38 85 - www.restaurant-leromuald-lislesurtarn.fr - closed Tue. eve. and Sun. eve. - lunch deal €16 - menu: €32.

④ LISLE-SUR-TARN

Bike hire. Electric mountain bikes and hybrid bikes, beside the station. The Tarn Valley cycle route between St-Sulpice-sur-Tarn and Albi (63 km) passes via Lisle-sur-Tarn and Gaillac.

Les Vélos de Léonce - 8 quai Pasteur - 05 63 33 35 06 - lesvelosdeleonce.com - €30/€60 per 1/2 day.

On an isle. Situated on the Tarn river, this bastide town, created in 1229, became a true island when a ditch was dug to ensure its defence. Hence its name ("Lisle": literally, "the island"). This large village in Albigensian country has preserved from its past a large square with a

⑤ GAILLAC

Bike hire. The La Bonne Échappée bike-café hires out road bikes and tandems, and proposes wine tours.

La Bonne Échappée - 20 r. des Frères-Delga - 06 50 89 92 76 - labonneechappee.com - closed Sun.-Mon. - €25/€35/day.

Dolce vita in the air. Situated on the banks of the Tarn, this small town's prosperity was long linked to its bustling port. Today, the town is proud to represent the Gaillac PDO, comprising mainly red, but also white, rosé, sweet white, and sparkling wine. Stroll at leisure through the narrow streets lined with the old houses of ancient Gaillac, where brick and wood blend harmoniously. With its brick and stone walls, the gothic-style St. Peter's church is adorned with a superb 14th century portal. Go down to the Place du Griffoul, with its pleasant arcades and 16th century fountain. The splendid French and Italianate gardens of the 17th century Parc de Foucaud are terraced above the Tarn.

Tourist office - abbaye St-Michel - ✆ 0 805 40 08 28 - www.tourisme-vignoble-bastides.com.

Dining and overnighting. In a former 19th century glassworks surrounded by a park, this charming hotel is an ideal stopover, near the station (7 min. walk). In the restaurant, bistronomy is the order of the day and vegetarians are welcome.

Hôtel-restaurant La Verrerie - 1 r. de l'Égalité - ✆ 05 63 57 32 77 - www.laverrerie81.com - 14 rms. €95/€130 - 🍽 €11 - ✗ closed Sun. eve. - lunch deals €18/€23 - menu €25/€40.

Discover the wines of Gaillac. This winery on the banks of the Tarn presents the production of 95 wine estates and 3 cooperative cellars. For tastings and direct sales, a presentation of the vineyard and an introduction to tasting.

Maison des vins de Gaillac - Caveau St-Michel - abbaye St-Michel - ✆ 05 63 57 15 40 - www.vins-gaillac.com - closed Sun. p.m. off season - wine tasting initiation 2h20/€30.

❻ CORDES-VINDRAC

➜ The station is at Vindrac-Alayrac. To reach Cordes-sur-Ciel (4.5 km on a steep slope): liO 707 coach or on-demand taxi service.
Info: www.mairie.cordessurciel.fr (in French: "Vie pratique" ("Practicalities") tab, "Au quotidien"("Daily life") section).

Closer to the stars. Perched on the summit of the Puech de Mordagne, in a beautiful setting, Cordes-sur-Ciel is a medieval town overlooking the Cérou valley. The town that is also known as the "city of a thousand arches" is a town out of time, stranded, according to Camus, "on the border of another universe", where the light plays on the pink and grey tones of the sandstone facades. Visiting Cordes means above all strolling as the fancy takes you through the upper town's cobbled streets, among an exceptional collection of Gothic houses (13th-14th century), admiring the sculpted decoration of their facades and lingering in front

Cordes-sur-Ciel.
H. Lenain/hemis.fr

of the shop windows of craftspersons, some of which are highly original to say the least!
Tourist office - 38-42 Grand-Rue Raimond-VII - Maison Gaugiran - 0 800 400 828 - www.cordessurciel.fr.

Dining and overnighting. This 13th century building is arranged around a charming patio, shaded by a wisteria several hundred years old. A fine spiral staircase leads to the perfectly kept, personalised rooms, some with spectacular views over the surrounding countryside. Traditional cuisine with a particular focus on foie gras, served in a dining room-terrace overlooking the valley, or in the patio.
Hostellerie du Vieux Cordes - 21 r. St-Michel - 05 63 53 79 20 - www.hotelcordes.fr - 11 rms. €90/€150 - €20 - €39.

Sweet or savoury snack. Desserts, fruit tarts, local specialities (croquant and pavé de Cordes), homemade ice creams (traditional or more original flavours), and other delicacies await you in this pastry shop, which also doubles as a tea room that serves lunches too (savoury tarts, pies, pizzas, etc.)
Maison Moulin - 1 av. du 8-Mai-1945 - 05 63 56 00 41 - closed Wed. from Nov. to Mar.

Heavenly music. This festival celebrates classical music in the 2nd fortnight of July. A melting pot for young soloists, as well as for violin and bow makers.
Info: www.festivalcordessurciel.com.

⑦ LAGUÉPIE

➔ See this stopover on p. 95. 🚴 It marks the end point of a nice cycling tour in the Aveyron gorges.

⑧ NAJAC

➔ The station is located on the other side of the Aveyron river, so it takes 20 min to walk to the old town. It is a very up and down place, so wear sensible shoes!
On-demand transport service (TAD in french) - lio-occitanie - booking required by calling 05 65 73 40 49 - Mon.-Fri. 9 a.m.-noon, 1:30-5 p.m.

What a site! Perched on its promontory overlooking a meander of the Aveyron, the old town (13th-16th century) seems to slumber beneath its slate roofs, which are still dominated by the

Najac and its castle.

towers of its formidable fortified castle. A masterpiece of 13th century military art, the fortress of Najac has retained an incredible fortified system flanked by large round towers. The southeast tower, the biggest one, was the keep, from which the views are magnificent. The ruined parts owe their condition mainly to the use of the stone as a quarry in the 19th century.
Tourist office - 25 pl. du Faubourg - ℘ 05 36 16 20 00 - www.tourisme-villefranche-najac.com.
Fortress - rue du Château - ℘ 05 65 29 71 65 - closed Nov.-Mar. - €6.50 (ages 7-16: €5).

Dining and overnighting. Just 4 minutes' walk from the station, on the banks of the Aveyron, the Belle Rive hotel, overlooked by the castle, is ideal for a nice quiet stopover. The rooms are functional and well kept. Dining room with large shady terrace. Traditional cuisine.
If you prefer to be in the heart of the village, check in at L'Oustal del Barry, which borders the central square. The owner concocts fine cuisine with regional accents that you can enjoy in the "rustic chic" dining room. Lovely summer terraces and comfortable rooms.
Hôtel Belle Rive - 4 r. Roc-du-Pont - ℘ 05 65 29 73 90 - www.le-belle-rive.fr - 🛏 - closed Nov.-Mar. - 17 rms. €78 - ⌑ €10.50 - ✕ €27/€31.
L'Oustal del Barry - 2 pl. Sol-del-Barry - ℘ 05 65 29 74 32 - www.oustaldelbarry.com - closed from end Dec. to mid-Feb. - 17 rms. €75/€95 - ⌑ €10 - ✕ lunch deal €17 - €21/€60.

For a picnic. This is a grocery-cum-delicatessen that sells more or less everything, preferably organic and locally produced: fruit, vegetables, eggs, meat, cheese, bread.
L'Épicerie du Coin - 33 pl. du Faubourg - ℘ 06 10 84 94 06 - Apr.-Sept.: variable opening times.

9 VILLEFRANCHE-DE-ROUERGUE

Villa Franca, the "free town". The town owes its name to the fact that it once granted franchises and privileges to new residents. Nestled between Rouergue and Quercy, Villefranche is a bastide town, founded in 1252, whose roofs crowd around at the foot of the imposing tower of the Church of Notre-Dame (13th-15th century) and whose narrow streets lend themselves admirably to a discovery stroll. Although Villefranche has since lost some of its medieval appearance with the destruction of its moats, ramparts and fortified gates, its identity as a bastide can still be clearly seen in its stone and cob houses, and its checkerboard layout with streets leading to the covered central square, and whose arcades shield the traders.
Touris office - prom. du Guiraudet - ℘ 05 36 16 20 00 - www.bastides-gorges-aveyron.fr.

A bed for the night. This stone building has been turned into a refined hotel with a contemporary style marked by sleek decor, genuine comfort and a cosy atmosphere. Its proximity to the railway station (10 minutes' walk) and to the Chapelle des Pénitents Noirs in the town centre makes it an ideal location.
Les Fleurines - 17 bd de Haute-Guyenne - ℘ 05 65 45 86 90 - www.lesfleurines.com - 24 rms. €61/€181 - ⌑ €13.

Dining. What you can be sure of at the Pied de Poule is that everything is home-made, using local produce. Find out for yourself when you sit down to eat: the house rule here is fresh daily, and where inspiration leads! You can bank on it!
Le Pied de Poule - 52 r. de la République - ℘ 07 66 80 57 80 - closed Mon-Thurs eve., Sat-Sun. - meal deals €15/€17.

For a picnic. In addition to the big Thursday morning market, this is the place to go to for local produce, including the famous Causse hams, which hang above the entrance. Very nice butcher's, delicatessen, dairy, cheese and preserves (ceps, duck fritons, etc.) sections, as well as local wines.
Pavillon du Causse - allée Aristide-Briand - ℘ 05 65 81 25 11 - www.fontalbat-mazars.com - daily exc. Sun.

THE CATHEDRALS LINE

From nowhere came the train of the cathedrals... After leaving behind Saint-Étienne de Toulouse, Sainte-Cécile, on its rocky outcrop, reveals its silhouette as you approach Albi. The line terminates at the foot of Notre-Dame de Rodez, one of the largest cathedrals in southern France. On the way, you will feel closer to the sky and hold your breath as you leave Tanus, when the line crosses the famous Viaduc du Viaur railway bridge, whose metal arch extends 116 m above the valley floor.

★ TOULOUSE TO RODEZ - 9 DAYS

- Non-stop trip: 2h20
- Frequency : 8 liO trains/day
- Timetables: www.ter.sncf.com/occitanie/se-deplacer/fiches-horaires
- Non-stop trip: €27.50
- Onboard services: bicycle transport authorised
- Connected lines: Pyrenees, Lot and Dordogne, Canal du Midi, Piémont and Gers lines from Toulouse; Causses of Quercy line from Rodez; the Bastides and most beautiful villages line shares the same route start.

Where best to sit to admire the landscape? On the right of the train, in the direction of travel.

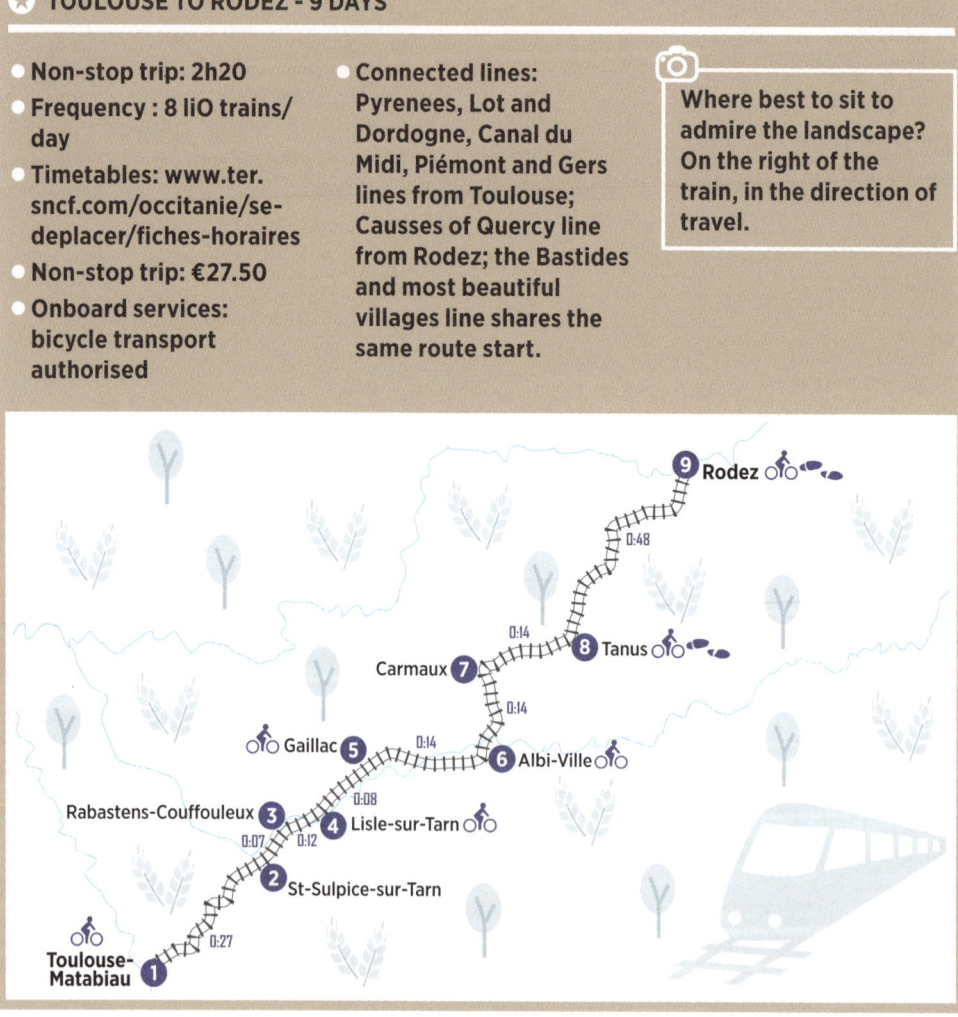

Albi, the cathedral.
Christophe Bouthé-Pierre Behar Balloïde Photos/Ville d'Albi

THE CATHEDRALS LINE

❶ TOULOUSE-MATABIAU

See the Pyrenees line p. 84.

❷ ST-SULPICE-SUR-TARN

See the Bastides line p. 97.

❸ RABASTENS-COUFFOULEUX

See the Bastides line p. 97.

❹ LISLE-SUR-TARN

See the Bastides line p. 98.

❺ GAILLAC

See the Bastides line p. 98.

❻ ALBI-VILLE

➜ Albi-Ville station is a 15-minute walk southwest of the cathedral.

🚲 Bike hire. 15 minutes' walk from the station, with hybrid bike, MTB and e-bike hire for adults and children.
L'Occ Bike - 1 r des Catherinettes - 📞 05 63 76 55 20 - www.locc-bike.com - hybrid and mountain bikes: €15 per 1/2 day, e-bikes from €25.

All clad in brick. The episcopal city is an imposing site atop its promontory, with its archetypal feel of the southern climes. Yet the town below is also ripe for discovery, passing via the banks of the Tarn with superb views of its ancient fortifications. Make sure to take a stroll through the old town, with its many townhouses, testifying to its prosperity from the 15th century onwards, built on the trade in saffron and woad. Not forgetting the Palais de la Berbie where an important collection of works by Toulouse-Lautrec, a native son, is on display.
Tourist office - 2 r. Mariès - 📞 05 63 36 36 00 - www.albi-tourisme.fr.

Toulouse-Lautrec Museaum - pl. Ste-Cécile - palais de la Berbie - ☏ 05 63 49 48 70 - www.musee-toulouse-lautrec.com - 10 a.m.-6 p.m.; Oct.-May: Daily exc. Mon. 10 a.m.-12:30 p.m., 2-6 p.m. - €10 (under 13s: free entry).

A bed for the night. A 15-minute walk from the station and ideally located on Albi's finest square, the Hôtel du Vigan offers simple and colourful rooms at reasonable prices. At the back of the square, the venerable 18th century Hostellerie Saint-Antoine has its spacious and quiet rooms arranged around a charming garden.

Hôtel du Vigan - 16 pl. du Vigan - ☏ 05 63 43 31 31 - www.hotelvigan.com - 37 rms. €70/€90 - 🍽 €10.

Hostellerie Saint-Antoine - 7 r. St-Antoine - ☏ 05 63 54 04 04 - www.hotel-saint-antoine-albi.com - closed from early Nov. to Easter weekend - 44 rms. €116/€168 - 🍽 €14.50.

Rich interior, sleek exterior. It can be admired from the Pont du 22-Août bridge or from the streets of old Albi as you enter the square. The apparent simplicity of the cathedral, whose construction began in 1282, does nothing to suggest the incredible richness of its interior. Once you have passed through the monumental portal completed by Bishop Dominique de Florence at the end of the 14th century, you need to climb the majestic staircase that leads to the baldachin-shaped porch (1520-1535). The choir was built between 1474 and 1484 under the patronage of Louis Ist of Amboise. The late Gothic style is fully on show here, with an abundance of intertwined motifs, artfully arranged pinnacles and arches, and vaults with richly decorated keystones. The huge painting on the western wall (under the great organ) is one of the largest depictions of the Last Judgement in the world. Completed between 1474 and 1484, the central part of the cathedral was unfortunately damaged in 1693 when the wall was pierced to give access to the chapel of St Clair. Louis II of Amboise called upon Italians to decorate the walls and the vault (1509-1512). The artists from the region of Bologna (Carpi) who adorned the vault of the cathedral's nave with dazzling frescoes took their inspiration from the splendours of the Quattrocento (15th century), the great century of the Italian Renaissance.

Cathédrale Ste-Cécile - ☏ 05 63 38 47 40 - www.cathedrale-albi.com - 10 a.m.-6:30 p.m., Sun. 12-4:30 p.m.

Dining. Near the cathedral, Au Hibou is a charming little establishment much appreciated by the people of Albi for its creative regional market cuisine. Le Lautrec also offers impeccable local cuisine (including a cassoulet with cod and Tarn saffron), a stone's throw from the artist's childhood home.

Au Hibou - 21 r. St-Julien - ☏ 05 63 76 38 99 - daily exc. Wed. 7:30 a.m.-5 p.m. - lunch menu €18.

Le Lautrec - 13-15 r. Henri-de-Toulouse-Lautrec - ☏ 05 63 54 86 55 - www.restaurant-le-lautrec.com - Tues.-Sat. 12-2:30 p.m., 7:30-10 p.m. - lunch deal €18 - menu €26/€48.

Taking a "gabare". These flat-bottomed boats, used for transporting goods until the 19th century, now carry tourists on the river. After leaving the old port at the foot of the ramparts of the Palais de la Berbie, along the Tarn you will discover the Albigensian mills, and the locks of the Gardès and Mothe mills.

Albi Croisières - berges du Tarn - ☏ 05 63 43 59 63 - www.albi-croisieres.com.

Sweet snack. Right next to the cathedral, this tea room offers excellent pastries, homemade ice creams and a selection of teas and coffees, as well as homemade lemonades, to be enjoyed on the terrace or in the attractive cement tiled room.

Au Moulin à Café - 1 r. de l'Oulmet - ☏ 05 63 43 15 51 - Tues.-Sat. 10 a.m.-7 p.m., Mon. 2-7 p.m.

⑦ CARMAUX

➔ **The station is a 10-minute walk from the small centre, which can be reached via Boulevard Augustin-Malroux.**

A hint of Zola. This town in the Tarn is now looking to promote its heritage, which is certainly different, but just as representative of the region's history as that of its prestigious neighbours. The town owes its fame to its coal mining history, with deposits exending to the south-west of the town over a length of about 10 km and a width of between 1 and 3 km.

Fabulous Journeys

Discovering the Tarn Ségala without a car

➜ From Albi, you can walk or cycle along the "Chemin du mineur" ("Miner's trail") greenway.

To discover this hidden facet of the region, you leave the Tarn valley as soon as you are out of town, then head up to the heights across the mining landscape. First stop at Cagnac-les-Mines, to immerse yourself in the daily life of the miners of old with a visit to the Departmental Mine Museum *(closed for renovation, to be reopened in 2023)* and the Homps mining estate, built after the First World War to house foreign workers. You can then picnic in the Cap'Découverte leisure park, established in a former opencast coal mine. Alpine coaster, roller skating or water sports on the lake are the activities on offer: there's something for everyone! A few kilometres further on, you arrive in Carmaux, the town synonmous with Jean Jaurès.

After spending the night in this town, take the GR® 36 to Monestiés, one of the "most beautiful villages of France". The Château de Combefa, former summer residence of the bishops of Albi, and the Chapelle St-Jacques are worth a visit. You can also visit the Bajèn-Vega Museum, which contains works by both artists. Then it's time to turn around and return to Carmaux by the same route.

Finally, on the last day, you can go to Tanus to discover two wonders of the region: the Viaur viaduct and the chapel of Las Planques, a jewel of Romanesque art dating from the 11th and 12th centuries, hidden in the woods.

3 days, 2 nights - approx. €60 per night in hotel - trip to be made in spring, summer and autumn.

Monestiés
H. Lenain/hemis.fr

Tourist office - pl. Gambetta - ✆ 05 63 76 76 67 - www.tourisme-tarn-carmaux.fr.

A bed for the night. A 10-minute walk from the station, this hotel is conveniently located in the town centre. Warm, homely welcome. Full and generous breakfast. A very good choice for a stopover.
Hôtel Gambetta - 1 r Voltaire - ✆ 05 63 76 51 21 - www.hotelgambetta.info - 13 rms. €69 - 🍽 €7.

Dining. A nice surprising place with home-made dishes. Menu with organic produce or produce from sustainable agriculture. Hearty, original and excellent dishes. Flawless, fast service.
Chez Martine - 16 pl. Jean-Jaurès - ✆ 05 63 76 51 08 - daily exc. Sun. 12-2:30 p.m. - menu €18.

Mine of attractions. Families can spend a few hours in an amazing amusement park on the site of a former open-cast mine, closed in 1997. This huge space is dedicated to the environment, sports, heritage, entertainment, and science. Picnic area, snack bar and restaurant.
Cap'Découverte - 20 min from the station by liO 711 coach - ✆ 05 63 80 29 01 - www.capdecouverte.com - free-access leisure area with paid activities - Jul.-Aug.: 12-6:30 p.m.; Mar.-Jun. and Sept.-Oct.: contact for details.

⑧ TANUS

➜ The station is in the centre of the village, 3.5 km south of the Viaur viaduct.

🚲 **Bike hire.** Electric bicycles are available for loan (reservation required) to the guests of this 3-room B&B near the station.
La Voie du Viaur - 19 av. Paul-Bodin - ✆ 06 36 73 28 96 - www.lavoieduviaur.com.

A break at the bridge. This charming and typical village of Ségala is also worth a stop. From Tanus, you can get to the Viaur viaduct, a famous railway bridge, whose metal arch rises 116 m high. This 3,734 t structure, the work of engineer Paul Bodin, a pupil of Gustave Eiffel, has spanned the river since 1902 over a length of 460 m. With its central arch spanning 200 m in a verdant setting, this metal feat of engineering, listed as a historic monument, has its own particular elegance and allows the Carmaux-Rodez railway to cross the river. Getting the railway into the region at the beginning of the 20th century did much to open up the Ségala.

Dining and overnighting. A mere 3-minute walk from the station, this is a nice surprising place to come to, practical and comfortable, with a pool in the garden area. Your hosts, David and Cécilia, also serve hearty cuisine with a local flavour (such as cassoulet, tête de veau in vinaigrette, duck confit in puff pastry), just the thing after a bit of a walk.
Hôtel des Voyageurs - av. Paul-Bodin - ✆ 05 63 76 30 06 - www.hoteldesvoyageurs-tarn.fr - 🏊 - 15 rms. €46/€50 - 🍽 €7 - 🍴 open every lunchtime Tue.-Sun. and Sat eve. - menus €27/€35.

💬 **Walk to the viaduct.** On its website, the Tarn Découverte et Loisirs association presents several hiking circuits, between 1h30 and 5h30 in duration, and suited to all walkers exploring the Ségala. Special mention goes to the "Circuit du Vieux Tanus" ("Circuit of Old Tanus"): this 2-hour loop takes in its famous viaduct and runs along the Viaur.
Tarn Découverte et Loisirs - ✆ 05 63 38 30 45 - www.tanus-decouverte-loisirs.com.

⑨ RODEZ

See the Causses of Quercy line p. 26.

Viaur viaduct.
Leonid Andronov/Getty Images Plus

Excursion from Rodez

Pierre Soulages at Rodez and at Conques

➜ From Rodez, Conques can be reached by liO 223 coach every day (between April and October). Ticket price: €2.
Info: lio-occitanie.fr

Opened in 2014 in the town where Pierre Soulages (1919-2022) was born, the Soulages Museum in Rodez was built thanks to two donations of over 500 of the artist's works. The exhibition covers the artist's entire career and how his techniques evolved. Organised chronologically, it allows visitors to discover his early works, the sure strokes of his walnut stain, the material of his acid etchings and heavy bronzes drawn from their matrices, before tackling the large formats. The museum tour ends in a room imagined as a nave, where the life-size cartoons of the stained glass windows of Ste-Foy de Conques (1987-1994) are displayed. You can then head to Conques to see the originals. This town, 38 km from Rodez, has a special place in the artist's life. "When I was fourteen," Soulages once confided, "it was in front of the Abbey Church of Sainte-Foy in Conques that I decided that art was the only thing that interested me in life." Between 1987 and 1994, he designed the 104 stained glass windows of the church, creating a colourless and translucent glass to respect the variations of the natural light and the grand Romanesque sobriety of the site.

Musée Soulages de Rodez - jardin du Foirail, av. Victor-Hugo - ☏ 05 65 73 82 60 - www.musee-soulages-rodez.fr - Jul.-Aug.: 10 a.m.-6 p.m.; rest of the year: daily exc. Mon. 10 a.m.-1 p.m., 2-6 p.m., w'end 10 a.m.-6 p.m. - €11 (under 18s free) - ticket giving access to the Fenaille museum (see p. 26).

Abbatiale Ste-Foy à Conques - ☏ 05 65 72 85 00 (tourist office) - May-Sept.: : 8 a.m.-10 p.m.; rest of the year: 8 a.m.-8 p.m.

Pierre Soulages' stained glass windows in the Abbey Church of Sainte-Foy.
Ch. Bossieux/hemis.fr/Adagp, Paris, 2023

THE AUBRAC LINE

This line, otherwise known as the "Causses" line and emblematic of the French railway network, links the Mediterranean to the Massif Central. For a very modest price, it offers a route with remarkable landscapes, allowing access to superb and preserved areas, between Grands Causses, Margeride and Aubrac. It terminates in style with the crossing of the Truyère via the Garabit viaduct, a remarkable structure courtesy of Gustave Eiffel.

⭐ **BÉZIERS TO ST-FLOUR - 9 DAYS**

- Non-stop trip: 4h30
- Frequency : 1 to 2 trains per day (Intercity or liO trains)
- Timetables: www.ter.sncf.com/occitanie/se-deplacer/fiches-horaires
- Non-stop trip: €10.
- Onboard services: bikes carried free of charge
- Connected lines: Mediterranean line from Béziers; Lozère line from Marvejols

📷 Where best to sit to admire the landscape? Right-hand side of the train in the direction of travel after Tournemire.

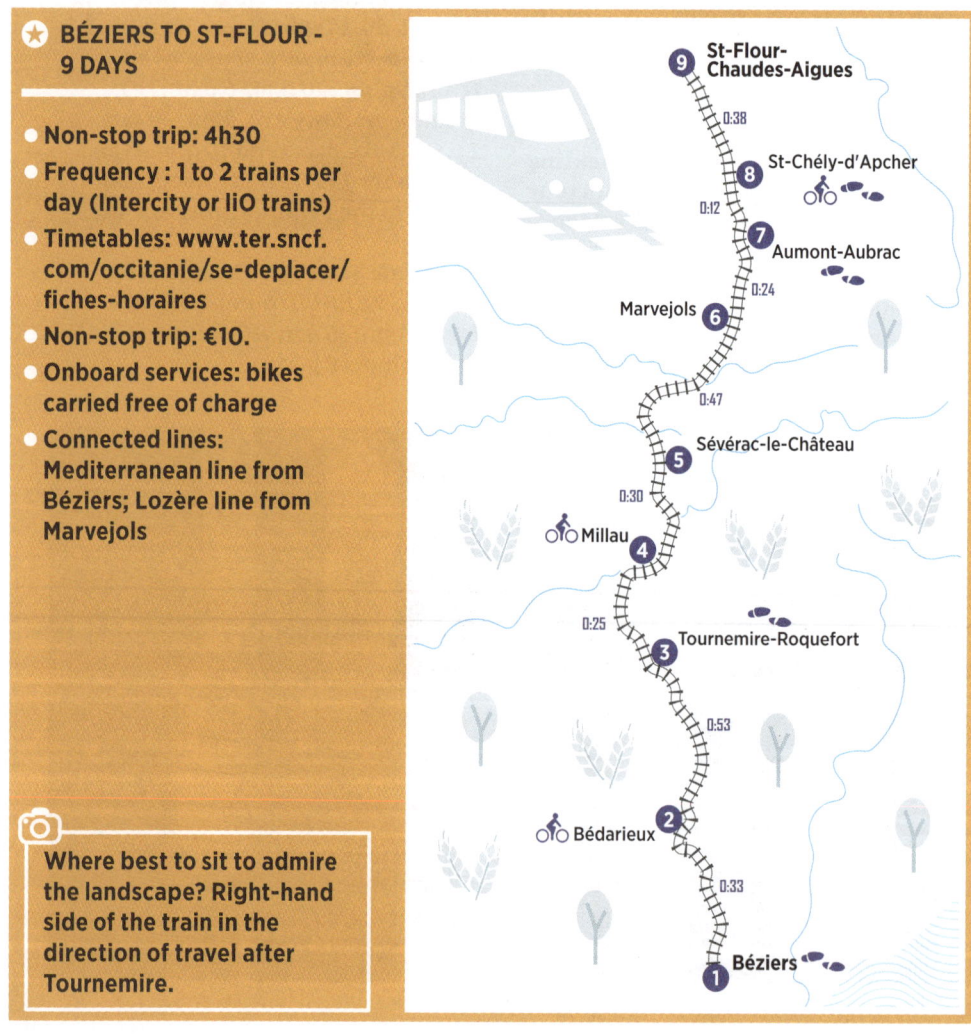

*Hiker in Aubrac.
M. Cavalier/hemis.fr*

① BÉZIERS

See the Mediterranean line p. 50.

② BÉDARIEUX

➜ **The station is a 15-minute walk from the town centre.**

🚲 **Bike hire.** Hybrid bikes, MTBs and e-bikes from Cycles Horizon. Take advantage of the greenway from Haut-Languedoc, dubbed the Passapaïs, which runs for nearly 75 km from Bédarieux to Mazamet (see p. 184).
Cycles Horizon - 13 av. Abbé-Tarroux - ✆ 04 67 95 34 25 - www.monde-du-velo.com.

Iconic viaduct. This former industrial and mining town still retains some traces of its former activities (gristmills, tanneries, cutlery factories, cloth factories, biscuit factories), as well as a spectacular viaduct (1853), the longest bridge (710 m) on the Graissessac-Béziers railway line, which was used to transport coal. The former St-Louis hospice (1828) houses the Maison des Arts, dedicated to temporary exhibitions of contemporary art, as well as the Musée du Patrimoine et du Rail (Heritage and Railway Museum).
Tourist office - 1 r. de la République - ✆ 04 67 95 08 79 - www.bedarieux.fr.
Musée du Patrimoine et du Rail - Maison des Arts - 19 av. Abbé-Tarroux - ✆ 04 67 95 48 27 - www.bedarieux.fr - School hols.: Wed. and Sat. 3-6 p.m.; rest of the year: Sat. 2-6 p.m. - free entry.

A bed for the night. A simple hotel located 5 minutes south of the station and close to the PassaPaïs greenway. It also offers triple and family rooms (4 people).
Hôtel de l'Orb - rte de St-Pons - ✆ 04 67 23 35 90 - www.hotel-orb.com - 28 rms. €68 - ☕ €12 (buffet).

Eat in or take away. This organic grocery store, full of fine regional produce, doubles as a restaurant area where you can enjoy a nice drink or a snack during the day. At lunchtime, you can order a dish of the day, a crepe or an omelette, all made with the grocery's fresh produce.

Le Local - 3 r. de la République - ☎ 09 53 80 28 30 - takeaway: daily exc. Sun. 9 a.m.-6 p.m. (9 p.m. Wed.) - eating in: Mon.-Sat. lunch - €5/€10.

3 TOURNEMIRE-ROQUEFORT

➔ The station is in Tournemire, a small town at the foot of the Larzac plateau, the starting point for many hikes. It takes about 30 minutes to walk to Roquefort-sur-Soulzon. Otherwise, you need to call a taxi when you arrive at Tournemire station.
Taxi Garde: ☎ 06 31 78 33 21 (call to book). Cost around €10/€15.

➔ No accommodation near the station; you can do the stage as a day trip and stay in Millau.

The village with natural cellars. At Roquefort-sur-Soulzon, the Combalou limestone ridge collapsed long ago, creating cracks in the underground rock where the wind infiltrates to form natural aerated cavities called "fleurines". It is to these natural cellars that we owe the famous Roquefort, the "king of cheeses", in the words of Diderot. Discover the village and its famous cheese cellars, and enjoy some beautiful walks in the surrounding area.
Tourist office - av. de Lauras - ☎ 05 65 58 56 00 - www.roquefort-tourisme.fr.

Dining. To savour Roquefort cheese in all sorts of ways: in a salad, on a platter, in ice cream, inside a crepe... as well as lots of other Aveyronnais produce. And always the taste of the terroir!
Restaurant des Fleurines - r. des Baragnaudes - ☎ 05 65 62 38 94 ou 06 30 52 90 58 - daily exc. Wed. - lunchtime only - €20/€22.

The secret of Roquefort production. Make sure to come with warm clothing, as the temperature in the cellars is 10-12°C. Open to the public since 1957, the Caves Société cellars offer a true discovery of the world of Roquefort cheese: fleurines, Penicillium, cellar workers and cheese maturation will have their mysteries unveiled to you during a fascinating exploratory walk (animated mockup, sound and light show, video, etc.).
Other cellars can be visited, including those of the century-old cheese factory founded by Paul Alric (the famous Papillon brand): you can discover the different stages of ripening of Roquefort cheese, a tour enhanced by the projection of a film and a free tasting.
Caves Société - 2 av. François-Galtier - ☎ 05 65 58 54 38 - www.roquefort-societe.com - 1h guided tour: 10 a.m.-noon, 1:30-5 p.m. - €7.50 (under 17s: €4.50).
Roquefort Papillon - 8 bis av. de Lauras - ☎ 05 65 58 50 00 - www.roquefort-papillon.com - guided tour on request (45 min) 10 a.m.-6 p.m. - free of charge.

💬 **Sensory stroll around the village.** An original way of discovering the village thanks to the work done by the children of Roquefort school, who collected numerous testimonies in order to restore the collective memory and

THE KING OF CHEESES

"Roquefort", named after the fortified castle that existed on the rock of Combalou in the 11th century ("roque" for "rock" and "fort" for castle), gave its name in turn to the famous cheese. Such is the fame of this cheese that the town also gave its name to the fungus that turns the curd into cheese: "Penicillium roqueforti". The legend goes that Roquefort cheese was born from the love affair between a shepherd and a shepherdess, who met in one of the countless caves of Combalou. The young shepherd left behind there his bag containing a piece of rye bread and sheep's curd. A few days later the shepherd found his bag again: he took out a piece of bread and a cheese covered with green-blue mould. The cheese had changed in taste and odour, but the two lovers devoured it with delight! "Et roquefortum fiat" (And so there was Roquefort)! »

Fabulous Journeys

Sporty weekend in Millau

In the heart of the Grands Causses Regional Nature Park, nestled in a meander of the Tarn, Millau undoubtedly deserves its title of regional outdoor sports capital.

Paragliding near Millau
P. Jacques/hemis.fr

The famous viaduct of the same name, designed by Norman Foster, has a prominent place in this landscape. You will discover it from every angle: from afar, after a 26 km trail that takes you through the Cade forest to the Causse Noir plateau, with an unrivalled viewpoint over the town and the valley and ideal for mountain biking; from up close, during a paragliding flight (thrills guaranteed!); from below, from a canoe during a trip on the Tarn, starting out from Peyre, classified as one of the "most beautiful villages of France". For the night, why not take to the canopy and enjoy the comfort of an overnight stay in a tree house. For gastronomy and local specialities, at least three food stops are a must: sample the "Aligot" dish in one of the many restaurants of Millau; call in at the Aire du Viaduc de Millau, where you can taste the famous stuffed "capucins", a kind of garnished crepe cone, from the great chef Michel Bras, while admiring once again the majestic structure from close up; and, of course, you must pay a visit to Roquefort-sur-Soulzon, the capital of the famous blue-veined ewe's milk cheese, for a visit and tasting (see box insert opposite).

2 days, 1 night - accommodation from €119 per night for 4 persons - to be done in spring, summer and autumn. Contact: Millau tourist office.

THE AUBRAC LINE

portray the men and women of the Roquefort AOC territory. This educational project has resulted in a exhibition of photos, sculptures and sounds (QR codes installed in various places make it possible to download extracts of personal accounts), which can be discovered along a walking route. There are also several waymarked hiking trails with interpretation panels around Roquefort.
3 km - 2h30 - leaving from the tourist office.

④ MILLAU

 Bike hire. MTBs, road bikes and e-bikes for hire, minimum half-day, from Cycles Arcuri (300 m from the station). You can pass under the Millau viaduct by mountain bike via the "Trace Verte du Viaduc" (Green track of the viaduct) along the Tarn (note: some sections are very steep).
Cycles Arcuri - 2 r. du Barry - ☎ 05 65 60 28 23 - closed Sun.-Mon.

A town at the heart of the Grands Causses. A strategic crossroads at the intersection of the roads to Albi, Clermont-Ferrand and Montpellier, the town, which has developed over the centuries around pottery, then leather tanning and glove-making, is well worth a visit with its harmonious combination of cultural heritage and outdoor activities. Millau is also famous for its elegant viaduct (8 km out of town), a great asset for traffic and communication, and which holds the world record for the highest pier! Stroll through the medieval streets and visit the Tower of the Kings of Aragon: from the top you can enjoy a superb panorama of the town's rooftops and the Causses, with the viaduct in the distance. For another great view of the famous viaduct, walk along the riverside to the Lerouge bridge (15-20 mins from the station).
Tourist office - 1 pl. du Beffroi - ☎ 05 65 60 02 42 - www.millau-viaduc-tourisme.fr.

A bed for the night. This centrally located hotel was given a facelift by its new owners in 2021. Modern style. An 8-minute walk from the station.
Hôtel La Capelle - 7 pl. de la Capelle - ☎ 05 65 60 14 72 - www.hotel-millau-capelle.com - 40 rms. €68/€88 - 3 family suites €98/€150 - ☕ €9.90.

Memory of the Grands Causses. Housed in the Pégayrolles mansion (18th century), the museum has some rich and varied collections. In addition to numerous fossils of Mesozoic Era fauna and flora, the palaeontology section contains the almost complete skeleton of an elasmosaurus from Tournemire. The basements contain a remarkable collection of Gallo-Roman pottery found on the Graufesenque site. And part of the building is dedicated to Millau's two traditional industries: tanning, which transforms a perishable, raw animal hide into a high-quality, rot-proof product; and glove-making.
Musée de Millau et des Grands Causses - pl. du Mar.-Foch - hôtel de Pégayrolles - ☎ 05 65 59 01 08 - www.millau.fr - 10 a.m.-12:30 p.m., 2:30-6 p.m.; Jul.-Aug.: Tues.-Sun.; mid-Apr.-Jun., and Sept.: Wed.-Sun.; Oct.-mid-Apr.: Tues.-Sat. - free entry, audioguide €2.50

Dining. In the vaulted dining room there is a large fireplace where the chef grills fish and meat. Bar and tables set up in a pleasant courtyard (former "jeu de paume" court).
Au Jeu de Paume - 4 r. St-Antoine - ☎ 05 65 60 25 12 - www.aujeudepaume-millau.com - closed Sun.-Mon. and for lunch on Sat. - meal deals €26/€29/€32.

For a picnic. Wednesday morning market and a larger Friday morning market for sampling produce both local and from further afield.
Les halles - pl. du Mar.-Foch and in the old town centre - morning: Wed.-Sat. (Sun. in summer); in Jul.-Aug.: evening market 1 Mon. in 2.

Exercise in the heart of nature. Hiking, climbing, via ferrata, caving, mountain biking, canyoning, canoeing, aquatic adventure, hot-dog, rafting, adventure course, bungee jumping, electric bike hire... More than a dozen activities led by qualified instructors. Equipment hire.
Roc et Canyon - 55 av. Jean-Jaurès - summer base: 155 av. de l'Aigoual - ☎ 05 65 61 17 77 - www.roc-et-canyon.com.

Sweet or savoury snack. A beautifully decorated tea room (small lamps, engravings, gingham tablecloths). Sweet or savoury: everything is home-made. The people of Millau flock to it! Book for a spot of lunch.

Millau Viaduct.
CEVM Eiffage/Foster+Partners/Allard1/Getty Images Plus

THE AUBRAC LINE

<u>Cak'T</u> - 1 r. de la Capelle - ℘ 05 65 60 13 82 - *www.restaurant-salondethe-millau.com* - Mon.-Sat. 10:30 a.m.-7 p.m.

Millau Jazz Festival. In mid-July, the streets resound to the sounds of concerts and musical events.
Info: millaujazz.fr.

⑤ SÉVÉRAC-LE-CHÂTEAU

➔ The station serves Sévérac-d'Aveyron, a village made up of two distinct districts: the station district and the medieval castle district on the hill. Allow for a 15-20 minute uphill walk to reach the medieval town and a further 5 minutes to the castle. liO 214 coach reaches the castle district ("Embranchement le Massegros" stop) from the SNCF station.
Info: lio-occitanie.fr

Straight out of the Middle Ages. On the horizon, a steep rock bears the remains of an imposing castle… This is Sévérac-le-Château! This once fortified village stands on the slopes of an isolated hill in the middle of the depression that is irrigated by the sources of the Aveyron river and their tributaries. In the narrow streets and vaulted passages leading to the castle stand old houses (15th-16th century) with mullioned windows, corbelled turrets, and timber-framed facades. You will also come across a beautiful Romanesque fountain. La Maison de Jeanne is said to date from the 11th century and is considered to be the oldest house in the ancient province of Rouergue.

<u>Tourist office</u> - 5 r. des Douves - ℘ 05 65 47 67 31 - *www.tourisme-aveyron.com* - *maps available even outside opening times.*

A bed for the night. Just opposite the station, the Hôtel de la Gare is a long yellow stone building dating from the 19th century. Since then, the hotel has been modernised and has decent rooms with a slightly old-fashioned decor. Otherwise, a 20-minute walk from the station, La Bergerie is a quiet address below

Sévérac-le-Château.
glanceofthefox/Getty Images Plus

the old town. This establishment also has a restaurant renowned for its fine Aubrac meat, with regional cuisine based on local produce. Don't miss its rib of beef served on a hot stone!
<u>Hôtel de la Gare</u> - 1 av. Pierre-Semard - ☎ 05 65 47 64 28 - www.hotel-severac.fr - 8 rms. €53/€75 - ☕ €9 - half and full board possible.
<u>La Bergerie</u> - 24 r. du Barry - ☎ 05 65 60 22 42 - www.hotellabergerie.fr - 30 rms. €59/€85 - ☕ €9 - menus: €29.50/€35.

Conquering the castle. The 17th century entrance takes you into the main courtyard. Older constructions are at the northern end (13th and 14th century): remains of curtain walls, three watchtowers, and a chapel; at the southern end, there is the Renaissance facade and the remains of a monumental double-flight staircase. From the terrace, situated to the east of the main courtyard, you can take in a magnificent view of the town and the upper Aveyron valley, the causses of Sévérac and Sauveterre, and the foothills of the Cévennes. From the watchtower of the western rampart, you can admire the panoramic view over the Aveyron valley.
<u>Château</u> - ☎ 05 65 47 67 31 - www.tourisme-aveyron.com - free access to the main courtyard all year round - Castle opening times Jul.-Aug.: 10 a.m.-7 p.m. - €3 entry (under 6s free).

Dining. La Maison de Sévérac offers, in the elegant setting of an old town house, bistronomic cuisine that gives pride of place to local produce.
<u>Maison de Sévérac</u> - 15 r. Amaury-de-Sévérac - ☎ 05 63 00 01 02 - www.maisondeseverac.com - closed Sun. eve. and Mon. - gourmet platters from €19, menus €18/€35.

For a picnic. Traditional market on Thursday mornings on the Place de la Gare.

Art in the old town. During the summer, artists and craftspersons present their creations in pop-up shops.

Sound and light show. In late July – early August, the sound and light show in the main courtyard of the castle brings the site to life. *www.spectacle-son-lumiereaveyron.fr* - €18 (ages 4-13: €10) - at 22h (time 1h40).

6 MARVEJOLS

See the Lozère line p. 32.

7 AUMONT-AUBRAC

Where territories meet. At the crossroads between the Margeride and the Aubrac, Aumont-Aubrac is known for its long-distance footpaths crossing splendid territories: the village is a stage on the Way of St. James pilgrimage route (GR 65) and on the tour of the Aubrac mountains (180 km), and is also the starting point for the long-distance walk to St-Guilhem-le-Désert (240 km). You can cover a little of this on foot or by bike. In the centre of the town, you will be able to see the Maison du Prieuré (17th century) and its beautiful vaulted cellars, the church of St-Étienne (12th century), the statue of the Beast of Gévaudan which sits above the fountain in the Place du Portail, and the "mysterious stone". For a panoramic view of the village, climb the Truc Del Fabre, a knoll atop the Place du Foirail, with the statue of Christ the King at its summit.

Tourist office - Maison du Prieuré - 04 66 42 88 70 - www.ot-aumont-aubrac.fr.

A bed for the night. This small establishment, 5 minutes from the station, has several contemporary and comfortable rooms, one of which can accommodate 3 to 4 people. The restaurant offers simple and tasty home cooking: pizzas, and dishes featuring the famous Aubrac beef (hamburgers, parmentier de bœuf aligoté, etc.).

Hôtel-restaurant Linette - 10 rte du Languedoc - 04 66 42 85 88 - www.hotel-restaurant-linette.com - 3 rms. €82/€87 - €10 - lunch deal €15.50, pizza €13.

Dining. The ideal way to taste Cyril Attrazic's local cuisine at moderate prices, Le Gabale brasserie has a modern decor with panoramic photos of the Aubrac countryside. Fine terrace. And if you like the setting, why not spend a night in one of the contemporary rooms?

Le Gabale - 10 rte du Languedoc - 04 66 42 86 14 - www.camillou.com - meal deals €19.80 € (lunch)/€21.80 - menus €29/€33 - 37 rms. €110/€148 - €14.50.

For a picnic. Market on Friday morning on the Place du Foirail and, on other days, everything you need in the town's various shops to stock up on fine local specialities.

On the legendary GR 65. From Aumont-Aubrac, set off on the Way of St. James in the direction of Nasbinals. Shortly after leaving La Chaze-de-Peyre (4.5 km from Aumont), many pilgrims tarry a while at the small chapel which stands alone on the roadside. Founded in 1525, it was originally dedicated to the Holy Cross, and pilgrims came here to gather strength and courage before facing the rigours of winter on the Aubrac plateau. Since 1868, the edifice has been placed under the protection of Our Lady of La Salette. From there, you can continue toward the sublime Aubrac plateau: there is little gradient but a long walk to Nasbinals (6h30 from Aumont-Aubrac).

VAST EXPANSE OF AUBRAC

Since 2018, Aubrac has been listed as France's 53rd Regional Nature Park. This volcanic and granite plateau is located in the centre of the Massif Central, on the borders of two regions. It is bordered to the northwest by the Cantal mountains, to the east by the Margeride, and to the south by the limestone plateaus of the Grands Causses. It is superb mid-mountain livestock rearing country - with its herds of fine Aubrac cattle - where water is abundant, and which has a rich architectural heritage. It is also the realm of hikers and pilgrims.

THE AUBRAC LINE

8 ST-CHÉLY-D'APCHER

→ The station is less than 10 minutes from the town centre. Walk through the Péchaud park, a pleasant green spot for a picnic (with pond, playgrounds, exercise equipment).

Bike hire. Passion Vélo hires out mountain bikes and e-bikes. From St-Chély-d'Apcher, you can join the GTMC mountain bike trail that crosses the Massif Central through pine forests and pastures in the Margeride.
Passion Vélo - 38 bis av. de la République - 04 66 31 18 15 - www.passion-velo-lozere.fr.

Between Auvergne and Languedoc. This industrial town (manufacture of magnetic sheet metal for transformers) has been very well renovated and has a beautiful historic centre with many shops. You will discover the perimeter wall (13th century), the Aniers fountain, the Place du Foirail, the watchtower, and the half-timbered Bonnet house, one of the oldest residences in the town. The industrial heritage can be discovered at the Metallurgy Museum, where former metalworkers will tell you, in a fun and fascinating way, about the production tools, the life of the workers, and the history of this industrial town, which is still very much an active place. Lastly, there are many possibilities for walks in the magnificent, unspoilt natural surroundings between Margeride and the Aubrac plateau.
Tourist office - 48 r. Théophile-Roussel - 04 66 31 03 67 - www.margeride-en-gevaudan.com.
Musée de la Métallurgie - rte de Fournels - 04 66 31 29 38 - Apr.-Sept.: contact for opening times. - Guided tour (1h) €7 (under 16s: €4).

Dining and overnighting. Centrally located (11min from the station), family-spirited and friendly address for a simple and comfortable stay. The restaurant is renowned for its traditional and generous cuisine based on local products.
Le Lion d'Or - 132 r. Théophile-Roussel - 04 66 31 00 14 - www.margeride-en-gevaudan.com - 24 rms. €70/€90 - €8 - menus €20/€30.

For a picnic. Thursday morning market, with many local producers. The market place is next to the tourist office, so take the opportunity to get all the information you need!

Heritage and nature. Several walks of varying lengths and levels (7.5 to 24 km) are signposted from the town centre. One of them leads you to Apcher castle, one of the highest points of the Margeride.
Maps and leaflets can be downloaded from the tourist office website or are for sale on site.

9 ST-FLOUR-CHAUDES-AIGUES

→ The station serves both towns. Chaudes-Aigues is 28 km away (not dealt with here).

Perched on high. St-Flour occupies a basaltic plateau with large mineral columns (dubbed "organs"), dominating the valley of the Ander. The square towers of the town's St. Peter's Cathedral, which once stood guard over the route leading from Languedoc to the former kingdom of France, reach for the sky. This lively consular and episcopal town has a lot of charm, especially in the high part of town. You will walk along Rue Marchande with your gaze drawn upwards to take in some remarkable old houses before reaching the cathedral. Behind its apse, the Terrasse des Roches, situated on the old ramparts, offers a beautiful view of the lower town, the valley of the Ander, and the hills of the Margeride.
Tourist office - 17 bis pl. d'Armes - 04 71 60 22 50 - www.pays-saint-flour.fr.

A bed for the night. For three generations, the Grand Hôtel de l'Étape, a 5-minute walk from the station, has stoutly defended its corner. The rooms are large and irreproachable. For the view, choose the rooms overlooking the mountain if possible. In the restaurant you can enjoy copious regional dishes.
Grand Hôtel de l'Étape - 18 av. de la République - 04 71 60 13 03 - www.hotel-etape.com - 22 rms. €73/€142 - €12.50 - menus: €34/€39 - closed Sun.-Mon.

*Garabit Viaduct.
Sablin/Getty Images Plus*

Dining. Chez Geneviève, they often play to a full house. The reasons for the success of this small restaurant, located in the upper town: a friendly atmosphere and generous, inventive local cuisine using fresh produce.
Chez Geneviève - 25 r. des Lacs - 04 71 60 17 97 - www.restaurant-saint-flour.com - daily in Jul.-Aug.; winter: closed Sun.-Mon. and Wed. eve. - menu €31.50.

For a picnic. Here you will find here a large choice of Auvergne PDO cheeses directly from the producer, but also products from the Cantal region, the eponymous blonde lentils of St-Flour, Planèze peas, apple juice and cider from the Upper Auvergne, jams, and a smiling welcome!
Crèmerie des Lacs - 53 r. des Lacs - 04 71 60 08 20 - Tues.-Sat. 9 a.m.-12:30 p.m., 2:30-7 p.m., Sun. and public hols. 9 a.m.-12:30 p.m. - closed Mon.

GARABIT VIADUCT.

Between St-Chély and St-Flour, you will have the pleasure of passing 95 m above the waters of the Truyère via the famous Garabit viaduct. This exceptional structure, repainted in red (its original colour), stands out against the green of the steep slopes, sometimes covered in woods, sometimes bristling with rocks. It owes its design is to engineer Léon Boyer, and its construction to Gustave Eiffel. Eiffel drew on the experience he acquired on the Garabit (1880-1884) for designing and building his famous tower in Paris for the 1889 Universal Exhibition.

THE AUBRAC LINE

THE PONT DU GARD AND RHÔNE LINE

There is just one line between Nimes, a relatively short distance from the illustrious Pont du Gard, and the Pont-St-Esprit, famous for another audacious feat of engineering. And between the two lies yet another famous "Pont" (bridge): the Pont d'Avignon. Between these stops, the train carries you along, following the winding path of the Rhône. Along the way, it also skirts a slope of its illustrious vineyard, the Côtes du Rhône Gardoises, in the peaceful valley of the Cèze, named after the river that runs through it.

★ NIMES TO PONT-ST-ESPRIT - 6 DAYS

- Non-stop trip: 1h16 (with a connection at Avignon)
- Frequency: 13 liO trains/day, but only 5 between Avignon and Pont-St-Esprit
- Timetables: www.ter.sncf.com/occitanie/se-deplacer/fiches-horaires
- Non-stop trip: €17.60
- Onboard services: bicycle transport authorised
- Connected lines: Cévennes, Mediterranean, Camargue lines from Nimes

Where best to sit to admire the landscape? On the right-hand side, in the direction of travel.

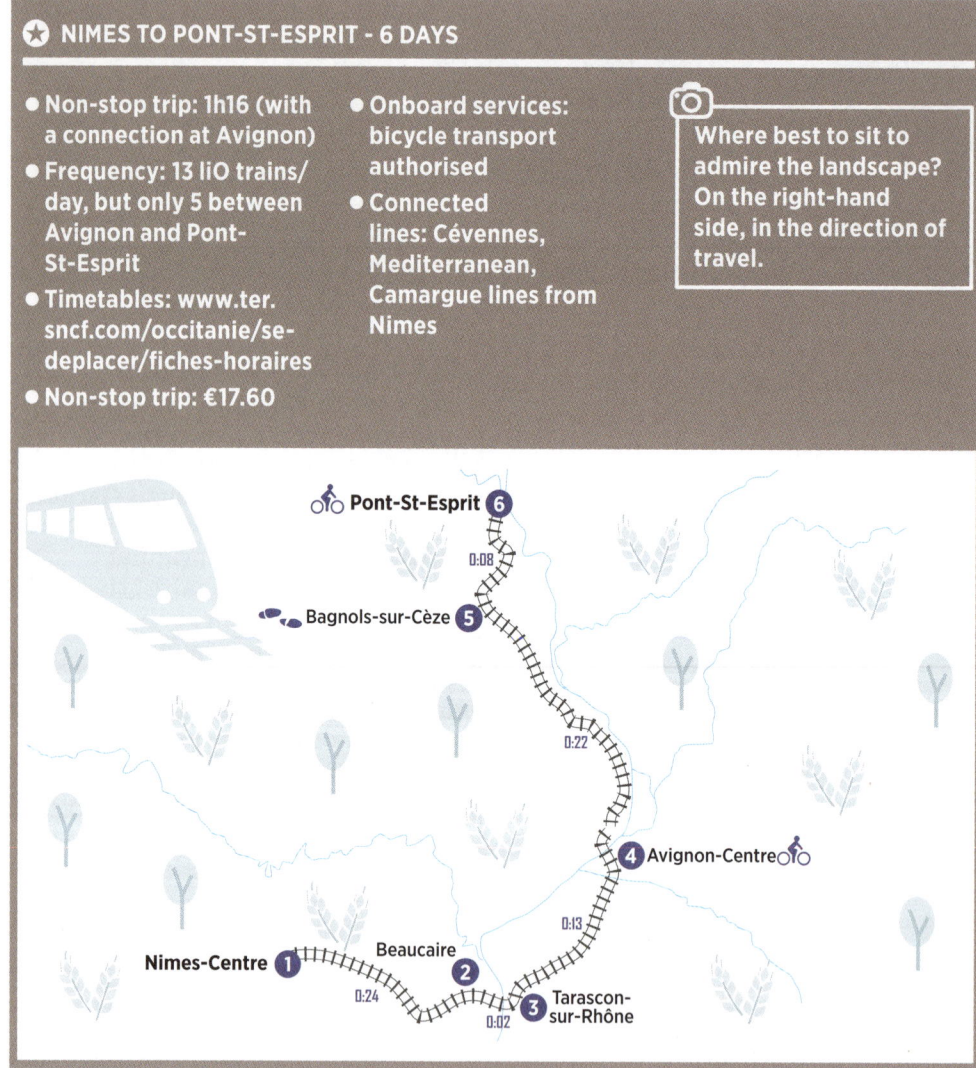

The rooftop of the Musée de la Romanité, Nîmes.
Olivier Arquès/CRT Occitanie

① NIMES-CENTRE

See Cévennes line p. 39.

② BEAUCAIRE

➔ **The station is a 20-minute walk from the fortress. It is also a 20-minute walk from the next station, at Tarascon.**

The Camargue spirit. Standing proud across the river from imperial Tarascon, Beaucaire was famous throughout Europe until the 18th century for its fair. Today, the citadel of the Counts of Toulouse is a quiet little town that is pleasant to walk around. Starting out from the river port, on the Rhône-Sète canal, you climb up through the cobbled streets of the old centre, lined with superb townhouses, to the fortress that towers over the town.
Tourist office - 8 r. Victor-Hugo - ☏ 04 66 59 26 57 - www.provence-camargue-tourisme.com.

A bed for the night. It is a 30-minute walk from the station or a taxi ride to this pleasant hotel with restaurant and pool. If you want to stay close to the centre, it's best to settle in Tarascon, our next stop, just across the bridge.
Les Vignes Blanches - 67 av. de Farciennes - ☏ 04 66 59 13 12 - www.lesvignesblanches.com - 🛏 ✗ - 57 rms. €85/€89 ☕.

Higher. Built in the 11th century on the site of a Roman castrum (fortified camp) and modified in the 13th century, the fortress of Beaucaire was later dismantled by Richelieu. Its remains stand on the top of the hill, protected by a wall. Shaded by pines and cypresses, resplendent with irises and Spanish broom, it has a strange and rare polygonal tower set on a rocky spur, curtains that run flush with the cliff, and a beautiful round corner tower.
Fortress - pl. Raymond-VII - ☏ 04 66 59 90 07 - Jul.-Aug.: 9:30 a.m.-6 p.m.; rest of the year: daily exc. Mon.-Tues. - free entry excluding events.

Dining. In a relaxed atmosphere, on a nice square with arcades and plane trees, you are treated to creative, seasonal cuisine. On the menu: a single starter and a choice of two

Excursion from Nimes

Pont du Gard

➜ From the Nimes bus station, liO 121 coach takes 45 minutes to reach the Pont du Gard. The same line passes via Bagnols-sur-Cèze and Pont-St-Esprit.
Info: lio-occitanie.fr

A marvel of antiquity and a grandiose structure built in the 1st century, the Pont du Gard, encrusted in a superb setting, would almost justify a trip to the region in itself! Simply admire: the bridge is built of colossal blocks weighing between 6 and 8 tonnes, hoisted more than 49 metres above the low waters of the Gardon. To break up any sense of monotony, the three levels of arcades are recessed relative to each other. The architect was able to vary, on the same level, the size of the arches. The arches are made of independent rings joined together, which gives the mass a lot of elasticity in case of settlement. Rarely has a feat of human engineering slotted so "naturally" into the landscape. Yet technical performance is not all there is to it. You will also experience an odd sense of lightness, unexpected for such a colossal structure, with its arches' reflection glittering in the green waters below. It's a sight you never tire of, visible from various perspectives: the bridge itself, the banks, and the hills around. On the right bank, there are stairs and footpaths that allow you to pass under the bridge or climb up and admire it from on high.

While the bridge may be the real star of the place, the museum and cultural areas along the left bank allow you to acquire a more in-depth understanding of this extraordinary edifice.

📞 04 66 37 50 99 - www.pontdugard.fr - Jul.-Aug.: 9 a.m.-7:30 p.m.; Apr.-Jun and Sept. 9 a.m.-6:30 p.m.; rest of the year: contact for details - €6.50 (under 18s free admission), the ticket includes access to both the bridge and the museum areas - bridge illuminated until midnight in season.

Pont du Gard. kavram/Getty Images Plus

dishes of the day. Everything is home-made, and served up generously with a smile.
L'Épicerie - pl. de la République - 📞 07 85 40 38 20 - closed Wed. and Sat. lunch - menu €22/€25.

Strolling along the banks. The "Vendredis de Beaucaire" ("Fridays at Beaucaire") weekly event livens up the marina and town centre every Friday in July and August. Craft market and musical events.

❸ TARASCON-SUR-RHÔNE

➜ **The station is a 10-min. walk from the castle.**

Check it out! Besides its imposing castle, looming over the waters of the Rhône, the town has preserved its old centre with streets lined with arcades and yellow stone houses. The sun reveals here and there a cornice, a portal or a frieze, and above all, small streets lined with hotels often boasting very well restored facades. The Collégiale Royale Ste-Marthe, a beautiful and inviting church built in the 12th century, is worth a visit. Fashion lovers can visit the Souleiado Museum, which is housed in the fashion chain's first factory, opened here in 1806.
Tourist office - 62 r. des Halles - 📞 04 90 91 03 52.

A bed for the night. Centrally located, a 3-minute walk from the station, this hotel occupies a building typical of the region, and has smart and well-kept rooms. When the weather is nice, breakfast is served on the terrace by the small swimming pool. Friendly welcome.
Hôtel du Viaduc - 9 r. du Viaduc - 📞 04 90 91 16 67 - www.hotelduviaduc.com - 🏊 - 20 rms. €72/€100 - ☕ €8/€11.

Castle of art. Its massive presence on the banks of the Rhône, the unannounced elegance of its interior architecture and its exceptional state of conservation make it one of the most beautiful medieval castles in France. The present building is the successor to a fortress, itself built on the site of the Roman castrum that guarded the border with Provence. Purchased by the State in 1932, it has since undergone major restoration work in order to have its medieval identity restored. It now houses the René d'Anjou art centre, dedicated to contemporary creation.
Château de Tarascon - bd du Roi-René - 📞 04 90 91 01 93 - chateau.tarascon.fr - May-Sept.: 9:30 a.m.-12:30 p.m., 1:45-6:30 p.m.; rest of the year: contact for details - €7.50 (ages 10-17: €3.50).

Dining. A nice address for its quirky decoration and its summer terrace installed on the town hall square. Copious main courses, savoury pies, salads and daily specials depending on what's picked up from the market.
Le Bistrot des Anges - 20 pl. du Marché - 📞 04 90 91 05 11 - every lunchtime Mon.-Sat. and evenings Mon., Wed., Fri. and Sat. - dishes €14/€23.

Tarasque festival. The four-day "Fêtes de la Tarasque" festivities begin on the last Friday of June. The Tarasque monster appears in a grand parade, led by its knights and accompanied by the personage of Tartarin. A succession of musical and folkloric events culminate in a fireworks display on the banks of the Rhône.

❹ AVIGNON-CENTRE

🚴 **Bike hire: see p. 126.**

On the bridge. During its prestigious festival in July, the town comes alive to the frenzied rhythm of entertainments that attract a dense and colourful crowd. But as soon as the festival is over, the town settles back into its lazy routine, ideal for embarking on a discovery of its other treasures: palaces, gardens, ramparts, bell towers, townhouses and tiled roofs are all just waiting to be seen as you wander the streets. Not forgetting its famous Pont St-Bénezet bridge, originally 900 m long and with 22 arches (only 4 of which remain).
Tourist office - 41 cours Jean-Jaurès - 📞 04 32 74 32 74 - www.avignon-tourisme.com.

A bed for the night. A 5-minute walk from the station, Le Colbert offers competitively priced

Excursion from Avignon

Villeneuve-lez-Avignon

➜Villeneuve is a 40-minute walk from the centre of Avignon. You can also take the liO 122 coach from the Avignon-Centre station, which gets you there in 20 minutes, or the No. 5 bus from the town centre. *Info: lio-occitanie.fr*

Only the Rhône separates them, but history links them forever. It was King Philip IV, known as Philippe-le-Bel ("Philip the Fair") who, in the 13th century, founded a "new town" ("ville neuve") in the plain facing Avignon. Start the visit at the Philippe-le-Bel tower to understand why. You have to climb to the upper terrace (176 steps) to see its strategic importance: this key structure defended the entrance to the St-Benezet bridge (the famous "Pont d'Avignon"). Today, it also offers a superb view of the Rhône, Avignon and the Palace of the Popes, the Montagnette and the Alpilles. Continue your walk via the Fort St-André, built in the 14th century by John II and Charles V on Mount Andaon. Its twin towers remain one of the finest examples of medieval fortification. At the top of the 85 steps, you will be rewarded with a splendid view of Mont Ventoux. Just next door, the St-André Abbey, founded by the Benedictines in the 10th century, was partially destroyed during the French Revolution. After visiting the abbey, you are sure to be impressed by its Italian and Mediterranean gardens, with an olive grove worthy of a Van Gogh painting! Among fountains, statues, ponds and great cypresses, deckchairs are available for you to relax and savour the moment. As for the view…

Lastly, you can end the day at the museum. The Pierre-de-Luxembourg Museum has a number of exceptional works of art on show. *The Coronation of the Virgin* (1454), a masterpiece of Gothic art painted by Enguerrand Quarton, is of particular note. *Avignon Tourist Office - pl. Charles-David - ☏ 04 90 03 70 60 - www.avignon-et-provence.com.*

St-André Abbey gardens.
K. George/age fotostock

accommodation. Ideally located a stone's throw from the Place de l'Horloge (about 15 minutes from the station), the Hotel de l'Horloge offers a welcoming and traditional setting.

Hôtel Le Colbert - 7 r. Agricol-Perdiguier - ✆ 04 90 86 20 20 - www.avignon-hotel-colbert.com - Apr.-Oct. - 13 rms. €78/€154 - ⌑ €10/€12.

Hôtel de l'Horloge - 1-3 r. Félicien-David - ✆ 04 90 16 42 00 - www.hotel-avignon-horloge.com - 66 rms. €99/€113 - ⌑ €20.

UNESCO listed. It took 30 years to build the Palais des Papes (palace of the Popes), a prestigious 15,000 square metre papal residence, which is actually composed of two distinct buildings: the Old palace and the New palace. The first was built under Benedict XII in 1334, and the second under Clement VI between 1342 and 1363. Its main courtyard hosts the Avignon festival every summer, receiving thousands of visitors every year. Its exceptional cultural value earned it a place on the UNESCO World Heritage list in 1995, along with the famous bridge.

Palais des Papes - 6 pl. du Palais - ✆ 04 32 74 32 74 - www.palais-des-papes.com - Jul.-Aug.: 10 a.m.-6 p.m.; rest of the year: 10 a.m.-5 p.m. - €12 (ages 8-17: €6.50).

Dining. At the Moutardier du Pape, you can enjoy regional cuisine and, above all, take in the sights while sitting on the shady terrace, which faces the Palace of the Popes. At L'Agape, the Provence region is showcased with fine and sophisticated culinary compositions.

Le Moutardier du Pape - 15 pl. du Palais - ✆ 04 90 85 34 76 - www.lemoutardierdupape.fr - menu €35.

L'Agape - 21 pl. des Corps-Saints - ✆ 04 90 85 04 06 - www.restaurant-agape-avignon.com - closed Sun.-Mon. - lunch deal €24/€29, evening tasting menus: €35/€80.

Canoe trip. In summer, you can hire canoes, kayaks and paddleboards to paddle under the famous Pont d'Avignon bridge or take a trip down the Rhône to explore the riverbanks.

Canoë Vaucluse - allée Antoine-Pinay - île de la Barthelasse - ✆ 06 11 52 16 73 - www.canoe-vaucluse.fr - from €8 per half-hour.

Aperitif time. In the basement of this magnificent building (which used to house the Banque de France), the former treasury room has traded gold for wine. Showcasing Côtes-du-Rhône and Rhône Valley AOCs, this establishment has a fantastic menu and a priceless view of the square in front of the Papal Palace. The tasting cellar, where some 10,000 bottles are kept, can be visited on request outside the restaurant's busiest times.

Le Carré du Palais - 1 pl. du Palais - ✆ 04 65 00 01 01 - www.carredupalais.fr.

Illustrious festivals. It was Jean Vilar (1912-1971), director of the Théâtre national populaire de Chaillot until 1963, who created the Avignon Festival in 1947. From 1968, the "Festival Off" transformed the pioneering festival into an immense theatrical extravaganza where more than 1000 different shows are staged every year.

Festival d'Avignon - www.festival-avignon.com.

Festival Off - www.festivaloffavignon.com.

⑤ BAGNOLS-SUR-CÈZE

Art in the Gard. With its ring of boulevards and ancient houses, old Bagnols is full of charm. Its museum of modern art occupies the second floor of the town hall, a beautiful building dating from the 17th century, with works by Monet, Marquet, Signac, Bonnard and above all Renoir. As for nature lovers, they will find themselves well catered for all along the peaceful valley of the Cèze, with lots of fine hiking possibilities.

Musée d'Art moderne Albert-André - pl. Auguste-Mallet - ✆ 04 66 90 75 80 - www.musees-mediterranee.org - Jul.-Aug.: 10 a.m.-12:30 p.m., 2:30-6:30 p.m.; rest of the year: 9:30 a.m.-noon, 1:30-5 p.m. (Wed. 9:30 a.m.-1 p.m.) - closed Mon. and pub. hols., Feb. - free entry.

A bed for the night. Just a 10-minute walk from the station, treat yourself to a charming break in the salons of this 18th century country house. The regional-style rooms are located in modern buildings in the grounds of the chateau.

Château du Val de Cèze - 69 r. Léon-Fontaine (setting off from Route d'Avignon) - ☎ 04 66 89 61 26 - www.chateauvaldeceze.fr - 22 rms. €80/€110 - 🍴 €12 - rest. closed w'ends - lunch deal €17/€21, dishes €18/€21.

Dining. Right in the centre of town, Ô Pas Sage offers tasty and inventive cuisine (Gascon platter with foie gras, tapas of duck heart, etc.) as well as lighter salads. The wine is from local producers, with advice from the sommelier at the table.
If you happen to be more a fan of the Aveyron and its gastronomy, another restaurant, L'Aveyronnais, will cater to your tastes with its dependable aligot, served with almost every dish on the menu!
Ô Pas Sage - 16 pl. Auguste-Mallet - ☎ 04 30 39 04 05 - closed Sat.-Sun., Mon. eve. and Wed. eve. - menu €16.
L'Aveyronnais - 2 av. Léon-Blum - ☎ 04 66 50 84 46 - closed Mon., Tues. eve., Thurs. eve., Sun. eve. - meals approx. €25.

Summer beach. In summer, head for... Bagnols-"sur-Mer"! Bars and foodtrucks, concerts and DJ (Fri.-Sat.), sports activities. The town makes up for the absence of the sea with children's play facilities and sports activities (zip line, treetop challenge, bouncy castles, etc.) installed along the river. You can also quench your thirst in three bars: a wine bar, a craft beers bar, and a soft drinks bar.
Bagnols Plage - parc Arthur-Rimbaud - www.bagnolsplage.fr.

Sweet snack. It is so hard to make a choice in this craft chocolate factory, where everything is so tempting! The establishment, run by Daniel Clavier, is known for its two specialities which are well worth the detour in themselves: the Raviole de Bagnols, a marzipan confection garnished with dark chocolate ganache, and the Croquant de Gicon, a biscuit based on Chusclan wine, crushed almonds and hazelnuts, and flavoured with vanilla, coffee, chocolate or rose.
Chocolaterie Daniel Clavier - 8 pl. du Château - ☎ 04 66 89 41 46 - Tues.-Sat. 8 a.m.-12:30 p.m., 2:30-7:30 p.m., Sun. 8 a.m.-1 p.m.

Feast your eyes. The Visorando website identifies two walks in the vicinity: a shorter one (6.45 km, 2h15) passing via the St-Pierre-de-Castres chapel with beautiful views over the valley, and another, longer one (20.35 km, 6h15), but without any particular difficulty, along the heights and passing along the Santiago de Compostela pilgrim trail.
Bagnols-sur-Cèze hikes - www.visorando.com/randonnee-bagnols-sur-ceze.html.

❻ PONT-ST-ESPRIT

🚲 **Bike hire.** A shop 6 minutes' walk from the station offers bikes for hire in the holiday season.
Cycling Génération - 59 av. Gaston-Doumergue - ☎ 04 66 89 39 05 - www.facebook.com/cyclinggeneration - Jun.-Sept.- hybrid bikes €25/day, e-bikes €40.

A bold bridge. Almost 1km long, there remain 19 arches of the original 25. From the bridge, you can enjoy a beautiful view downstream over the Rhône and of the town. From the centre of the esplanade, you will see the flamboyant portal (15th century) of the old collegiate church, as well as the remains of the citadel fortified in the 17th century by Vauban. Built between 1265 and 1309 on the Rhône, a little upstream from the confluence with the Ardèche, this handsome structure boosted the fortunes of this small trading town, which has preserved some magnificent old houses and maintained its status as a market town.
Tourist office - Caserne Pépin - bd Gambetta - ☎ 04 66 39 44 45 - www.provenceoccitane.com.

A bed for the night. A 5-minute walk from the station, Le Mas de l'Olivier is a hotel with rooms overlooking the wooded grounds and swimming pool. Ideal for a stopover on the holiday trail.
In a somewhat different vein, a little further away (12 minutes from the station), the charming Domaine La Vigie guest house offers modern and nicely decorated rooms overlooking the wooded gardens. Here too there is a swimming pool.
Hôtel-restaurant Le Mas de l'Olivier - 138 av. du Gén.-de-Gaulle - ☎ 04 66 89 12 38 - www.mas-olivier.com - 🍴 - 28 rms. €75/€85 - 🍴 €10 - menu €20.

The Rhône at Pont-Saint-Esprit.
Max Labeille/Getty Images Plus

Domaine La Vigie - 526 ch. de Gaujac - ☏ 07 69 44 31 14 - www.domainelavigie.fr - 🍴 - 3 rms. and 2 cottages (4/6 pers.) - €75/€95 - ☕ €7.50.

Spiritual. This museum reveals the significance of the sacred artworks that make up its eclectic collection, familiarising the public with somewhat arcane rites. Discover nativity scenes and their figurines, dating from the 18th and 19th centuries, in the old tower. You will also see domestic reliquaries, including examples of "quilling", i.e.: pictures made of rolled paper. Observe also a moving *Agony of Christ* (17th century), the *Adoration of the Magi* by Nicolas Dipre (circa 1495), and paintings by Benn (1905-1989).

Musée d'Art sacré du Gard - 2 r. St-Jacques - ☏ 04 66 39 17 61 - www.musees.gard.fr - Jul.-Aug.: 10 a.m.-12:30 p.m., 3-6:30 p.m.; rest of the year: 10 a.m.-noon, 2-6 p.m. - closed Mon. - free entry.

Dining. In the town centre, you can enjoy delicious and aromatic bistronomic cuisine (7-hour slow-cooked lamb, slow-roasted rack of pork), served in a cosy dining room or on the patio, in a friendly and relaxed atmosphere. Bar area for a coffee, a local beer, or a glass of wine. The establishment also has a delicatessen, where you can pick up something to go with your aperitif.

La Taverne aux Épices - 17 bd Gambetta - ☏ 04 30 39 90 05 - www.lataverneauxepices.com - closed Thurs. eve. and Sun.-Mon. - lunch deal €18.90, menu €38.90/€40.

Aperitif time. This brewery and wine shop boasts 500 different local and northern beverages on its shelves. Dish of the day at lunchtime and snacks at any time (croque-monsieur, charcuterie plancha, pancakes, waffles, etc.). Entertainment at the weekends.

Le Caviste de la Bourse - 8 pl. de la République - ☏ 04 66 33 85 51 - Facebook page - open year round, 7 a.m.-1 a.m. in the holiday season.

Playing in the cellar. An old cooperative cellar from 1929 has been transformed into a playground for young and old. You can now play escape games in this underground maze. Meals available on site.

KavKop - 232 r. du Commando-Vigan-Braquet - ☏ 04 66 89 61 58 - www.kavkop.com - closed Sat.-Sun. - 2 p.m.-midnight - from age 12 upwards - from €23/pers. acc. to the game and number of participants.

A biking tour

The Provence of the Gard

75 km in 3 stages, from Avignon to Uzès.

From the city of the Popes to the ducal city of Uzès, this bike tour of the Gard region includes the added attraction of passing under the Pont du Gard, the Roman aqueduct that is a masterpiece of ancient architecture. An easy itinerary, between vineyard and garrigue, which follows part of the ViaRhôna before joining the greenway of the Pays d'Uzège and which you can complete in two stages, but whose rich heritage treasures you will appreciate all the more by taking three days to do it.

Avignon to Beaucaire - 40 km

Leaving the City of the Popes behind, cross the Édouard-Daladier bridge to reach Villeneuve-lez-Avignon, on the right bank of the river. From there, the itinerary runs along a first section of shared roadway on little-used local roads, then joins the ViaRhôna, a greenway with a smooth or stabilised surface, running between the river and the D2 road. From Aramon, you cycle the 16 km to Montfrin along a temporary shared road section to the point where the ViaRhôna links up to the "Rétro Littorale" which runs south to Beaucaire (5 km).

Beaucaire to Pont du Gard - 20 km

Turning back the way you came, take the "Rétro Littorale" (V66) greenway to the outskirts of Montfrin. From Sernhac, this route extends into the new greenway leading to Uzès via the Pont du Gard, along a beautiful, safe, smooth metalled cycle path. This allows you to breeze along to the southeast end of the Roman aqueduct. Rarely has a human construction blended so "naturally" into the landscape. This is one sight you will never tire of contemplating.

PRACTICAL INFO

- **Bike hire in Avignon**
  Provence Bike – 7 av. St-Ruf - ✆ 04 90 27 92 61 - www.provence-bike.com. Hire of road bikes, mountain bikes and hybrid bikes (classic or electric), trailers, panniers and child seats. From €15 per day. Can arrange transport of luggage and return by minibus to Avignon.

- **Where to stay?**
  At Beaucaire: see p. 119.
  At Remoulins (Pont du Gard): Hôtel-restaurant Le Colombier - 24 av. du Pont-du-Gard - ✆ 04 66 37 05 28 - www.hotelrestaurant-pontdugard.fr - 🛏 - 17 rms. €65/€89 - 🍽 €9/€12 - ✖ closed Mon. and Tues. lunchtime - lunch deal: €15, menus: €20/€35.
  At Uzès: Le Patio de Violette - 8 ch. de Trinquelaïgues - ✆ 04 66 01 09 83 - www.lepatiodeviolette.fr - 🛏 - 25 rms. €94 - 🍽 €13.50.

- **And for the return trip?**
  To get back to Avignon from Uzès, take the liO 115 coach (lio-occitanie.fr). Please note that the coaches are not equipped with bicycle racks and bicycles are only accepted in the luggage compartment if space is available.

Pont du Gard. P. Jacques/hemis.fr

Pont du Gard to Uzès - 15 km

This stretch of the route, easy and pleasant to ride, continues along the greenway constructed on an old railway line. Only the last two kilometres are on a shared road (be aware, it's quite a steep climb!), but the crossing of the D981 is safe. With its shaded boulevards, medieval streets and beautiful houses with bronze-coloured facades, built in the 17th and 18th centuries, when cloth, serge and silk brought wealth to the town, Uzès exudes a radiant and serene beauty that will reward all your efforts in getting here.

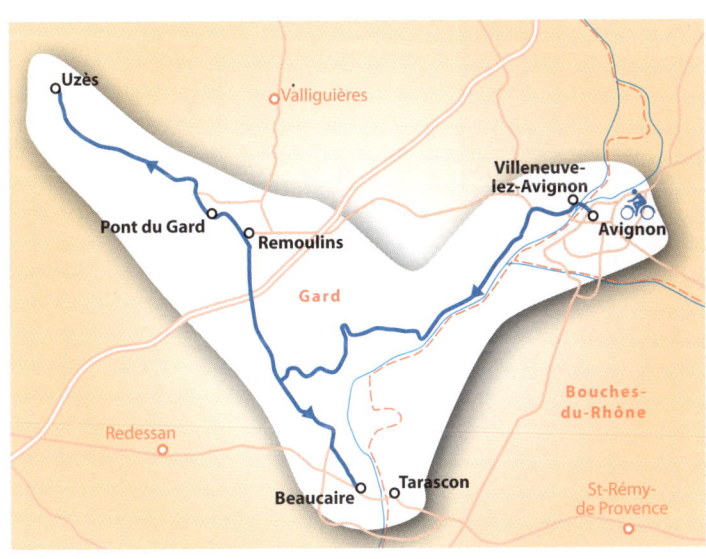

THE CAMARGUE LINE

No sooner has it left the town than the train enters the Gard-country Camargue, land of marsh and reedbed. In less than an hour, it crosses three protected designation of origin areas: the Costières de Nîmes vineyards, the Vins des Sables vineyards, and the rice fields of the Camargue. Aigues-Mortes emerges like a mirage, its long honey-coloured city walls hoving into view, bathed in pink by the setting sun. The train terminates at Le Grau-du-Roi, 400 m from the beach. Magical!

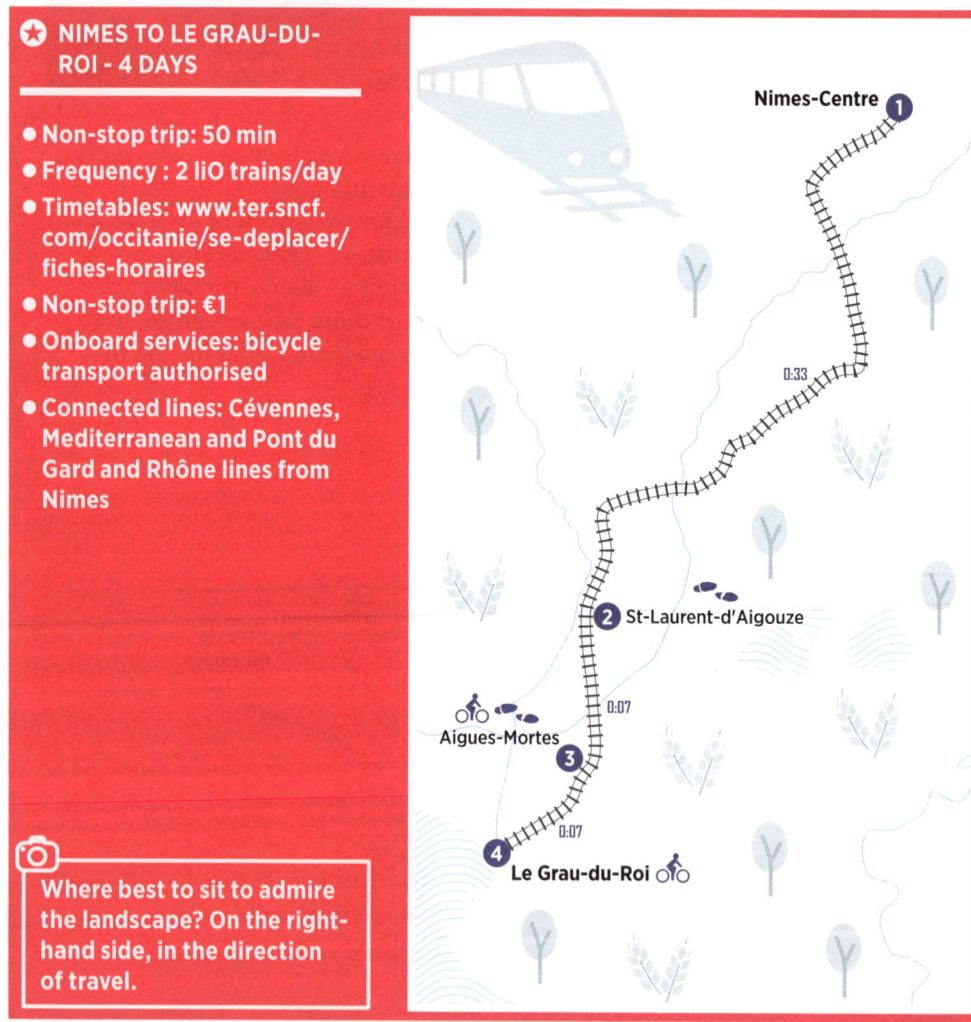

⭐ **NIMES TO LE GRAU-DU-ROI - 4 DAYS**

- Non-stop trip: 50 min
- Frequency : 2 liO trains/day
- Timetables: www.ter.sncf.com/occitanie/se-deplacer/fiches-horaires
- Non-stop trip: €1
- Onboard services: bicycle transport authorised
- Connected lines: Cévennes, Mediterranean and Pont du Gard and Rhône lines from Nimes

📷 Where best to sit to admire the landscape? On the right-hand side, in the direction of travel.

*Pink flamingoes.
Agaeta/Getty Images Plus*

1 NIMES-CENTRE

See Cévennes line p. 39.

2 ST-LAURENT-D'AIGOUZE

➜ **The station, slightly out of town, is a 15-minute walk from the bullring, on the other side of the D979.**

As seen on TV. Every evening, almost 4 million fans keep coming back for more. Welcome to the village where they film the series *"Ici tout commence"*, broadcast on TF1. In the series, St-Laurent-d'Aigouze has been renamed "Calvières" – a nod, no doubt, to the Bernis-Calvières family, owners until the 19th century of the chateau, the main backdrop of the series. But the visit does not stop there. This wine-growing village also boasts an astonishing bullring, backed on to the church, in the village square, shaded by large plane trees. Decked out in wood, the bullring has all the air of a permanent open-air exhibition.

Tourist office - 247 bd Gambetta - ☏ 04 66 77 22 31 - tourisme-saint-laurent-daigouze.fr.

A bed for the night. A 15-minute walk from the station, this charming hotel promises calm and serenity, with the added bonus of its two swimming pools. Possibility to stay in a room with a private terrace (and to have breakfast there) or in an equipped studio. Restaurant and massage service available at the hotel.
Hôtel Lou Garbin - 210 av. des Jardins - ☏ 04 66 88 12 74 - www.lou-garbin.com - ✗ - closed from Oct. to mid-Mar. - 🛏 - 12 rms. €90/€130 - ☕ €14 - menu €26/€32.

Dining. In the centre of the village, this is a very pleasant restaurant with a small menu packed with home-made dishes. Tasty fare on the plate and a fine selection of wines.
Le Griffou - 146 pl. de la République - ☏ 04 66 80 38 19 - www.facebook.com/LeGriffou - closed Mon., Sat. lunch and Sun. evening - dish of the day €12.50, menu €15/€19.

A walk behind the scenes. The "Sur les traces d'ITC" ("In the tracks of ITC") tour will take you to the heart of the TV series, *"Ici tout*

THE CAMARGUE LINE

Aigues-Mortes and the Salt Ponds of the Midi.
Pascale Gueret/Getty Images Plus

commence", broadcast Mondays to Fridays on TF1. Although the current filming locations, the chateau and the park remain off-limits, you will recognise the main sites of the series from the outside as you wander through the typical streets of a Camargue village.

"Sur les traces d'ITC" - tours (2h) at 10:30 a.m. and/or 3 p.m. or 4:30 p.m. - 📞 04 66 77 22 31 - bookings on the site www.jachete-en-terrede camargue.com - €14 (ages 6-16: €11).

❸ AIGUES-MORTES

➔ The station is on the left bank of the Rhône Canal, 5 minutes from the town centre on the opposite bank.

🚲 **Bike hire.** There is an e-bike rental shop a 5-minute walk from the station.
Aigues Bike - 1 bis bd Diderot - 📞 09 50 46 81 26 - www.aigues-bike.com - from €22 for 1 to 4 hours.

Behind the ramparts. "A veritable man'o'war", to paraphrase Chateaubriand's description of its fortified aspect, grounded between salt ponds, marshes and canals, Aigues-Mortes, in the lee of its ramparts, no longer appears entirely reminiscent of the Camargue or entirely reminiscent of Languedoc. Protected from the briny wind by its high walls, the town seems to have escaped the wear and tear of time. You will enjoy exploring its grid-plan streets, characteristic of the new towns of the Middle Ages. You will also come across lots of cafés, craft shops, souvenir shops and art galleries around Place St-Louis and in the main streets.
Tourist office - pl. St-Louis - 📞 04 66 53 73 00 - www.ot-aiguesmortes.com.

A bed for the night. Just a 7-minute walk from the station and around the corner from Place St-Louis, Chez Carrière is an unpretentious hotel that allows you to sleep within the confines of the town's fortifications. You may choose to spend the night in its "Le Mazet" suite with its pleasant private patio (€105/€115). The bright restaurant, all dapper in blue and yellow, offers local specialities such as fish soup en croûte and stuffed squid. Not far away and hard by the ramparts, the Hôtel St-Louis is an elegant 18th century building with colourful rooms and a spa. In the evening, tapas are served in the wine bar or on the shady patio, a must in the summer.
Chez Carrière - 18 r. Pasteur - 📞 04 66 53 73 07 - www.hotelrestaurant-chezcarriere.com - 🍴 - 10 rms. €92/€105 - ☕ €11 - menus €19/€27.

<u>Hôtel St-Louis</u> - 10 r. de l'Amiral-Courbet - 📞 04 66 53 72 68 - www.lesaintlouis.fr - ✖ - 22 rms. €86/€118 - ☕ €15 - lunch deal €24, menu €32/€50.

Royal attributes. The visit begins with the Governor's lodge, built in the 17th century on the site of the former royal castle, where a film illustrating the history of Aigues-Mortes is shown. The Constance tower, an imposing circular keep 40 m high (including the turret) was built between 1240 and 1249; the entrance gatehouse and the bridge linking it to the ramparts date from the 16th century. A tour of the ramparts via the sentry walk then offers a high vantage point for discovering the town, with beautiful views of the maritime channel (today a marina) and the Aigues-Mortes salt ponds. Built from 1270 onwards, the walls of Aigues-Mortes (made of Beaucaire and Baux stone) have survived intact, making them the finest example of military architecture of the 13th century.

<u>Towers and ramparts of Aigues-Mortes</u> - access via the Governor's lodge, pl. Anatole-France - 📞 04 66 53 61 55 - www.aigues-mortes-monument.fr - May-Aug.: 10 a.m.-7 p.m.; rest of the year: 10 a.m.-5:30 p.m. - €8 (under 18s free).

Dining. All aboard the Ni vu Ni connu: here, a shellfisher offers razor clams, tellinas and other seafood for your culinary delectation in a charming boat moored in the Aigues-Mortes basin. Back on dry land, try a table at the Villa Mazarin. Renovated into a charming establishment, this 16th century manor house offers fine and delicious market cuisine in its dining room or in its superb interior garden. A particular treat is the 5-hour slow-cooked lamb shank with the flavours of Provence. To extend your enjoyment, you can spend the night in one of the rooms, with their 17th century furnishings, ideal for a romantic tryst.

<u>Ni vu Ni connu</u> - bassin d'Aigues-Mortes - 📞 07 71 94 30 29 - closed Mon.-Tues. (exc. Jul.-Aug.) - dishes €19/€25.

<u>Villa Mazarin-La Table</u> - 35 bd Gambetta - 📞 04 66 73 90 48 - www.villamazarin.com - rest. closed Mon.-Fri. lunch - dishes €25/€30 - 23 rms. from €140 - ☕ €24.

Sweet snack. The multicoloured mosaic facade of this bakery, located a stone's throw from the Place St-Louis, is sure to catch the eye. But what it is particularly famous for is its fougasse, a tasty speciality flavoured with orange blossom. <u>Boulangerie-pâtisserie Olmeda</u> - 32 r. Émile-Jamais - 📞 04 66 53 73 42 - 6 a.m.-1 p.m., 4-7 p.m. - closed Tues.

💬 **Excursion into the Gard Camargue.** Not far from the ramparts of Aigues-Mortes, the Maison du Grand Site de France offers an excellent introduction to the Camargue of the Gard. On the first floor, a fine exhibition space presents the four types of landscapes that make up the area: freshwater marshes (Scamandre lake); reed beds and salt marshes (Marette lake); salt ponds (étang de la Ville); and seashore and dunes (Espiguette beach), as well as a focus on the people who have shaped these landscapes. Outside, an interpretation trail (1.6 km) on the Marette lake allows you to find out about the surrounding plant and animal life. Lots of events all year round.

<u>Maison du Grand Site de France de la Camargue gardoise</u> - rte du Môle - 📞 04 66 77 24 72 - www.camarguegardoise.com - Jul.-Aug.: 10 a.m.-12:30 p.m., 1:30-7 p.m.; rest of the year: 10 a.m.-12:30 p.m., 1:30-5 p.m. or 6 p.m. acc. to season - closed Mon.-Tues., pub. hols. and Oct.-Feb. - free entry.

④ LE GRAU-DU-ROI

🚲 **Bike hire.** Bikes (city and electric) are available for hire 5 minutes from the station. <u>Le Grau Vélo</u> - 4 bis r. du Cdt-Marceau - 📞 09 73 23 45 15 - regular bike from €8€/h (€11 for an e-bike).

Under the rails... The arrival of the railway gave the people of Nimes access to the beach. Built on both sides of a "grau" (a coastal inlet opened naturally around 1570, at a place called Gagne-Petit), between the mouths of the Vidourle and the Rhône, this resort has 18 km of fine sandy beaches by the sea. Until the middle of the 19th century, this humble port was populated by fishermen, often of Italian origin, living in modest shacks. Today, the nerve centre remains the canal, with its swing bridge, its pontoons and the old lighthouse topped by its lantern, the symbol of the town. Fishing boats are moored along the quays, where there are lots of quayside restaurants too. From the end of the jetty, you get a view of the Gulf of Aigues-Mortes with, to the left, the Pointe de l'Espiguette (and Port-Camargue) and, to the right, La Grande-Motte, seemingly overshadowed by the Pic St-Loup mountain, the Gardiole Massif and Mont St-Clair, which overlooks Sète.

Tourist office - Villa Parry - r. du Sémaphore - ℘ 04 66 51 67 70 - www.letsgrau.com.

A bed for the night. An 8-minute walk from the station, close to the port and 50 m from the beaches, the family-run Les Acacias hotel offer contemporary rooms in grey tones and a pleasant shaded terrace for breakfast.

Ideally located, a stone's throw from the centre and 10 minutes from the station, the Café Miramar has direct access to the beach. The rooms with a balcony and sea view are very pleasant. As for the restaurant, you can enjoy fish, shellfish, grills and tapas to share... all facing the sea!

Les Acacias - 21 r. de l'Égalité (right bank) - ℘ 04 66 51 40 86 - www.hotel-les-acacias.fr - closed Dec.-Jan. - 28 rms. €70/€109 - ☕ €9.

Café Miramar - 25 av. Frédéric-Mistral - ℘ 04 66 51 40 51 - www.cafe-miramar.fr - ✖ - 17 rms. €80/€115 - ☕ €12 - lunch deal €22, menu €35.

In the big blue waters. Sharks, jellyfish, seals, sea lions, Mediterranean fish and tropical pools will amuse or impress young and old alike in this vast space organised into seven themes. Interactive screens and video projections provide information about the lives of fish and shellfish, while games and tactile spaces help children discover the underwater world. Apart from the ever-popular seal and sea lion tank, the star attraction here is undoubtedly the shark aquarium ("Requinarium"). Measuring 1000 m² and containing a million litres of sea water, it is unique in Europe. It can hold 30 species of sharks and rays in several tanks (including one giant 80,000-litre tank, that can be viewed on two levels).

Seaquarium - av. du Palais-de-la-Mer - ℘ 04 66 51 57 57 - www.seaquarium.fr - Jul.-Aug.: 9 a.m.-11:30 p.m.; rest of the year: 9 a.m.-7:30 p.m. - €15 (ages 5-15: €11).

Dining. A seafood bistro, Le Dauphin, stands out from the crowd, with a terrace on the quayside. Run by a family of fishers-restaurateurs, the owner takes care of the service, her son works in the kitchen, and her husband owns a trawler! You couldn't hope for fresher fish!

Otherwise, L'Oasis is also a friendly family restaurant that has been run for over twenty years by Géraldine, a very bubbly character, and Gilles, her husband, who runs the kitchen. On the menu: tuna tataki, cuttlefish a la plancha, grilled fish, bull's beef ribs, all accompanied by regional and organic wines. To be enjoyed on the terrace, facing the boats.

Le Dauphin - 48 quai du Gén.-de-Gaulle - ℘ 04 66 53 91 44 - closed Mon. (exc. Jul.-Aug.) and Dec.-Feb. - menus €24/€31.

L'Oasis - quai d'Honneur - ℘ 04 66 53 07 08 - closed Mon. eve., Tues. eve. and Wed. (exc. Jul.-Aug.) - lunch deal €12.50, menu €25.

Aperitif time. This local institution plies its trade both summer and winter. Its blue and white decor is very easy on the eye, and from its terrace, overlooking the canal, you can watch the returning trawlers, mobbed by seagulls. Great for enjoying a few tellinas or other molluscs, washed down with a glass of sangria...

Café de la Marine - 31 quai Colbert - ℘ 04 66 51 40 33 - Summer: 9 a.m.-9 p.m.; rest of the year: 9:30 a.m.-8:30 p.m.

Walking in the sand. Le Grau-du-Roi is largely frequented for its beaches. From north to south, first you have the beach at Boucanet, which stretches from the residential areas to the shops; on the other side of the canal is the northern beach, skirted by a pedestrian promenade that extends all the way to Port-Camargue; the southern beach fronts the marina, while beyond the southern channel begins the long beach of Espiguette, the wildest of the beaches.

Fabulous Journeys

Active discovery of the Gard Camargue

It would be hard to find a better haven for an immersive stay in the Camargue than a thalasso hotel in Le Grau-du-Roi, the base for the largest marina in Europe. A magnificent view, relaxation and fitness areas will help recharge the batteries after days of high activity and intense stimulation.

Let's start with a bike ride on the ViaRhôna, which passes close to the salt marshes and lakes populated by pink flamingos, to bring you to the walled town of Aigues-Mortes. Continue your ride along the fringes of these wild spaces where horses and bulls roam free (no, it's not just a Camargue cliché!), and finish with a walk in the Scamandre nature reserve, a mecca for ornithologists.

During your stay, you could take a sea trip in the Gulf of Lion or try your hand at big game fishing (for bluefin tuna, swordfish, etc.) An invigorating horseback ride on the Espiguette, one of the largest beaches in Europe, is also well worth the experience! And since epicurean pleasures are also highly appreciated in the Camargue, why not pay a visit to an eco-responsible beach hut for dinner. Don't forget, either, to pick up some souvenir local specialities (oil, rice, salt) at the Maison Méditerranéenne des Vins. You're in for a variety-packed stay!

3 days, 2 nights - accommodation from €90 per night for 2 pers. - trip to be made in spring, summer and autumn.
Contact: Le Grau-du-Roi tourist office.

THE CAMARGUE LINE

Horseback ride on Espiguette beach at Le Grau-du-Roi. Richard Sprang/Ouvert au Public/CRT Occitanie

THE CÔTE VERMEILLE LINE

Anem a la platja ! The target destination is Spanish Catalonia for this cross-border line departing from Perpignan. After Argelès-sur-Mer, the train approaches the Côte Vermeille, with its sun-drenched terraced vineyards. Here the mighty Mediterranean takes centre stage, with the line running like a thread along the coastline. From one town to the next, the heritage shines through in a panoply of colour, with colours and light that are forever an artist's delight.

⭐ PERPIGNAN TO PORTBOU - 8 DAYS

- Non-stop trip: 50 min
- Frequency: approx. 9 liO trains/day
- Timetables: www.ter.sncf.com/occitanie/se-deplacer/fiches-horaires
- Non-stop trip: from €5
- On-board services: possibility to travel with your bicycle folded in a carrier case (no special carriage)
- Connected lines: Mediterranean and Catalan country lines from Perpignan

Where best to sit to admire the landscape? Left-hand side in the direction of travel.

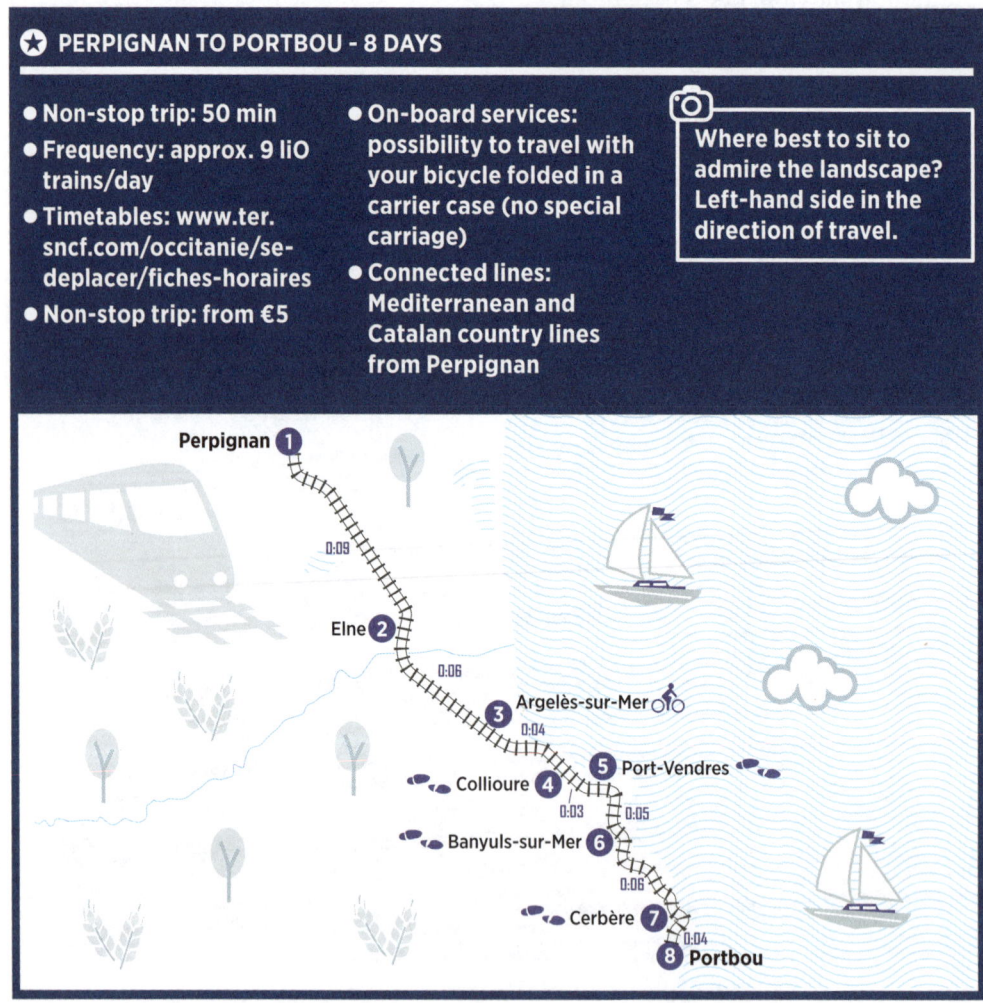

*The Côte Vermeille.
C. Deschamps/CRT Occitanie*

THE CÔTE VERMEILLE LINE

① PERPIGNAN

See the Mediterranean line p. 56.

② ELNE

Episcopal heritage. Surrounded by hills covered with apricot and peach trees, the upper town still sits protected behind its ramparts. The oldest town in Roussillon was also its spiritual capital: it had the great privilege of hosting the episcopal see of the region, from the 6th to the 17th centuries, thereby stealing some of Perpignan's thunder. Today, Elne is a sleepy little town, but the cloister of Elne cathedral, a magnificent example of Catalan Romanesque art, bears witness to its past influence. Take time to admire the capitals, where griffins, rams, peacocks and lions rub shoulders with figures from Genesis; the centrepiece is capital 12, which depicts Adam and Eve. The cathedral, begun in the 11th century and completed in the 14th and 15th centuries, show the phases in the development of Gothic art. A spiral staircase leads up to a terrace from which you can see the cathedral bell towers, the Albera Massif and the Mediterranean.
Tourist office - 2bis r. du Couvent - ☎ 04 48 98 00 08 - tourisme-pyrenees-mediterranee.com.
Elne Cathedral - plateau des Garaffes - ☎ 04 68 22 70 90 - Apr.-Sept.: 10 a.m.-6 p.m. (7 p.m. in summer); rest of the year: daily exc. Mon. 10 a.m.-12:30 p.m., 2-5 p.m. - €4.50 (under 10s free entry).

Dining and overnighting. In the heights of Elne, 10 minutes from the station, a charming hotel offers impeccable rooms with panoramic views of the Albera Massif and the Canigou. In the restaurant, the cuisine is based on fresh produce and local wines. On fine days, the meals are served on the terrace overlooking the valley.
Hôtel Cara Sol - 10 bd Illiberis - ☎ 04 68 22 10 42 - www.hotelcarasol.com - 15 rms. €72/€109 - ☕ €9 - half board €136/€172 - ✕ daily lunch and eve. - menu €17.

For a picnic. There is a small market every Monday and Wednesday, but the big market day is Friday, with the market on the main road.

③ ARGELÈS-SUR-MER

➜ Argelès-sur-Mer station is 2 km from the beach. A little train shuttle (Apr. to Sept.) links up the different parts of town. Info: www.trainbus.fr.

🚲 Bike hire at Argelès-Plage.
Argelès Vélos - 30 allée Jules-Aroles - ☎ 06 19 76 27 51 - www.argelesvelos.com - from €13.50 /day (sliding scale of prices).

Camping, beach and souvenirs. A large seaside resort, Argelès has beaches and campsites as far as the eye can see, making it the European capital of camping. But there is more to the town than the sunny, festive atmosphere: it bears the marks of a tragic history. In 1939, during the Retirada (retreat), thousands of Republicans fleeing Franco's troops were interned in what was the first Spanish refugee camp. Its Memorial recounts this history, as well

Collioure.
H. Arcence/OT Collioure

as that of the 160,000 men, women and children who passed through the Argelès-sur-Mer camp from February 1939 to early 1942.
Tourist office - pl. de l'Europe - 04 68 81 15 85 - www.argeles-sur-mer.com.
Argelès-sur-Mer Camp Memorial - 26 av. de la Libération - 04 68 95 85 03 - www.memorial-argeles.eu - Jul.-Sept.: 10 a.m.-6 p.m.; Oct.-Jun.: Tues.-Sat. 10 a.m.-1 p.m., 2-6 p.m. - €2 (under 18s free).

A bed for the night. Located 6 minutes from the station, L'Hostalet is a charming guest house with a warm welcome and comfortable rooms. In the morning, a delicious smell of homemade cakes will wake you up, announcing breakfast time, which is taken on the terrace on the Place de la République, in the shade of the plane trees. Delectable from every point of view!
L'Hostalet - 32 r. de la République - 04 68 95 76 54 - hostalet.fr - 5 rms. €73/€100 - €12.50.

Dining. This is an address that fans of good food will be keen to share. And with good cause: the chef, Thibaut Lesage, and his wife Stéphanie, a pastry chef, delight the taste buds by giving their own inspired touch to classic favourites. A real treat! Attention: advance booking a must.
La Bartavelle - 24 r. de la République - 06 19 25 70 13 - www.restaurant-labartavelle.fr - closed for lunch (exc. Wed.) in Jul.-Aug., Sun.-Mon., Tues. lunch, Thurs. lunch and Fri. lunch the rest of the year - menus €42/€52.

For a picnic. Weekly market in Rue de la République and Place de la République on Wednesday and Saturday mornings in the village and in the Platanes car park during the season (from mid-June to mid-Sept.) on Monday, Wednesday and Friday mornings.

Sea and tramontane. Take advantage of the winds that blow along this coastline to try your hand at sailing in all its forms. Catamaran, windsurf, paddleboard and sea kayak rental.

Central Windsurf - plage des Pins - ☏ 07 50 60 57 61 - www.centralwindsurf.com - May-mid Sept.: 9 a.m.-7 p.m.

Aperitif time. An ode to the sea and to local wines in this charming and friendly establishment, set back from Racou beach. The chef concocts delicious dishes for the restaurant, but you can also sit at the bar and enjoy wine and appetizers at cocktail hour.
Le Menje Ecaille - 29 av. de la Torre-d'en-Sorra - Le Racou - ☏ 04 68 81 41 23.

Sardana. The Foment de la Sardana was founded in 1958 at the initiative of the Argelès-born musician, Jordi Barre (1920-2011). Since 1976, this association has organised the *aplech*, a rural gathering of dancers and musicians, every first Sunday in September, in the Parc de Valmy.

 # COLLIOURE

→ **Collioure is the gateway to the magnificent Côte Vermeille ("Vermilion coast"), which stretches to the Spanish border, between terraced vineyards and the Mediterranean. The liO line crosses these landscapes by following the coastline or passing through tunnels in the hills.**

The colours of Collioure. Its fortified church stands so close to the sea that it appears to have emerged from the waves. Its bell tower, with its distinctive pink dome, was actually once a lighthouse in the old port. In the two small ports, separated by the old royal castle, you may well spot a number of "barques Catalanes", the traditional Catalan fishing boats, recognisable by their bright colours and typical masts. The fortified castle is built on the rocky spur separating the two coves, around the square keep constructed by the kings of Majorca. Charles V and Philip II transformed it into a citadel, reinforced by Fort Saint-Elme *(see p. 138)* and Fort Miradou. Ancient streets with floral balconies, interspersed with staircases, a seaside promenade, café terraces and shops with colourful windows complete the picture of this small medieval town which attracted many painters in the 20th century,

including the Fauvist artists, led by Matisse, who sought to capture its palette of light.
Tourist office - pl. du 18-Juin - ☏ 04 68 82 15 47 - www.collioure.com.

A bed for the night. Nestled in the heart of the village, a 5-minute walk from the station and 200 metres from the beach, the hotel offers pleasantly renovated and functional rooms.
Hôtel Princes de Catalogne - rue des Palmiers - ☏ 04 68 98 30 00 - www.hotel-princescatalogne.fr - 30 rms. €79/€152 - ⌑ €10.

Dining. Chef Victoria Robinson has made slow food her credo. Hardly surprising then to find lots of fresh produce from small local producers in the fare on offer, whether for eating or drinking. The chef is also keen to select products that are organic, or the produce of sustainable fishing and ethical farming.
La Cuisine Comptoir - 2 r. Colbert - ☏ 04 68 81 14 40 - lacuisinecollioure.com - lunch and evening - menus €25/€40.

Choice souvenir. Since 1870, Anchois Roque has been perpetuating the traditional preparation of anchovies. Shop on the ground floor and workshop on the 1st floor to watch expert hands at work preparing the small iconic fish of Collioure.
Anchois Roque Collioure - 17 rte d'Argelès - ☏ 04 68 82 04 99 - anchois-roque.fr - Mon.-Sat. 8 a.m.-7 p.m.; Sun. 9 a.m.-noon, 2-7 p.m. - tours: Mon.-Fri. 8:15-11:45 a.m., 2:05 -4:45 p.m.

Dive into the azure waters of the Vermilion Coast! This diving centre provides professional equipment and supervision for learning and practising this sport.
CIP-Collioure - 24 r. Ravin-du-Coma-Xeric - ☏ 04 48 89 19 99 - www.cip-collioure.com - 9 a.m.-noon, 2-5 p.m. - closed from start of Sept. to end of Jun - initiation €70, snorkelling excursion €55.

Aperitif time. The greatest artists (Derain, Picasso, Matisse) have visited this now legendary bar: the paintings on the walls bear witness to this. An authentic place where you can enjoy a good AOC Collioure wine with tapas.
Bar des Templiers - 12 quai de l'Amirauté - ☏ 04 68 98 31 10 - www.hotel-templiers.com - 8 a.m-2 a.m. (closes earlier off-season).

Patronal festival. The Festival of St. Vincent (Fêtes de la St-Vincent), an event eagerly anticipated throughout the region, takes place from 14 to 18 August. The crowds gather for the bullfight, the balls, and the procession of the relics of Saint Vincent on the sea, on 16 August, which culminates in a magnificent sound and light show.

Climbing up to Fort St-Elme. The defensive role of this high hill goes back almost 1,000 years. Perched on the summit, the fort occupies a strategic position, overlooking Collioure and Port-Vendres, and controlling the road to Barcelona. It was Emperor Charles V who decided to build the present fortress, in its six-pointed star configuration, the walls of which are almost 8 m thick. These walls could withstand any artillery fire. Seized by the troops of Louis XIII in 1642, the bastion remained a border checkpoint until the French Revolution. Remarkably restored and with activities all year round, it contains a fine collection of firearms from across the ages, presented in the vaulted rooms, and offers a magnificent panorama of the surrounding area.
1h hike from Collioure - average difficulty.
Fort St-Elme - www.fortsaintelme.fr - 10:30 a.m.-7 p.m. (5 p.m. off-season) - €8 (ages 6-18: €5).

⑤ PORT-VENDRES

The port of Venus. Port-Vendres (*Portus Veneris*, the "port of Venus") grew up around a cove where galleys took shelter. From 1679 onwards, the town was developed by Vauban as a military port and citadel. It is today the most active fishing port on the Rousillon coast. It is popular with visitors for its fish market, or as a place to take it easy after some great walks around the Côte Vermeille.
Tourist office - pl. du 18-Juin - 04 68 82 15 47 - collioure.com.

A bed for the night. This charming hotel is located on the quayside, just a 5-minute walk from the station, and offers renovated rooms, some of which have a sea view for taking in all the port's hustle and bustle.
Hôtel sur le Quai - 2 quai Pierre-Forgas - 04 11 96 00 80 - hotelsurlequai.fr - 22 rms. €73/€110.

Dining. A restaurant right in heart of the port: the chef has only to step out of doors to find the finest catches of the day at the fish market, which he cooks up with a Mediterranean flavour. Particularly appealing is the terrace overlooking the sea, where the atmosphere is more relaxed than indoors.
La Côte Vermeille - quai Fanal - near the fish auction - 04 68 88 85 05 - www.restaurantlacotevermeille.com - closed Sun. eve. and Mon. (off season) - lunch deal €28, lunch menu €32, eve. €48/€66, menu €48/€66.

Discovering the marine reserve. This diving centre provides equipment and professional supervision for practicing this sport in complete safety: an opportunity to discover the Cerbère-Banyuls marine nature reserve, protected since 1974 for its exceptional biodiversity. Snorkelling excursion for those preferring to stay on the surface.
Centre d'Activité Plongée Port-Vendres - Gerbal cove (old fish auction) - 07 80 97 46 38 - www.plongee66.com - daily exc. Sun. 9 a.m.-6 p.m. - initiation €80/€180, snorkelling excursion €30.

Closer to the heavens. The hike up to the Madeloc tower takes you from Port-Vendres station through the vineyards and garrigue of the hinterland, up to 652 m above the sea (6h - 950 m ascent, strenuous in places). This rubble-stone tower, round and ringed with machicolations, is an ancient signal tower which, along with the Massane tower to the west, was part of a watchtower network during the time of Aragonese and Majorcan sovereignty. The Massane tower watched over the Roussillon plain, while the Madeloc tower looked out to sea. Along the way, the path passes by old batteries, including Battery 500, a remnant of Port-Vendres' fortifications to control the hinterland. Once you reach the belvedere in front of the tower, your efforts will be rewarded with absolutely spectacular views of the sea, the Côte Vermeille, the Roussillon and part of the Albera Massif.

6 BANYULS-SUR-MER

→ The station is high above the village; you get down from it (and back up to it) via the stepped streets. Allow 20 minutes to return from the village to the station if you don't want to miss your train!

Sea, bronze and wine. The peaceful seaside resort of Banyuls is wrapped around a pretty bay, sheltered from the tramontane wind and overlooked by a beautiful landscape of terraced vineyards, from which the famous AOC dessert wine is made. The main (pebble) beach has a wooden promenade running alongside it, where you can stroll among statues of Aristide Maillol, a native son. Opposite the marina is the facade of the first aquarium in France, the Biodiversarium (1885). Banyuls is also the site of France's first natural marine reserve (1974), and the only exclusively marine reserve to date. Extending along 6.5 km of coastline between Banyuls and Cerbère, it covers an area of 650 hectares of sea, aimed at protecting species threatened by both intensive fishing and by pollution and tourist traffic.

Tourist office - av. de la République - 04 68 88 31 58 - www.banyuls-sur-mer.com.

A bed for the night. A welcoming hotel located on the seafront, on Elmes beach, and 10 minutes' walk from the station. Renovated rooms in a nautical style. Fish and shellfish star on the menu at the restaurant (La Littorine), with its terrace overlooking the sea. Spa, relaxation and fitness area.

Hôtel Les Elmes - Elmes beach - 04 68 88 03 12 - www.hotel-des-elmes.com - 33 rms. €70/€243 - €12/€16 - menu €35/€58.

Dining. This friendly restaurant is hidden away in the village, set back from the seafront. The young and dynamic team runs a wine shop there with a focus on natural local wines, a delicatessen area offering regional organic products and a restaurant with a delicious menu, all in an old building with charming architecture. Not to be missed!

The Cerbère-Banyuls natural marine reserve.
Damocean/Getty Images Plus

Personal account

The buffets at Cerbère and Perpignan stations

Jean-Charles Sin is the great-grandson of the founder of the Le Belvédère hotel, which is inextricably linked to the railway station of Cerbère. Very attached to the rail history of his town, he recalls how it was: "I remember the steam locomotives that made a lot of smoke and noise: that was life back then! When we were children, we had an understanding with the transhipment workers handling the Valencia oranges that passed via Portbou and Cerbère before being shipped around Europe. These women carried the oranges around in big baskets, and occasionally the odd orange would fall out..."

For 45 years, Jean-Charles Sin was the manager of the buffet at Cerbère station and for 28 years managed the Perpignan station buffet too. "The buffets were passed down from generation to generation, like a legacy: my family ran the buffet at Cerbère station for 104 years, a national record!" Harking back to the great era of station buffets, he recounts the splendour of the meals organised on the days of the orange auctions when whole truck-loads of citrus fruit were negotiated around a big banquet: "At the Cerbère station buffet, the service was gargantuan, and just reading the auction menu was enough to give you indigestion!" During his 28 years at the Perpignan buffet, he organised meetings between places proclaimed to be "the centre of the world": "One day, Salvador Dalí was wandering around the public lobby when he went into raptures about a piece of plaster, shaped like a cabbage, that had fallen from the ceiling. This had him declaring that Perpignan station was the '*centre of the world*'. Later, I came to realise that there were lots of other 'centres of the world', and I invited them to come join us in ours." »

Hôtel du Belvédère in Cerbère.
A. Abad/age fotostock

Les 9 Caves - 56 av. du Gén.-de-Gaulle - ☏ 04 68 36 22 37 - 9caves.com - daily exc. Tues. and Wed. for lunch and Sun. eve. - menus €24/€48.

AOC wine to go. The oldest wine cooperative in the town (1921) specialises in Old Banyuls and produces a dozen recognised varieties. Red and rosé AOC Collioure wines are another speciality.
Cave L'Étoile - 26 av. du Puig-del-Mas - ☏ 04 68 88 00 10 - www.banyuls-etoile.com - 9:30 a.m.-6 p.m. (8 p.m. in season).

Aperitif time. Enticing wine cellar and tapas bar with cuisine cooked up according to the seasons and the mood of the chef, Manu. He prepares with gusto dishes based on ultra-fresh produce, to be shared among friends: charcuterie, carpaccio or fish tartars, accompanied by a very nice selection of natural wines, many of them local. Guaranteed to win you over! There aren't many tables, so remember to book in advance.
El Xadic del Mar - 11 av. Puig-del-Mas - ☏ 04 68 88 89 20 - 10 a.m.-3 p.m., 5 p.m.-2 a.m. - tapas €16/€35.

Sardana Festival. 2nd weekend in August. Dancing and concerts in the square in front of the beach.

👣 Coastal path. This coastal walk links Banyuls to Cap Béar, passing through the site of Paulilles. Setting off from Elmes beach, you are in for a delightful day of walking, swimming and culture, amidst terraced vineyards, prickly pear trees, garrigue and - everywhere - the sea! About halfway along the route, you can visit the site of Paulilles, in the magnificent bay of the same name, previously known for its dynamite factory, created in 1875 in association with the man responsible not only for inventing dynamite but also for creating the peace prize: Alfred Nobel. After absorbing the industrial history of this listed site, the walk can resume at a leisurely pace. You can stop off at one of the pretty secluded coves you come across after passing Bernardi beach. At the end of the path (clearly marked) you will reach the Santa Catarina cove and its several "shacks". The path then climbs to the Cap Béar lighthouse, built in 1905 out of Villefranche pink marble, where the strongest winds in the region are recorded. *10 km - approx. 3h30 one-way - no particular difficulty, but to be avoided in case of strong winds.*

⑦ CERBÈRE

➜ **Cerbère is the last French station for the liO train, which then continues on to the Spanish village of Portbou.**

👣 **Other options for getting to Portbou:** a footpath links Cerbère to Portbou in 1h30 via the Balistres pass and the old border post (see p. 142).

Last stop before Spain. On the border between France and Spain, Cerbère is served by an international railway station. It has had its moments of glory since its inauguration in 1878, and for much of the 20th century, despite the tragedies of the Spanish Civil War and the Second World War. An obligatory stop between France and Spain for transhipment (the rails of the two countries do not have the same gauges), it remained for a long time an unavoidable stopover to wait for visas and passes necessary to enter Spain, before the country joined the EEC (in 1986). Without the railway viaduct and its remarkable infrastructure, Cerbère would only be a small isolated port, hemmed in between the mountains. Well sheltered at the back of its cove, it has a pleasant shale beach. In the narrow streets of the village, the café terraces and pedestrian alleys already have a Spanish feel.
Tourist office - av. du Gén.-de-Gaulle - ☏ 04 68 88 42 36 - www.cerbere-tourisme.com.

A bed for the night. Overlooking the sea and the railway, this Art deco hotel, not to be missed, is the heritage gem of Cerbère. With its unique architecture, in the shape of an ocean liner, it was built in 1932 as an extension of the station at a time when commercial and rail traffic was at its peak in Cerbère. Its founder decided to turn it into a luxury venue with a cinema in an Italian-style theatre, a restaurant, a bar and a games room, while the spacious and modern rooms welcomed the stars of the day, including Orson Welles and Michèle Morgan. The establishment (which is listed) is gradually regaining its magnificence thanks to the current owner *(see box p. 140)*: 9 apartments with kitchenette, most with a sea view, have been refurbished, combining modern comfort with old-fashioned elegance.

Hôtel Le Belvédère du Rayon Vert - av. de la Côte-Vermeille - 04 68 88 41 54 - hotel-belvedere-cerbere.fr - 9 studios - €110/€180.

Dining. On Peyrefite beach, this pleasant restaurant lives up to its name: you have the feeling of being at the end of the world in this last part of France, between sea and mountain. Under the reed canopy, almost with your feet in the water, you can enjoy fish tartar or cuttlefish a la plancha while sipping a nice beverage. Note that in season the place gets very busy, so it is better to book in advance.

Le Bout du Monde - plage de Peyrefite - 04 68 88 47 33 - daily exc. Mon. - menus €28.

Beaches and an underwater trail. While the beach of the village is pleasant enough, you ideally want to get to the beaches in the protected zone of the natural marine reserve: to the north of the village, via the coastal path, the beaches of Terrimbo and Peyrefite await (20 and 35 minutes' walk). From Peyrefite beach, you can explore the reserve's underwater trail, with its submerged information panels, equipped with mask, fins and snorkel. The 250-metre-long route is dotted with five observation stations. Marked by a buoy, each one allows you to observe a different biotope, whether among seagrass, rocks or pebbles. With a bit of luck, in addition to seabream, bass, wrasse and red mullet, you might get to see a dolphin, a loggerhead turtle, or a long-snouted seahorse!

Underwater trail - Peyrefite beach - 04 68 88 09 11 - Jul.-Aug.: noon-5 p.m. - fins-mask-snorkel hire €7/€9.

To the outskirts of Portbou. This 3 km loop (allow 2 hours) ends up skirting the Spanish border. From the town centre, walk along the seafront on the pedestrian path until you reach the cemetery, then keep left to reach Cap Cerbère where the solar lighthouse stands.

From here, the view of the Spanish coastline stretches as far as the eye can see, with the high cliffs of Bou Fallut in the foreground. Walking alongside these cliffs, you branch off toward the track that leads up to the Balistres Pass. The old border post is marked by a monument to the exiles of the Retirada, the retreat of the Spanish Republicans who took refuge en masse in Cerbère. To go back down, take the steps near the border post and follow the path that leads to the village. Another option is to take this path to reach Portbou, on the Spanish side, for an hour and a half's walk over the Balistres Pass.

8 PORTBOU

→ **The Spanish station of Portbou is the terminus of the liO line. For day trips between Cerbère and Portbou, the train makes 7 daily return journeys.**

Catalan terminus. The small Spanish town of Portbou is best explored on a day trip from Cerbère, its French counterpart, but you can also opt for an overnight stay to enjoy the local evening entertainment. During the day, take a stroll along the beach promenade or the shaded rambla with views of the surrounding cliffs. The imposing neo-Gothic church of Santa Maria towers over the incredible network of railway lines: it was built for the railway workers when the station was constructed. Portbou is also the last resting place of the philosopher Walter Benjamin.

A bed for the night. The charming and pleasantly shaded Hotel Comodoro is located just 50 metres from the beach and a 5-minute walk from the station. You'll appreciate the warm welcome, the impeccably spotless rooms and the slightly old-fashioned atmosphere there.

Hotel Comodoro - carrer Mendez Nuñez, 1 - (+34) 609 47 15 04 - www.hotelcomodoroportbou.es - 16 rms. €80/€96.

Passages. History tells us that the German philosopher Walter Benjamin, a Jewish exile previously in Paris and close friend of Hannah Arendt and Adorno, tragically ended his days in Portbou. Fleeing the Nazis and French

Portbou station — MarcoZouvek/Getty Images Plus

collaborators, and cornered in Portbou without a pass from the Franco government, Walter Benjamin committed suicide on 26 September 1940, by taking a morphine overdose. 50 years after his death, a memorial was commissioned from the Israeli artist Dani Karavan. The corridor of glass and steel that plunges into the sea is a poignant allegory of what drives some exiles to choose the sea as their final refuge. It is a powerfully evocative place, in memory of all passages and passengers.
At the Portbou cemetery - passeig de la Sardana - free access.

Dining. Located on the promenade along the sea front, this restaurant has been given a fresh lease of life thanks to the new generation at the helm and a more gourmet offering. The quality of the products and the chef's skills make this a sought-after address: it is best to book, especially in the evening.
Voramar - passeig de la Sardana 6 - ℘ (+34) 972 39 00 16 - www.voramarportbou.com - daily exc. Tues.-Wed. 1-3 p.m., 8-10 p.m.; Sun. lunch only - menus €68/€112.

For a picnic. The market hall is open every morning (except Sunday) and offers all the fresh produce of the region (fruit and vegetables, local specialities).
Passeig Enric Granados.

Aperitif time. In the market square, the Catalan tapas of Casa David are renowned throughout the region: locals of all ages meet here at all hours to share a cold caña (beer), freshly caught calamari and local charcuterie that melts in the mouth.
Casa David - plaça del Mercat, 2 - ℘ (+34) 972 39 00 06 - daily exc. Mon. 8 a.m.-midnight - tapas €8/€15.

Festa Major de Sant Jaume. This great traditional celebration is held at the end of July and lasts three days. It culminates on the last day with the Catalan *correfoc* during which men dressed as devils run around with fireworks on sticks and throw firecrackers into the crowd.

A biking tour

The Catalan coast

95 km in 2 stages, from Argelès-sur-Mer to Narbonne.

A ride with a Mediterranean view! A breathtaking itinerary that takes in nature, gastronomy, sun and heritage. From Argelès-sur-Mer to Narbonne, there are paths to take your breath away, running through villages and seaside resorts. After Leucate and the nature reserves, the atmosphere changes as you follow the towpath. The locks punctuate the progression towards Narbonne, your final destination, where the Archbishops' Palace and the famous Belle Époque-style covered market await your discovery. Enchanting.

Argelès to Leucate: 55 km

A stage on a smooth surface, with the exception of the start of the cycle path along the D81, alternating between seafront in sections shared with pedestrians and cycle paths along the departmental roads. The Mediterranean route (EV8) is signposted. Note that between Canet-Plage and Canet-en-Roussillon you have to take a cycle track on the left of an open gate. The route through the Pointe de la Corrège, with its great views, takes you through the pine forest to the village of oyster huts, and then on to Port-Leucate, your stopover. Have your towel handy for taking a dip on the way! Along the route, Port Barcarès is a family resort dating back to the 1970s, the flagship of tourist development on the Roussillon coastline. Once you have completed this stage, you can also enjoy the beautiful beaches of Port-Leucate. And if you have the time, why not rent a paddleboard, a pirogue or a canoe?

Port-la-Nouvelle, Ile Sainte-Lucie.
A. Spani/hemis.fr

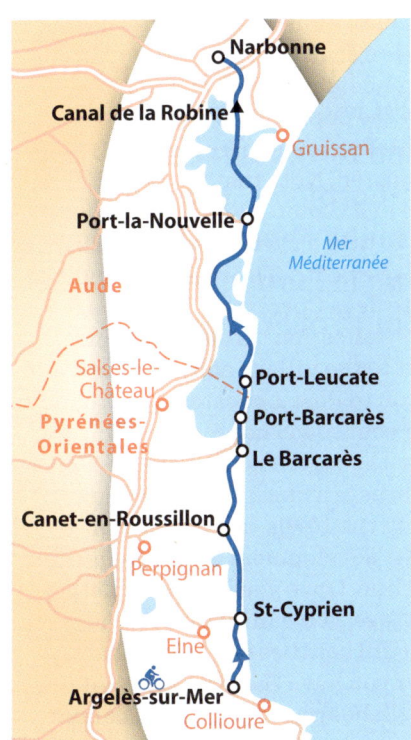

Leucate to Narbonne: 40 km

A second stage taking in sea, lakes, nature reserve and canal, a little more strenous than the first. The start involves a splendid climb up to the plateau, followed by a steep descent (a 50 m drop in elevation in one km!) which takes you on to the cycle track leading to the station of Leucate-la Franqui. You ride alongside the La Palme lake bordered by the salt ponds, before reaching the junction of the Robine canal and the towpaths to Narbonne. This canal follows the old course of the river Aude, which the Romans already used to sail along. Like the Canal du Midi, it is listed as a UNESCO World Heritage Site. Be aware that the path is strewn with pebbles just before Port-la-Nouvelle. After Mandirac, the towpath along the Canal de la Robine is very rural.

THE CÔTE VERMEILLE LINE

PRACTICAL INFO

- **Bike hire at Argelès and Narbonne**
Paulette, bike hire – 📞 05 82 28 05 10 - www.paulette.bike/fr. Argelès-sur-Mer agency: 8 r. Wilson - 📞 06 50 36 69 98; Narbonne agency: 11 bd Condorcet - 📞 04 68 42 43 92. This network of agencies in Occitanie operates like a car rental company: bookings on the website, one-way bike hire possible, wide range of bicycles. Lots of optional accessories. Luggage transfer possible. Budget for €60 for 2 days for an e-bike, leaving the bike in Narbonne.

- **Where to stay?**
At Port-Leucate: Hôtel des 2 Golfs - r. du Dour - 📞 04 68 40 79 79 - www.hoteldes2golfs.com - 30 rms. €102. Accueil Vélo ("Bikes welcome") label.

- **Useful to know**
It's better to choose a Gravel bike (all-terrain) or an MTB, as the second part of the circuit is fairly rough and uneven.

THE CANAL DU MIDI LINE

From Toulouse, the capital of Languedoc, to the bustling port of Narbonne, this line follows the Canal du Midi along towpaths fringed by ancient trees, old vineyards and towns steeped in history. Along the way are also Lézignan-Corbières, the mini-capital of the Corbières, at the gateway to the Minervois region, and Carcassonne, the largest fortress town in Europe. An enchanting trip with the accents of the South of France.

⭐ TOULOUSE TO NARBONNE - 6 DAYS

- Non-stop trip: 1h30
- Frequency : 14 liO trains/day
- Timetables: www.ter.sncf.com/occitanie/se-deplacer/fiches-horaires
- Non-stop trip: €26.50
- Onboard services: bike transport authorised on trains

- Connected lines: Pyrenees, Lot and Dordogne, Bastides and most beautiful villages, Cathedrals, Piemont and Gers lines from Toulouse; Mediterranean line from Narbonne

📷 Where best to sit to admire the landscape? On the left-hand side, in the direction of travel.

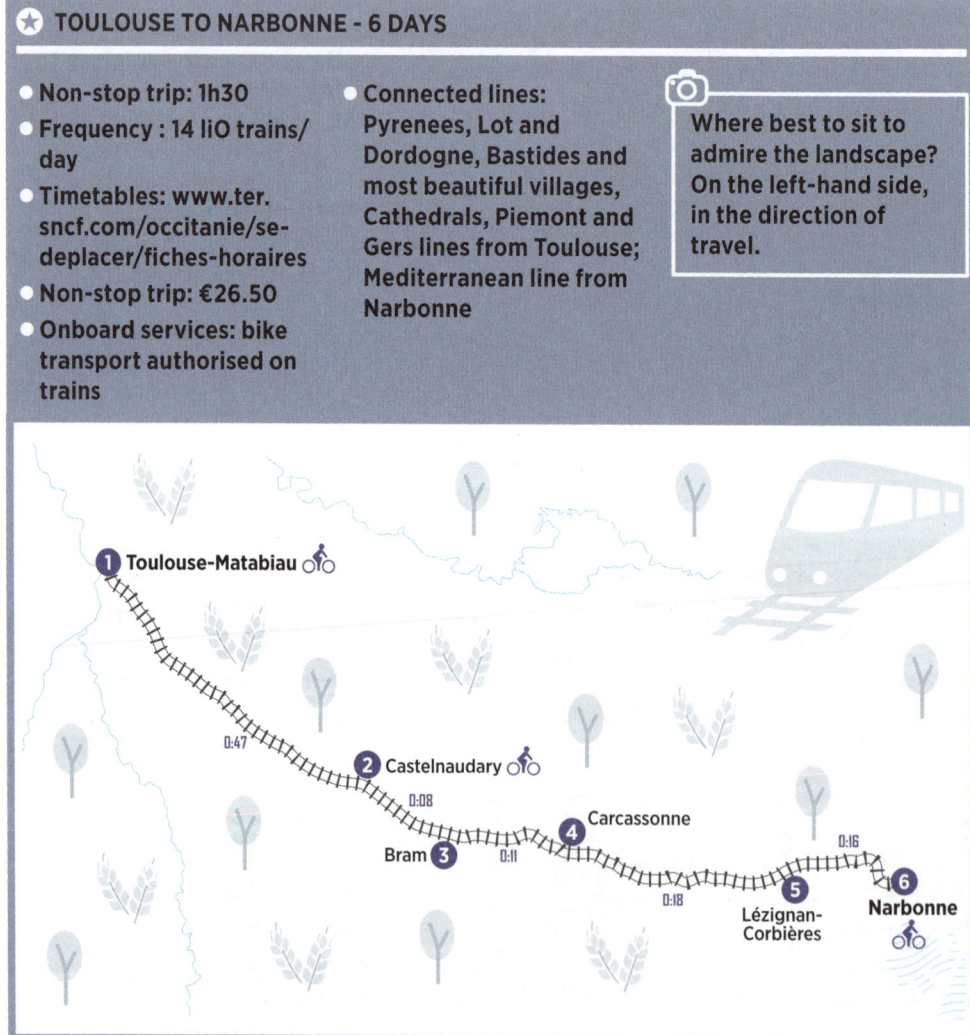

1. Toulouse-Matabiau
0:47
2. Castelnaudary
0:08
3. Bram
0:11
4. Carcassonne
0:18
5. Lézignan-Corbières
0:16
6. Narbonne

Canal du Midi between Carcassonne and Béziers.
J.-P. Lescourret/hemis.fr

① TOULOUSE-MATABIAU

See the Pyrenees line p. 84.

② CASTELNAUDARY

Bike hire. Just a minute's walk from the station, an association offers tourist bikes for hire.
<u>La Roue qui tourne</u> - 44 av. Paul-Riquet - ☏ 07 68 13 87 23 - www.larouequitourne011.wordpress.com - closed Sat.-Sun. - hybrids/MTBs €10 per half-day, e-bikes €22 per half-day.

In the land of cassoulet. What would Castelnaudary be without its cassoulet? Well, it would still be a quiet little town, sitting astride the canal. Today, commercial traffic has made way for pleasure boating, the waterway dotted with a pleasant series of locks and culverts. In fact, the Grand Bassin (7 ha) serves as a reservoir for the four locks of St-Roch, which make it possible to negotiate a difference in level of almost 10 m (passing via the eastern end, crossing the Avenue des Pyrénées and following the towpath). The town's beautiful Church of St-Michel, built in the 14th century, was reconstructed on the site of a previous building. The 50 m-high bell tower-porch, the north facade with its two portals (Gothic and Renaissance) and its openwork rose windows are remarkable.
<u>Tourist office</u> - pl. de la République - ☏ 04 68 23 05 73 - www.castelnaudary-tourisme.com.

A bed for the night. A 10-minute walk from the station, right in the town centre, the hotel offers spacious, functional and well-renovated rooms in a contemporary style. Traditional cuisine (with cassoulet, of course!) served in a baroque dining room.
<u>Hôtel-restaurant Le Centre</u> - 31 cours de la République - ☏ 04 68 23 25 95 - www.le-centre-hotel.fr - 10 rms. €69/€84 - ☕ €9 - 🍴 lunch deal €19.50/€24.50, menus €27/€31.50 - half-board possible.

Dining. Au Petit Gazouillis, right in the centre of town, is a nice find. After doing the rounds in French Guiana, the chef turned his hand to the recipes of this small corner of France. Simple, well-crafted food, low prices and a pastel-coloured dining room.

A little further out, Le Tirou is located inside a lovely menagerie. In the garden, you can enjoy 100% home-made dishes (the cassoulet is delicious), local produce and fine wines. This inn has all it takes to please, and you can buy tins and jars of home-made produce to take away.

Au Petit Gazouillis - 5 r. de l'Arcade - ☎ 04 68 23 08 18 - closed Wed. (in Jul.), Wed.-Thurs. (off-season), from mid-Dec. to mid-Jan. - menus €18/€23.50 - booking recommended.

Le Tirou - 90 av. Mgr-de-Langle - ☎ 04 68 94 15 95 - www.tirou.fr - closed Sun.-Mon. and Tue.-Fri. eve. - menus €38/€49.

Messing about in boats. Renting a houseboat, generally equipped to accommodate 6 to 8 people, offers a somewhat different way to discover the sites. These boats do not require a licence (max. speed: 6 kph), but you do get an initiation into what to do by the rental company before setting off. This is what is proposed by this particular company, the first licence-free boat rental company to be set up on the Canal du Midi in the 1970s. Choice of houseboats for between 2 and 12 people.

Le Boat - au Grand Bassin - quai du Canelot - ☎ 04 68 94 42 80 (booking centre) or ☎ 04 68 94 52 94 (Castelnaudary base) - www.leboat.fr.

Has beans. If you are in the area at the end of August, don't miss the Castelnaudary Cassoulet Festival. Expect lots of cassoulet, events on the canal, free concerts, street shows, bodegas, gourmet market, and a flower parade. Tradition dictates that the beans for the cassoulet need to have grown in the soil of Castelnaudary, that they are cooked in the very pure water of the town, and that gorse from the Montagne Noire feeds the fire in the oven.

Fête du cassoulet - www.fete-du-cassoulet.com - end of Aug.

Pedalling along the waterside. The Canal du Midi lends itself to mountain bike or hybrid bike rides, between Castelnaudary (from the St-Roch lock) and Bram, for example (16 km, 1h). Info: www.canaldes2mersavelo.com.

Castelnaudary.
L. Maisant/hemis.fr

③ BRAM

➜ The station is a 5-minute walk from the tourist office. Walk west along the D43.

Round and round. The birthplace of the journalist and writer Jean Cau (1925-1993), Bram is typical of traditional Languedoc town planning in "circulades", with villages built in concentric circles around the church. It was the scene of one of the most terrible episodes of the crusade against the Albigensians. In 1210, having taken Bram by siege, Simon de Montfort had the noses cut off and the eyes gouged out of 99 town inhabitants; the 100th was "lucky" enough to have "only" one eye gouged out, so that he could lead the others to the castle of Cabaret and instil fear in the local defenders. A more charming prospect is held out by three discovery trails in the town, inviting walkers and cyclists to follow the tracks of the town's Gallo-Roman past.
Tourist office - 3 pl. Carnot - ℘ 04 68 24 75 45 - www.collinescathares.com.

A bed for the night. A 15-minute walk from the station, this is the only accommodation close to the centre. It offers family rooms and a terrace. It also has a restaurant.
Le Clos Saint Loup - av. du Razès - ℘ 04 68 76 11 91 - www.le-clos-st-loup.fr/fr/hotel-restaurant - 10 rms. €70 - ☕ 6 € - 🍴 closed Fri. eve., Sat. lunch and Sun. - menus €15/€34.

In Gallo-Roman times. This archaeological museum is a 3-minute walk from the station. Paying tribute to the Gallo-Roman past of the town, which was at one time the largest settlement on the Aquitaine route between Toulouse and Narbonne, it exhibits the remains unearthed in the western part of the Aude region (amphoras, everyday objects, funerary artefacts, etc.).
Eburomagus - 2 av. du Razès - ℘ 04 68 78 91 19 - www.villedebram.fr - Apr.-Oct.: Tues.-Sat. 2-6 p.m. (+ Wed. 10 a.m.-noon) - closed Sun.-Mon. and Nov.-Mar. - €4 (ages 6-15: €1).

Dining. Beside the canal, Meg Pletts and Dave Welby offer cuisine perfect for summer days in an idyllic setting, with the canal, the harbour, the boats, and the terrace. On the menu: generous salads, razor clams, grilled tuna, cuttlefish a la plancha and the fish of the day... with homemade chips. The owners' origins give the place a British feel. This café-restaurant-ice cream parlour is therefore the ideal place to go for lunch or a refreshment. *Like home sweet home*!
L'Île aux oiseaux - lock house - ℘ 04 68 24 53 66 - closed Tue. eve., Wed., and from mid-Oct. to end Apr. - dishes €16/€27, menu €38.

④ CARCASSONNE

➜ The station is a 10-minute walk from the tourist centre, on the other side of the canal.

Exceptional site. How could you fail to admire this town, standing proud of the wine-growing plain, with the Corbières Massif looming in the background? Too bad for Viollet-le-Duc's detractors, who contend that he was not faithful to history when he restored his medieval city. Listed as a UNESCO World Heritage Site since 1997, it remains engraved in the memory of anyone who has walked the narrow streets of the fortified town, protected by its impressive double walls. The Saint Nazarius Basilica (11th-14th centuries) is, together with the castle, the town's other jewel: a resounding architectural success. On entering, you are struck by the contrast between the central nave, an example of southern French Romanesque art, simple and stark under its barrel vault, and the Gothic chevet, illuminated by the windows of the apse and six chapels. This building, its interior bathed in light, is perfectly proportioned, and handsomely decorated with pure lines and a light touch. The stained glass windows also form an exceptional ensemble, one of the most interesting in the South of France.
Tourist office - 28 r. de Verdun - Bastide St-Louis - ℘ 04 68 10 24 30 - www.tourisme-carcassonne.fr - annex in the medieval city (21 r. Cros-Mayrevieille).

A bed for the night. In the lower town, a 4-minute walk from the station, the Astoria is a small, simple and cheerful 2-star hotel. To stay within the city walls, the Best Western Hôtel Le Donjon offers another solution. A 15th century

orphanage, a medieval house and two pavilions in the garden make up this completely renovated hotel. Personalised rooms, some with a mini-terrace. Traditional cuisine in the brasserie opposite.
L'Astoria - 18 r. Tourtel - ☏ 04 68 25 31 38 - www.astoriacarcassonne.com - 19 rms. €81 - ☕ €9.
Best Western Hôtel Le Donjon - 2 r. du Comte-Roger - ☏ 04 68 11 23 00 - www.hotel-donjon.fr - ✕ - 61 rms. €140/€220 - ☕ €15.

Oh, my château! Make sure you visit this remarkable castle, which allows you to understand the history and architecture of Carcassonne. The former viscount's palace (12th century) was transformed into a citadel after Carcassonne became part of the royal domain in 1226. Highlight: the sentry walk, with a beautiful view of the town's rooftops, the Saint Nazarius basilica and the western and northern ramparts, from where you can take in the views over the Aude plain.
Castle of the Counts - 1 r. Viollet-le-Duc - ☏ 04 68 11 70 70 - www.remparts-carcassonne.fr - Apr.-Sept.: 10 a.m.-6:15 p.m.; rest of the year: 9:30 a.m.-4:45 p.m. - €9.50 (under 18s free).

Dining. In the lower town, at L'Agapé, a stone's throw from the Old Bridge, you can eat in a dining room with minimalist decor or, on fine days, enjoy your meal on the small sunny terrace. At lunchtime, a single menu changes daily according to what's available from the market and, in the evening, an "Aperitivo" formula proposes delicious tapas for sharing. On the menu: marbled Black Angus à la vénitienne, Aude pork in Vermouth sauce, spring risotto, etc. For dessert, don't miss the famous King Banoffee! Places are limited and sought after (twenty place settings), so book ahead.
Otherwise, in the medieval city, it is hard to find better value for money than at the Auberge des Lices. The delicious cuisine served up by Jean-Pierre Blasco lacks nothing in creativity; each dish is beautifully presented, and the service is impeccable. It is to be warmly recommended. Air-conditioned dining room and shady terrace.
L'Agapé - 15 r. des Trois-Couronnes - ☏ 04 68 72 12 10 - www.agape-carcassonne.fr - closed w'ends and Jan. - lunch deal: €15.50/€18.50.
Auberge des Lices - 3 r. Raymond-Roger-Trencavel - ☏ 04 68 72 34 07 - www.aubergedeslices.com - closed Tues.-Wed. off-season - menus €25/€46.

By boat around Carcassonne. For a pleasant escapade on the water, you can also try one of the cruises (with or without lunch, 1h30 or 2h45) on the Canal du Midi. For another perspective of the medieval city...
Carcassonne Croisière - prom. du Canal - ☏ 06 80 47 54 33 - www.carcassonne-navigationcroisiere.com - Mar.-Oct. - €8.50/€12.50 (children €6.50/€7.50), picnic hamper €11.90.

Aperitif time. The very convivial address of a lover of wine and truffles (black or white, depending on the season). Local vintages are matched up with truffle-based preparations: oysters, duck parmentier, brie, etc.
Barrière Truffes - 51 r. Trivalle - ☏ 04 68 25 92 65 - www.barriere-truffes.com - closed Mon., Tues. lunch and Wed. lunch.

Summer festival. Summertime theatre, circus, opera, dance, and concerts in an exceptional setting: the theatre of the medieval city. At the same time, the Festival Off lays on free concerts in different parts of town. On 14 July, don't miss "Carcassonne ablaze", one of the most spectacular fireworks displays in France.
Carcassonne Festival - www.festivaldecarcassonne.com.

⑤ LÉZIGNAN-CORBIÈRES

→ **The station is slightly out of town, a 15-minute walk to the east of the town centre. You get there by following the D611 towards Avenue Georges-Clemenceau.**

Striking bell tower-cum-keep. Within the rugged relief of the Corbières, halfway between Carcassonne and the sea, Lézignan-Corbières keeps busy with its vineyards and the wine trade. The medieval town layout is still visible, and is dominated by the church of St Felix, in the southern French Gothic style with a single nave, recognisable by its impressive bell tower.

City of Carcassonne.
G. Deschamps/CRT Occitanie

Its monumental appearance is a reminder that the church was once part of the town's fortifications. All around, side streets, squares and boulevards lined with impressive plane trees invite you to take a break in the shade.

Tourist office - 2 r. Guynemer - ✆ 04 68 93 78 18 - www.tourisme-corbieres-minervois.com.

A bed for the night. A 15-minute walk from the station, this is the only accommodation in the centre. It has very decent rooms and a restaurant. In terms of cuisine, the chef will regale you with his culinary specialities, in particular his home-made cassoulet.

Le Tournedos - rond-point de-Lattre-de-Tassigny - ✆ 04 68 70 29 19 - www.letournedos.fr - 15 rms. €59/€63 - ☕ €9.50.

Dining. An excellent restaurant and tapas bar in the centre of town. Generous and inventive dishes using local produce, or hearty platters of Iberian sausages and cheeses and delicious tapenades: the choice is yours!

L'Alégria Cathare - 7 cours de la République - ✆ 04 30 16 24 13 - www.facebook.com/tellezlionel - closed Thur., Wed. and Sun. eve. - dish of the day €11.90, menu €16.90.

Aperitif time. Before setting off again, you can stop off at this cellar located 4 minutes' walk from the station. The first cooperative cellar in the Aude department (created in 1909) offers AOP (Corbières) or PGI (Aude ou Pays Cathare) wines, in white, rosé and red.

Le Chai des Vignerons - 15 av. Frédéric-Mistral - ✆ 04 68 27 00 36 - www.chai-vignerons.com - closed Sun.

⑥ NARBONNE

See the Mediterranean line p. 53.

A biking tour

Canal du Midi

Carcassonne to Toulouse - 102 km - 3 stages.

Carcassonne to Castelnaudary - 41 km

This first stage consists of a 2h30 ride, climbing all the way. The slope is sometimes barely perceptible, but it is always there. Note that this brings you to the highest point of the Canal du Midi at the Seuil de Naurouze. Remember to take plenty of water on this stretch, as the topping up possibilities are scarce. Another difficulty is that you are cycling on an unpaved towpath. There are no motor vehicles, of course, but beware of other hazards (holes, stones, roots, etc.) which can make this section fairly tricky. The end of the route, on the greenway (3 km to Castelnaudary), is more comfortable. At the end of the journey you arrive at Castelnaudary, with its houses reflected in the waters of the Grand Bassin, the largest area of water on the canal.

Cycling along the Canal du Midi. elmvilla/Getty Images Plus

Castelnaudary to Montgiscard - 40 km

This second day is a more bucolic jaunt, shady and quite flat (a total 35 m of elevation gain). Running entirely along a greenway, the route is safe for cyclists. You almost get the impression of going back in time. On the first part of the route, there isn't a car to be seen. There isn't even any tarmac, truth be told! The only bugbear, and no minor one at that, is the Autoroute des Deux Mers (A61) motorway, whose din can be heard in the background once you are past the Seuil de Naurouze. Remember to request in advance a permit to cycle on the towpath (see box insert below). Here, the old towpath means you are cycling in a rustic environment, on a gently sloping earth track where the going is fairly easy. But beware of the potholes here and there.

Montgiscard to Toulouse - 21 km

Without particular difficulty and through a conservation area, this short stage offers a gentle way to finish off your excursion, and perhaps also to take advantage of all that Toulouse has to offer upon arrival. The greenway along the Canal du Midi runs northwards through the agricultural plain of the Lauragais, always safe for cyclists and on the flat, along the old towpath, which is well signposted. After an hour and a half in the saddle, you enter Toulouse via the quays, the last stretch of the canal, highly frequented by the people of Toulouse.

PRACTICAL INFO

- **Bike hire in Carcassonne**
  Évadéo Cycles – 14 r. Jean-Monnet (40 min. walk from the station or 10 min. by taxi) - 04 34 42 88 32 - www.evadeocycles.com/fr - daily exc. Sun.-Mon. From e-MTB to hybrid bike, a wide choice from €25/day.

- **Where to stay?**
  At Castelnaudary: Hôtel du Canal - 88-108 av. Arnaut-Vidal - 04 68 94 05 05 - www.hotelducanal.com - 43 rms. €78/€87 - €12. Accueil Vélo ("Bikes welcome") label.
  At Montgiscard: La Casanat guest house - 18 rte départementale 813 - 07 60 08 05 34 - www.lacasanat.com - 3 rms. €80. Secure parking for bikes.

- **Useful to know**
  From Carcassonne to the Seuil de Naurouze, you need a permit from Voies Navigables de France (VNF) to cycle on the towpath. It should be requested approximately one month in advance, by email (us.adve.dt-sud-ouest@vnf.fr) or by letter (VNF ADVE/Bureau des usagers - 2 port St-Étienne – BP 7204 – 31073 Toulouse cedex 7).

  Note that works carried out by VNF may result in the closure of certain sections, but alternative routes are then proposed. More info at www.vnf.fr.

THE PIÉMONT LINE

From Toulouse, the line runs south-west along the Garonne river, with a fine view of the first peaks of the Pyrenean Piémont on the left. Between Martres-Tolosane and Montréjeau, our train changes from one bank of the Garonne to the other several times as we keep an eye out for the Pic du Midi. These rugged contours announce the Hautes-Pyrénées. In a final dash, the line bypasses Tarbes from the west before reaching its terminus at Lourdes. Quite an apparition!

TOULOUSE TO LOURDES - 11 DAYS

- Non-stop trip: 3h10
- Frequency : 8 liO trains/day
- Timetables: www.ter.sncf.com/occitanie/se-deplacer/fiches-horaires
- Non-stop trip: €33.20
- Onboard services: bicycle transport authorised
- Connected lines: Pyrenees, Lot and Dordogne, Bastides and most beautiful villages, Cathedrals, Canal du Midi and Gers lines from Toulouse

Where best to sit to admire the landscape? On the left-hand side, in the direction of travel.

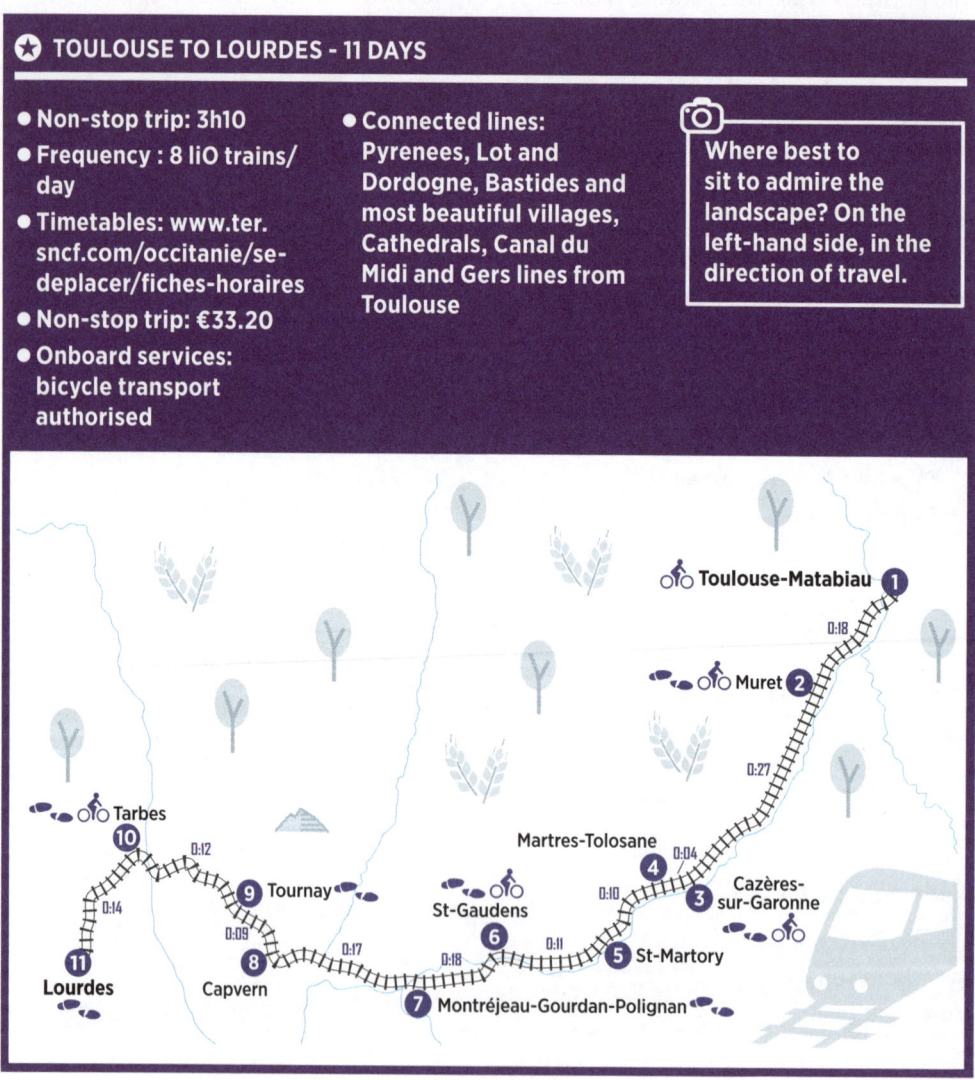

Place Saint-Georges, Toulouse.
J. Larrea/age fotostock

❶ TOULOUSE-MATABIAU

See the Pyrenees line p. 84.

❷ MURET

➜ **The station is located in the suburbs of Toulouse, with more than 30 connections per day, at 20-minute intervals. It is an easy trip from Toulouse itself, where there are more accommodation possibilities.**

🚲 **Bike hire. Take a bike in Toulouse and transport it on liO train.**

A bit of history. Two periods have left their mark on the town: the medieval period and the 19th-20th centuries, in particular the 1930s, under the impetus of Vincent Auriol, the former President of the Republic who was Mayor of Muret. Just imagine that Muret was the stronghold from which Simon de Montfort's three crusader corps sallied forth on 12 September 1213, at war against the massed might of Raymond VI of Toulouse and Peter II of Aragon. Yet within hours, the great dream of a Mediterranean kingdom under the leadership of the King of Aragon collapsed here, and the troops of Raymond VI were swept from the plain. In the chapel of the Rosary in the Church of St. James (12th century), where St. Dominic is said to have withdrawn to pray on the morning of the Battle of Muret, note the brick vaults enhanced with beautiful keys. Outside, a stone soldier continues to await the outcome of the battle…

A bed for the night. This is the only option within 15 minutes' walk from the station. It proposes clean and functional rooms and a restaurant.
<u>Hotel-restaurant Clément Ader</u> - 70 av. Jacques-Douzans - ✆ 05 34 46 06 86 - ✗ - 68 rms. €75 - 🛏 €8.

Place of Great Men. A 7-minute walk from the station, installed in the home of Vincent Auriol (1884-1966), this museum retraces the history of Muret and pays tribute to the personalities who left their mark on the town, such as the aviator, Clément Ader (1841-1925). A native son

of Muret, this brilliant inventor named his successive models "Avion" ("Airplane I, II, III…"). He first constructed a strange-looking machine, the *Éole*, which, on 9 October 1890, lifted off the ground to travel a distance of around 50 metres, to the astonishment of the observers present. Later, during a test run, his *Avion III* was buffeted by the wind to such dramatic effect that the authorities stopped funding his research.
Musée Clément-Ader et les Grands Hommes - 6 bd Aristide-Briand - 05 61 51 91 40 - www.mairie-muret.fr - Jul.-Aug.: 2-6 p.m.; rest of the year: 2-5:30 p.m. - closed Sun.-Mon. - €2.50 (under 16s free).

Dining. A delicious place to eat in the town centre, offering French cuisine made with seasonal products. A small family restaurant with a very warm welcome.
Les 2 Toqués - 46 r. Clément-Ader - 05 67 11 46 31 - www.les2toques.fr - closed Sun.-Tues. and Wed. eve. - lunch deal €12.90/€14.90, menus €23/€27.

Pedalling along the Garonne. From the station, follow the Avenue du Pic-du-Ger and go straight on at each intersection. This shared but little-used road follows the Garonne at a distance as it winds its way through the fields. When you reach Le Fauga, turn left towards the central square. You can take a diversion and cross the Garonne with the ferry to discover the charming Romanesque chapel of Alouach. After 1.5 km on a departmental road, you will find yourself riding on more rural roads (D53 and D10), which will take you through Mauzac and Noé. At Carbonne, you will reach the "Parcours cyclables de la Garonne" ("Garonne cycle path"), which you stay on for the rest of the way. You can ride on to the stations of Cazères *(40 km, see opposite)* or St-Martory *(64 km, see p. 158)*, before returning on the train or carrying on.

Walks in the Natura 2000 zone. The tourist office suggests several hiking paths. In addition to a walk around town, "Le sentier fleuri des Arts et des Inventions" ("Floral path of Arts and Inventions") is a signposted circuit for exploring the "banks of the Garonne and the hills of Muret" while enjoying a beautiful panorama from on high. Another favourite route, 16 km long and starting from the station, allows you to see the main sights, observe the preserved biodiversity, and visit artists' studios, particularly on the banks of the Garonne between Muret and Le Fauga.

Garonne Canal.
World Pictures/age fotostock

"Historic heart of Garonne and panorama" hike - downloadable from www.randohautegaronne.com/nos-randos.

③ CAZÈRES-SUR-GARONNE

➔ The station is a long way from any hotel, but the frequent connections mean that you should not be deterred from stopping for a day in the town before continuing your journey.

🚲 Cazères is also a possible departure or arrival point for a cycling trip to or from Muret or St-Martory: see "Pedalling along the Garonne" in Muret *(opposite)*.

In the footsteps of pilgrims. This former stopover for pilgrims and merchants on the Via Garona GR footpath is an important centre for inland waterway transport on the Garonne. New leisure opportunities have emerged ever since an EDF dam raised the level of the river, creating a body of water suitable for nautical activities, and thanks to its position on the gentle slope of a concave bank of the river. The church, dating from the 14th and 15th centuries, can be seen from afar, with its two towers rising above the brick and stone facade, and contains a wealth of liturgical objects. On the ten-sided baptismal font, note the sculpted Lamb and Cross of the diocese of Rieux. The tourist office and its exhibition room (on inland waterways) occupy the old Case de Montserrat (Montserrat hut) (1547), which housed pilgrims on their way to the eponymous abbey.
Tourist office - 13 r. de la Case - ☏ 05 62 02 01 79 - www.tourismecoeurdegaronne.com.

Dining. A 10-minute walk from the station, this address offers simple and good food, to eat in or to take with you on a walk.
L'Auberge ariégeoise - 4 pl. Henri-Barbusse - ☏ 05 61 98 52 59 - menu of the day €12/€14.

On the GR path. From Cazères, you can also join up with the Martres-Tolosane (7 km) or St-Martory (18 km) stages by following a fairly easy stage of the Via Garona hiking trail.

④ MARTRES-TOLOSANE

➔ The station is located between the Garonne and the town centre, an 8-minute walk via the Avenue de la Gare.

On an ancient Gallo-Roman estate. Known for its fine earthenware factory, the town is organised around its ancient centre, encircled by an emblematic "town ring". It stands on the territory of the former Gallo-Roman estate of Chiragan, whose villa has yielded up nearly 300 statues and busts, deposited in the Musée St-Raymond in Toulouse. The church of St. Vidian, which dates back to the 14th century, stands on the site of a funerary basilica, itself founded on an early Christian necropolis. In addition to the sarcophagi, the chapel of St. Vidian, which opens under the old portal of the Romanesque church, can be seen in the nave on the left. The martyr's relics are placed inside a stone monument in the flamboyant style.
Tourist office - pl. Henri-Dulion - ☏ 05 61 98 66 41 - www.tourismecoeurdegaronne.com.

A bed for the night. A 20-minute walk from the station, this campsite is the only accommodation option in the area. It offers chalets and a wide range of services as well as a swimming pool. You are quite some way from the centre, but in a pleasant rural setting, on the banks of the Garonne. The campsite owes its name to its 18th century watermill.
Camping Le Moulin - ☏ 05 61 98 86 40 - www.campinglemoulin.com - 🛏 - from €175 for 2 nights in a chalet.

The art of pottery. Housed in the tourist office, this heritage interpretation centre retraces the history of the town, which has been a centre of fine earthenware ("faience") production since the 18th century. On the ground floor, there is a presentation of the faience manufacturers still in operation. The first floor is devoted to the history of the village from the Gallo-Roman period (with the Chiragan site) up to the 18th century, and to the importance of earthenware in the town. On the second floor, you can admire a collection dating from the 18th, 19th and 20th centuries, as well as pieces resulting

THE PIÉMONT LINE

from collaboration between the Martres potters and the guests of honour of the "Salon des arts et du feu" plastic arts fair. Just alongside, the Grand Presbytère hosts quality exhibitions dedicated to arts and crafts.

Heritage interpretation centre - pl. Henri-Dulion - Jul.-Aug.: 9:30 a.m.-12:30 p.m., 2:30-6 p.m. - closed Mon. p.m. and Sun. p.m.; rest of the year: Tues.-Sat. 9 a.m.-1 p.m., 2-5 p.m. (Jan.-Feb. and Nov.-Dec.: closed Sat.) - €2 (under 12s free).

Dining. Who would have thought that this modern-looking venue, at some distance from the town centre, was once the station café? The chef places his faith in fine produce and a solid technique. You leave there in raptures. So get down there post-haste!

Le Castet - 44 av. de la Gare - ☏ 05 61 98 80 20 - www.maisoncastet.com - closed Sun. eve. and Mon. - lunch deal €19, menus €52/€110.

All fire and flame. Craftspersons from all over France gather here every year. This provides a reminder that, since the 18th century, Martres-Tolosane has been manufacturing fine earthenware using traditional techniques. Left to "rot" for nine months, the limestone clay is then kneaded and pressed into plaster moulds. After demoulding, trimming and drying, the piece is fired. The glazing is then done by dipping, followed by the application of decorations on the glaze, using the glost firing technique. The part then undergoes a second firing at 940 °C. In the past, the Martres-Tolosane earthenware factories supplied apothecaries with pots bearing inscriptions describing their contents.

Salon des arts et du feu - All Saints' w'end - www.salondesartsetdufeu.fr.

⑤ ST-MARTORY

→ The station is a 10-minute walk from the town centre, on the other side of the Garonne.

On the banks. The town's name evokes the martyrdom of Christians under the yoke of the Saracens. Squeezed between the Garonne and the steep-sided Escalère, St-Martory boasts a three-arched bridge, dated 1724, access to which is still governed by the old 18th century town gate. Unfortunately, the little town seems to have fallen somewhat into neglect. When passing over the bridge, take advantage of the rather lovely view of the river. A dam built a little downstream diverts part of the Garonne's waters into the St-Martory canal to irrigate the plains around Toulouse. On the right, note the Foulon mill, which used to produce oil and flour. Pass along the canal until you reach the church, which has retained its Romanesque portal. To the side of the church there is a neolithic menhir (6,000 years old), which was found on the Garonne plain.

Tourist office - 18 rte de Gascogne - ☏ 05 61 97 40 48 - www.opyrenees.fr.

Dining and overnighting. A mere 5-minute walk from the station, you won't find anything better! Bear in mind that there are only six rooms here, but they are both delightful and practical. As for food, the bistro serves family cuisine using fresh local produce from the market (duck, local cassoulet, etc.) in a friendly atmosphere.

Chez Kiki - 11 av. des Pyrénées - ☏ 05 61 97 23 33 - www.hotelrestochezkiki.com - 6 rms. €90 half-board.

⑥ ST-GAUDENS

→ The station is a 10-minute walk from the town centre, which can be reached via Rue Lamartine.

🚲 **Bike hire.** Electric mountain bikes are for hire an 18-min. walk from the station.

Impulsion Vélo - 121 av. F.-Mitterrand - ☏ 05 61 89 01 93 - www.impulsionvelo.fr - €45 per day.

A balcony on to the mountains. Halfway between Toulouse and Spain, in the Comminges region, St-Gaudens lies in a prime spot facing the central Pyrenees, which can be admired from its viewpoints. The Boulevard Jean-Bepmale, extended to the south-west by the Boulevard des Pyrénées, constitutes an almost 3 km panoramic promenade. From the viewpoints, especially next to the Three-Marshals monument, there are beautiful views of the Ariège Pyrenees stretching as far as the Maladetta massif, with an orientation table,

St-Gaudens collegiate church.
X. Subias/age fotostock

very useful for identifying the various peaks. St-Gaudens is also a choice stop on the Via Garona, a hiking route linking Toulouse to St-Bertrand-de-Comminges.
<u>Tourist office</u> - 2 r. Thiers - 05 61 94 77 61 - www.tourisme-stgaudens.com.

A bed for the night. A 15-minute walk from the station, in this modern building just a stone's throw from the town centre, the rooms are functional, furnished with individual style, and all with air conditioning. In the restaurant, you'll find bright and breezy colours, a mix of old and new, and a menu where cassoulet features prominently.
<u>Hôtel du Commerce</u> - 2 av. de Boulogne - 05 62 00 97 00 - www.commerce31.com - 50 rms. €79/€99 - €11 - menus €22 (lunch)/€30, half-board possible and well-being packages.

Going to church. This beautiful Romanesque building consists of a central nave with five bays and two aisles topped by half-barrel vaulted galleries. Numerous illustrated capitals crown the columns and beautiful 18th century Aubusson tapestries adorn the side aisles. The choir, with its 17th century choir stalls and gallery, is remarkable. Note the carved and partly gilded organ casing dating from the 17th century, which contains an instrument rebuilt around 1830 by Dominique-Hyacinthe Cavaillé-Coll. From the corner of Place Jean-Jaurès and Rue Thiers, there is a nice view of the church's apse.

Dining. Just outside St-Gaudens, a 15-minute walk from the centre, you will find this restaurant where you can enjoy almost 100% homemade recipes. The place can be a bit noisy in the summer, but the shady terrace is very inviting indeed.
<u>La Pyrène</u> - 60 av. Joffre - 05 61 89 60 98 - closed Tue. eve. and Sun. eve. - menu €25/€40.

Hiking around St-Gaudens. A free app provides access to more than 72 signposted hikes and 10 mountain bike circuits in the region.
<u>Info</u>: see the "Rando Comminges" app.

Excursion from Montréjeau

Bagnères-de-Luchon

➜ From Montréjeau station, 8 connections per day by liO 394 coach to Bagnères-de-Luchon (50 min.). www.lio-occitanie.fr

While its official name is Bagnères-de-Luchon, it is often referred to quite simply as Luchon. "Bagnères" is an allusion to the spa baths and "Luchon" refers to the town of Ilixo, the tutelary god of the baths. Here you find yourself in the liveliest spa town in the region! On a site halfway along the Route des Pyrénées, it overlooks valleys dotted with ancient marble quarries. Visitors here can find lots of things to do, as well as a wide choice of walks, in all seasons. The Allée d'Étigny, the avenue leading to the spa, is the main hub of activity. At No. 18, the 18th century hotel where the Duke of Richelieu was received was built in 1773 by Baron Bertrand de Lassus-Nestier, who also built the Château de Valmirande in Montréjeau. It houses the tourist office and the Pays de Luchon Museum. Opposite, next to the town hall (1840), the Castel or Hotel Boy dates from the late 18th century. Further on, at number 56, you can see the three Spont chalets built in the Swiss style. Constructed in 1848 by the architect, Edmond Chambert, on the site of the former Roman baths, the spa complex opens onto a hall decorated with stained glass windows and frescoes. More than 80 springs are channeled from the mountain at Superbagnères. If you are visiting in winter, the ski slopes (Superbagnères, Peyragudes or Mourtis) are not far away: from Bagnères-de-Luchon, you can take the gondola lift to reach the ski centre of Superbagnères (alt. 1804 m), situated above the forest tree line.

Tourist office - 18 allées d'Étigny - 05 61 79 21 21 - www.pyrenees31.com.

Herd of cows at Superbagnères. X. Sabias/age fotostock

Cycling to Montréjeau. A 17 km signposted path takes you to the next stopover. As you proceed, ahead you see the western Pyrenees with the majestic Pic du Midi. You can then make the return journey by train.
Info: *www.tourisme-stgaudens.com/ sejourner/activites/velo-vtt.*

❼ MONTRÉJEAU-GOURDAN-POLIGNAN

➜ The station is located between Montréjeau, described below, and Gourdan-Polignan.

Observation post. Built on a terrace overlooking the confluence of the Neste and Garonne rivers, this ancient bastide, founded in 1272, really comes to life on market days. Its position as an observation point justified the development of some beautiful esplanades and panoramic avenues: Place de Verdun (market hall and public garden), Place Valentin-Abeille (fountain in the centre, arcades on the sides, beautiful half-timbered house at No. 21), Boulevard de Lassus running along the escarpment. The views extend to the Pyrenees around Luchon, beyond the wooded hillsides of the Barousse. Note the Church of St. John the Baptist, built between the 13th and 15th centuries, which boasts a beautiful inverted ship's hull vault.
Tourist office - *6 r. du Barry* - ✆ *05 62 00 79 55* - *www.tourisme-stgaudens.com.*

A bed for the night. A 15-minute walk from the station, this is the only option nearby, yet it is perfectly charming, situated in a lakeside hotel residence at the foot of the Pyrenees.
Les Chalets Montréjeau - *at the lakeside* - ✆ *06 79 09 39 92* - *www.leschaletsmontrejeau. fr* - *€80/€110* - *4 nights min. in Jul.-Aug.*

View of the château. Built by Baron Bertrand de Lassus at the end of the 19th century on an estate hidden behind high walls, the Château of Valmirande (literally "the valley that amazes") offers an exceptional view of St-Bertrand-de-Comminges and, beyond, of the Pyrenean peaks: Pic du Midi, Cagire and Maladetta. It is topped by a 40 m-high viewing tower. Richly decorated, its architecture is reminiscent of the Renaissance residences on the banks of the Loire. The property, spread over some forty hectares developed by the Bühler brothers, includes a lake, a fountain, a trompe-l'œil well, a keep, and outbuildings forming a small hamlet. Although the interior of the château is closed to visitors, the guided tour of the property, which comprises a pleasant stroll in the landscaped park (more than 180 species of trees and shrubs), takes in the stables, the tack room and the chapel.
Château de Valmirande - *rte de Tarbes* - ✆ *06 21 05 40 16* - *guided tours only from mid-Jul. to end Aug.: 10 a.m. and 4 p.m.* - *€8 (ages 4-12: €5).*

Dining. Dominant yellow tones sprinkled with touches of blue… There can be no doubt, you're at the Citron Bleu. Here you are in for delicious regional cuisine. The restaurant also does take-away sandwiches.
Le Citron Bleu - *8 r. du Barry* - ✆ *05 61 89 08 38* - *Open for lunch Mon. to Fri. and by reservation evenings and w'ends* - *lunch deal €15.50/€18.*

Sweet snack. In 1871, the Suberbielle family developed the recipe for "millasson", which has become a regional institution: it is a kind of flan flavoured with orange blossom. The other home-made cakes and pastries are also worth the detour.
Pâtisserie Suberbielle - *29 r. du Barry* - ✆ *05 61 95 80 02* - *closed Tues.*

World festival. Montréjeau really comes alive for 4 days and 4 nights thanks to 500 participants from all around the world, with shows celebrating traditional customs (song, dance, music), and street entertainment.
Festival Folkolor - *mid-Aug.* - *www.festival montrejeau.fr* - *free access.*

💧 Walking around the lake or bathing in it. Facing the Pyrenees, the outdoor activities centre and its lake extend over 30 hectares. Fishing and free swimming with lifeguards in the summer. Onsite bar/restaurant.
Montréjeau Lake - *r. Salvador-Allende* - ✆ *05 61 94 77 61* - *www.hautegaronnetourisme.com/ activites/lac-de-montrejeau.*

8 CAPVERN

→ The station is some way away from certain places of interest such as the thermal health spa (40 minutes' walk). Thanks to the line's frequent connections, you can stop here with your bicycle (11 min. from the station to the health spa) and spend the night in Montréjeau or Tarbes. Otherwise, a taxi gets you to the spa in 7 min. The ride will cost between €25-€30.
Taxis Fourcade-Lestrade - 📞 *06 08 42 93 88.*

To the water! The spa resort of Capvern-les-Bains enjoys a temperate and windless climate. The two thermal springs of Hount Caouté and Bouridé, from which emerges water renowned for its exceptional virtues, are separated from each other by a few hundred metres. The residential area of Laca has been developed on a promontory overlooking the foothills of the Pyrenees-Baronnies (Haut-Arros hills), Arbizon, Pic du Midi, Montaigu. From the orientation table you get a great view of the Pyrenees and, in the foreground, the Château de Mauvezin perched on a hill.
Tourist office - 300 r. des Thermes - 📞 05 62 39 00 46 - www.coeurdespyrenees.com.

Dining and overnighting. For those keen to stay here, the nearest option is a 25-minute walk from the station, in the town's casino complex, with hotel and restaurant facilities.
Casino de Capvern-les-Bains - 1500 r. du Goutillou - 📞 05 62 39 04 13 - www.casino-capvern.fr - 23 rms. €75/€95 - ✕ menu €22/€24.

9 TOURNAY

Taking the bastide. Pronounce it "Turn-eye", to sound (a bit) like the locals! The gateway to the Baronnies, Tournay is a bastide with a regular checkerboard layout, founded in 1307. The devoutly religious poet, Francis Jammes, author of the *Christian Georgics*, was born here in 1868. On the outskirts of the village (towards Capvern) is the Notre-Dame Abbey, built in 1952 and belonging to the Order of St Benedict. The church and the cloister can be visited. The monks display and sell their products.
Tourist office - pl. d'Astarac - 📞 05 62 35 70 26 - www.ville-tournay.fr.

A bed for the night. A 7-minute walk away, this is the only option near to the station. It has simple, recently refurbished rooms and a restaurant. Takeaway meals.
Hôtel-restaurant Cazaux - 7 r. de la République - 📞 05 62 35 70 30 - www.hotel-restaurant-tournay.fr - 8 rms. €45 - ☕ €7 - ✕ closed Mon. - menu €13.50/€30.

Dining. On the main square, this unmissable village bistro has kept its 1900s feel. The bar is a popular place to go and have a chat, and on the terrace the regulars enjoy the dish of the day.
La Bastide - 19 pl. d'Astarac - www.facebook.com/LaBastideTournay - 7 a.m.-8 p.m. - dish of the day €9.50.

💬 **Natural grandeur.** The Tournay arboretum presents the origin and characteristics of each species. Spread over 9 hectares of an ancient fern heath, this park is home to more than 200 species from here and elsewhere: Serbian spruce, giant sequoia, Chinese palm, Atlas cedar, and so on. The educational trail is dotted with thematic breaks.
Arboretum - www.ville-tournay.fr/larboretum - free access.

10 TARBES

🚲 **Bike hire. The town runs a self-service bicycle scheme.**
Self-service e-bikes - pick-up points: Place Brauhauban, Place de Verdun, SNCF station - registration required on www.tlp-mobilites.com - (€1/30 min.).

Giddy up! Tarbes, the capital of Bigorre, is famous for its horses and its hussars, a reputation that is still relevant today, since its two important barracks now house the parachute hussars. The other star of the town is of course its beans, which are used in the recipe for cassoulet and whose production was revived in the 1980s. Finally, this dynamic town located near the Pyrenean winter sports resorts is also the birthplace of the novelist Théophile Gautier, author of *Captain Fracasse*, born in 1811, and Marshal Foch, born in 1851 (whose childhood home can be visited).
Tourist office - 3 cours Gambetta - 📞 05 62 51 30 31 - www.tarbes-tourisme.fr.

Rosary esplanade, Lourdes. Patrice Thebault/CRT Occitanie

A bed for the night. A 12-minute walk from the station, right in the centre, the Hotel Foch is a soundproofed establishment on a lively square, with stylishly designed and spacious rooms (some with a balcony).
The Rex Hotel, also centrally located, is a building with bold glass architecture, whose facade becomes multicoloured at night and where the ultra-modern rooms feature creations by Starck and Panton.
Hôtel Foch - 8 pl.de Verdun - 05 62 93 71 58 - www.hotel-foch.eu - 30 rms. €65/€120 - €9.
Rex Hôtel - cours Gambetta - 05 62 54 44 44 - www.lerexhotel.com - - 85 rms. €135/€195 - €19.

Remarkable garden. Located in the heart of Tarbes, around the Massey Museum, this beautiful English-style park has been listed as a "Remarkable Garden of France" and is full of lush vegetation, different types of trees, and a number of exotic species. It was designed by its owner, Placide Massey, a talented naturalist and landscape gardener, who bequeathed it to the town on his death in 1853. The orangery, a metal-structured greenhouse, has a fine collection of cacti, succulents and climbing plants. In the centre of the garden stands the neo-Byzantine building, topped by a Moorish-inspired observation tower, where Placide Massey lived. This building is said to be a copy of a palace in Cairo designed by the native Tarbes architect, Jean-Jacques Latour. It now houses the Massey Museum, which comprises two distinct entities: the International Hussars Museum (uniforms, equipment, weapons, etc.) and the Fine Arts Museum (with paintings from the Italian, Flemish and French schools of the 16th-19th centuries).
Jardin Massey - r. Massey - mid-Jun. to mid-Aug.: 7 a.m.-9 p.m.; early-Apr. to mid-Jun. and mid-Aug. to end Sept.: 8 a.m.-8 p.m.; Mar. and Oct.: 8 a.m.-7 p.m.; rest of the year: 8 a.m.-6 p.m. - free entry.
Musée Massey - r. Achille-Jubinal - 05 62 44 36 95 - www.musee-massey.com - daily exc. Mon. 10 a.m.-noon, 2-6 p.m. - €5 (under 18s free); €5 family ticket (2 adults + child).

Dining. At Le Fil à la Patte, there's no standing on ceremony, and the regulars know it! The atmosphere is friendly and down-to-earth in this restaurant, where local and market dishes fill the tables. Make sure you try the foie-gras andouillette!

Excursion from Tarbes

Pic du Midi de Bigorre

➔ From Tarbes, two liO coaches lines serve the Pic du Midi: line 960 (Tarbes-Bagnères-de-Bigorre) with a connection to the Pic du Midi on line 962.
Info: lio-occitanie.fr.

The Pic du Midi de Bigorre, or just Pic du Midi for short, is the highest point of the main foothills of the central Pyrenees. Its exceptional panorama, its pure, unchanging sky, and its state-of-the-art scientific facilities have all contributed to its reputation. A cable car leaves from the La Mongie station. The 15-minute ascent takes place in two stages, with a first cable car taking you to Taoulet (2341 m). This foothill of the Pic du Midi offers close-up views, to the south, of the Néouvielle massif and the Arbizon. To the north-east is the valley of Campan. You then ascend to the summit via a second cable car. From the 1,000 square-metre terrace, you can soak up a superb panorama of the Pyrenean mountain range. From east to west, the horizon extends over 300 km of mountains. Orientation tables allow you to identify the peaks: Crabère, Arbizon, Pic d'Aneto, Néouvielle, Mont Perdu, Vignemale, Balaïtous and Pic du Midi d'Ossau… Here there is a veritable bridge to the sky: you walk out over the void on a 12 m long metal footbridge. You can discover the entire site at your own pace using a HistoPad, a digital guide that offers real added value to the visit. An interpretation area and a planetarium complete the experience, with an immersive and educational journey into the history of the peak.

www.picdumidi.com - tickets can be booked online (recommended in high season).

Pic du Midi: a 360° view on Pyrenees. Atout France - @LittleFireSky/CRT Occitanie

In a slightly different vein is the L'Empreinte restaurant where, after valuable experience working alongside great chefs, Manuel Godet has chosen to set up shop in his native region in order to offer modern cuisine that is grounded in his own roots. Most of the produce comes from local suppliers.
Le Fil à la Patte - 30 r. Georges-Lassalle - ☎ 05 62 93 39 23 - closed Sun.-Mon. and Wed. eve.- dishes €11/€13.
L'Empreinte - 2 r. Gaston-Manent - ☎ 05 62 44 97 48 - www.restaurant-empreinte.com - closed Mon., Tues. and Sun. eve. - lunch menus €17/€29, dinner €35/€52.

Sweet snack. Located opposite the Marcadieu market halls, this tea room offers coffee roasted on-the-spot, a selection of 70 teas, and delicious chocolates. Convivial atmosphere and antique objects.
Nectar - 19 pl. Marcadieu - ☎ 05 62 44 19 44 - 9 a.m.-6 p.m. - closed Sun.-Mon.

Aperitif time. You can grab a table at any time, from morning coffee to nightcap. A must at aperitif time with a house cocktail and tapas. Diners' menu.
Chez Marcel - 5 pl. de Verdun - ☎ 05 62 56 99 31 - www.chezmarceltarbes.fr - 8 a.m.-midnight (to 2 a.m. Fri. and Sat.) - closed Sun. p.m.

A horse! A horse! More than 50,000 festival-goers gather in the sumptuous setting of the Tarbes stud farm. Equestrian shows with the "Night of Creations" and events across 4 rings (circus, acrobatics, pony rides, horse breed presentations). Equestrian cabaret, crafts, local produce, themed restaurants in the village.
Equestria, international festival of equestrian creation - 6 days late Jul.-early Aug. - www.festivalequestria.com - free entry.

Head for the Adour. A 15 km-long trail along the Adour river, between the Bours lake in the north and the Soues lake in the south, can be explored on foot or by bike. From the town centre, another route to the Soues lake (6 km there and back) is very picturesque with its views of the Pyrenees
CaminAdour - www.agglo-tlp.fr/caminadour.

11 LOURDES

→ The station is a 15-20 minute walk from the main tourist sites of the town (castle, grotto, etc.) located on the opposite bank of the Gave de Pau.

Faith of Bernadette. The second-most frequented Catholic pilgrimage site in the world after Rome, Lourdes welcomes millions of people from 170 countries every year - a true phenomenon for this small Pyrenean town, which had fewer than 4,000 inhabitants in the mid-19th century. Crowds began to flock here in 1858, when the young Bernadette Soubirous started reporting her visions of the apparition of the Virgin Mary. A walk around the town and the surrounding area will allow you to discover the places that marked Bernadette's childhood. The "Chemin de Bernadette" hiking trail proposed by the tourist office links up these different points of interest. The town, towered over by its castle, is in an ideal geographical location for walking: at the foot of the Pyrenees, with the Gave de Pau running through it, Lourdes is a good starting point for some superb hiking.
Tourist office - pl. du Champ-Commun - ☎ 05 62 42 77 40 - www.lourdes-info tourisme.com.

A bed for the night. A 15-minute walk from the station, at the foot of the castle and overlooking the Gave, the Mercure Impérial is a 1930s hotel that offers rooms in a retro style, with a panoramic roof terrace and a beautiful staircase. Close to the entrance of the Sanctuaries, the hotel La Solitude runs alongside the Gave de Pau. Modern rooms and panoramic views from the small rooftop pool area. Rotunda dining room with terrace overlooking the river.
Hôtel Mercure Impérial - 3 av. Paradis - ☎ 05 62 94 06 30 - www.mercure.com - closed mid-Dec. to end Jan. - ✕ - 88 rms. €121/€151 ☕.
Hôtel La Solitude - 3 passage St-Louis - ☎ 05 62 42 71 71 - www.hotelsolitude.com - closed mid-Nov. to mid-Apr. - ♨ ✕ - 24 rms. €70/€160 ☕.

Like an apparition. Along the Gave, the grotto, where the apparitions occurred, is a simple cavity in the "rock of Massabielle" ("old rock" in Gascon), which is no more than 10 m deep and wide. A Carrara marble Virgin, sculpted by Fabisch in 1864, marks the exact location of the apparitions. The spring that Bernadette caused to flow on 25 February 1858 can still be seen at the bottom of the grotto; underground pipes now carry the water to the fountains and pools where pilgrims are immersed. The first sanctuary of Lourdes, the crypt, dug into the rock of Massabielle, was consecrated on 19 May 1866. Above it, the Basilica of the Immaculate Conception, in neo-Gothic style, was inaugurated in 1871. The neo-Byzantine Rosary Basilica, blessed in 1889, is located between the two ramps of the hemicycle. The underground basilica of St. Pius X, consecrated on 25 March 1958 on the occasion of the centenary of the apparitions, is located under the esplanade at the edge of the southern avenue. Finally, two bridges provide access to the meadow on the right bank where, since 1988, the church of St Bernadette stands, built on the spot where Bernadette stood during the last apparition on 16 July 1858.

Estate of the grotto - *the two main ones, St Michael's Gate, which opens onto the Rosary esplanade, and St Joseph's Gate, which offers quicker access to the basilicas and the information centre, are open from 6 a.m. to midnight. Outside these hours, use the Lacets gate (open 24 hours), opposite the Chapelains' house.*

Castle. Built on a rocky outcrop towering over the town, this former residence of the Counts of Bigorre in the 11th and 12th centuries, and a State prison in the 17th and 18th centuries, has housed the Pyrenean Museum since 1921, which presents the region's popular arts and traditions. You will see beautiful collections relating to Béarn cuisine, costumes, musical instruments, "surjougs" and ceramics (magnificent Samadet fine earthenware service). The palaeontology and prehistory rooms bring together the discoveries made in various Pyrenean caves. Finally, a hall of honour is dedicated to Pyreneism. The castle chapel (on the east side) contains the woodwork, the altar and the 18th century polychrome wooden statues that adorned the former parish church of Lourdes. On the esplanade, several 1/10 scale models illustrate French and Spanish Pyrenean architecture.

Castle - Pyrenean museum - *access from Rue du Fort via the lift, the Sarrasins stairway (131 steps) at the level of the drawbridge, or via the ramp of the Fort from the Rue du Bourg - 05 62 42 37 37 - www.chateaufort-lourdes.fr - Apr.-Oct.: 10 a.m.-7 p.m.; rest of the year: 10 a.m.-6 p.m. - last admission 1h before closing - €7.50 (ages 6-17: €3.50).*

Dining. A nice place with straw-yellow walls, decorated with photos and prints. The pizzas are made in the first room. Take a seat in the second room, which is a lot quieter. Crispy pizzas and efficient service.

PizzaDaMarco - *45 r. de la Grotte - 05 62 94 03 59 - www.damarco.fr - closed Sun.-Mon. - pizzas €12/€18 - menu €28.*

Processions and celebrations. From April to October, masses are celebrated daily from 7 a.m. to 10:30 p.m. in the Sanctuary. International mass at 9.30 a.m. (underground basilica) on Wednesdays and Sundays. Every day, at 5 p.m., there is the Eucharistic procession and blessing of the sick (passing from the meadow to the underground basilica); at 9 p.m., a torchlight procession from the grotto to the Rosary esplanade.

Climbing to 948 m. You can go up to the Pic du Jer by the funicular (10 min., departures every 30 min.) or on foot by a path that winds along the mountain, partly through the undergrowth (1h30, 520 m elevation gain). Once you reach the upper station of the funicular, a botanical trail on a tarmac path leads to the summit, marked by a large metal cross that lights up at night (10 minutes' easy walking). You are then treated to a vast panorama of the town of Lourdes and the central Pyrenees. To extend the walk, leave the tarmac path in the first left-hand bend (in the downhill direction) to follow the narrow path leading to the southern peak of the mountain (approx. 30 min. walk there and back). You get a view of the confluence of the Argelès and Castelloubon valleys.

Pic du Jer - *1 km to the south of Lourdes - funicular departs from 59 av. Francis-Lagardère - 05 62 94 00 41 - www.picdujer.fr - Jul.-Aug.: 9:30 a.m.-7 p.m. (last descent); rest of the year 9:30 a.m.-6 p.m. (last descent) - closed from start Nov. to end Apr. (open Xmas school hols.) - €12.50 (ages 6-17: €10) - family ticket (2 adults + 2 children) €30 - possibility to board with your MTB.*

Excursion from Lourdes

Cirque de Gavarnie

➔ From Lourdes (bus station), liO 965 coach serves Gavarnie, but only in summer. *Info*: *lio-occitanie.fr*

Access to the cirque is on foot, via a picturesque and undulating path, passing along a river and through the undergrowth. The Hôtel du Cirque seems to appear out of the blue. You are initially struck by three superimposed tiers separated by luminous patches of snow, which contrast with the ochre hue of the limestone. And then you are simply blown away by such awe-inspiring beauty, almost beyond imagination! The cirque extends over a distance of 3.5 km at its base and 14 km along the ridge (from Astazou in the east to the Sarradets peak in the west). The average level at the floor of the cirque is 1,676 m. The altitude of the summits exceeds 3,000 m. The cirque owes its origin to repeated cycles of glacial scraping over millions of years. A resurgence here evacuated the waters buried in the Mont-Perdu massif and caused the head of the valley to recede, undermining its cliff top. The Gavarnie glacier, of which only small vestiges remain on the upper ledges, finally cleared out the cirque and evacuated the debris. You can but admire its majestic sheer walls and its tumbling silvery waterfalls. The biggest of the waterfalls, the Grande Cascade, fed by a resurgence of the waters of the frozen lake of Monte Perdido (alt. 2,592 m) on the Spanish side, leaps 422 m into the void. As donkeys and horses do not climb higher than the hotel, the rest of the way needs to be done on foot (1 hour there and back from the cirque).

A 2-hour walk from the village of Gavarnie. To get there on the back of a donkey: donkeys for hire from the Association des Loueurs de Montures de Gavarnie - 06 33 44 51 03 - €25 (2h) or €35 (3h). The 3-hour ride leaves an hour free for a picnic or to go higher up.

Path to the Cirque de Gavarnie.
bbsferrari/GettyImages Plus

THE GERS LINE

The train leaves the pink city and the Toulouse plain, teeming with wheat, orchards and vegetable gardens on the banks of the Garonne. Heading west, it crosses the Gascony region, with its delightful hilly landscapes. The train skirts L'Isle-Jourdain and passes alongside its large lake. After the Gimone valley, the line wends its way into elegant Auch, on the bank of the Gers, almost at the foot of its famous monumental staircase linking the lower town to its historic centre.

⭐ TOULOUSE TO AUCH - 4 DAYS

- Non-stop trip: 1h30
- Frequency : 7 liO trains/day
- Timetables: www.ter.sncf.com/occitanie/se-deplacer/fiches-horaires
- Non-stop trip: €16.40
- Onboard services: bicycles authorised onboard
- Connected lines: Pyrenees, Lot and Dordogne, Bastides and most beautiful villages, Cathedrals, Canal du Midi and Piémont lines from Toulouse

📷 Where best to sit to admire the landscape? Left-hand side in the direction of travel.

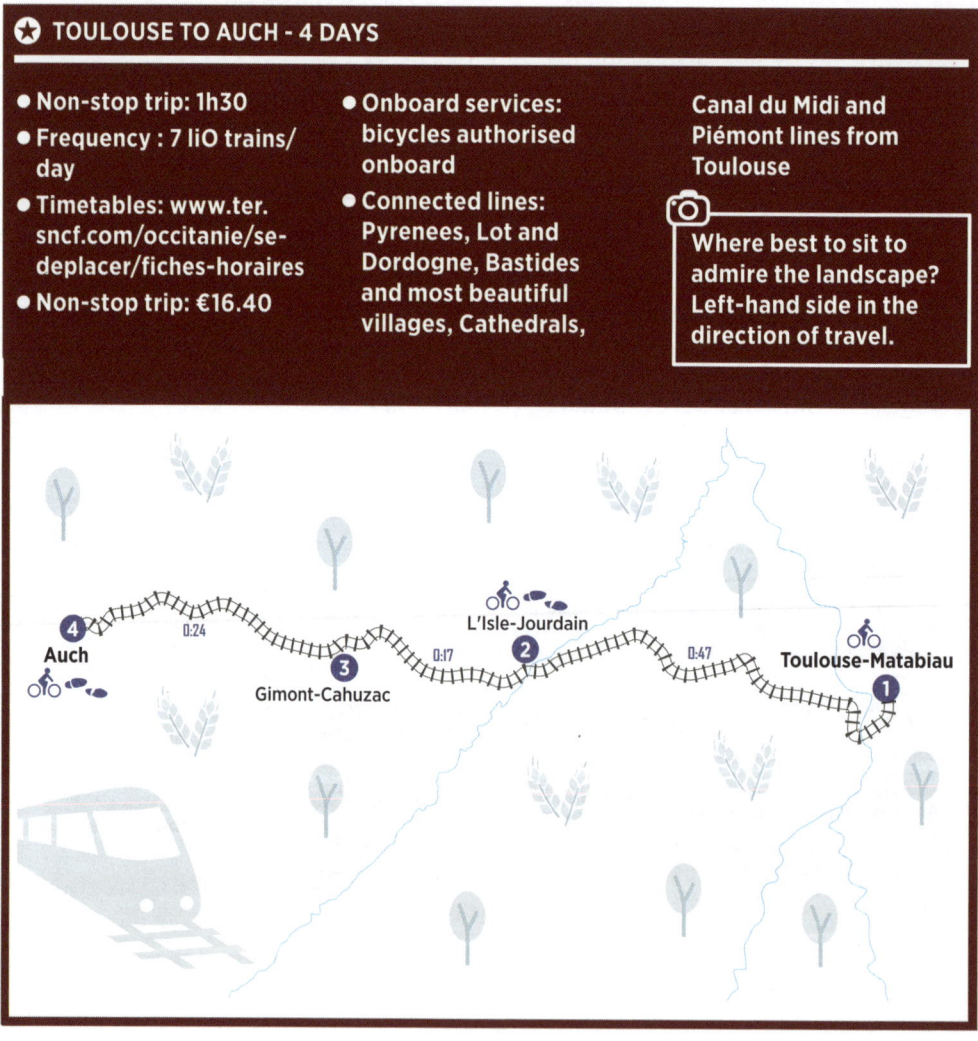

liO train between Toulouse and Auch.
Sébastien Lapeyrere/CRT Occitanie

❶ TOULOUSE-MATABIAU

See the Pyrenees line p. 84.

❷ L'ISLE-JOURDAIN

→ The station is a 10-minute walk from the centre and 20 minutes from the tourist office, on the edge of the lake.

🚲 **Bike hire.** The tourist office has a small fleet of 12 e-bikes for hire, a 20-minute walk from the station.
Tourist office - av. du Bataillon-de-l'Armagnac (at the lakeside) - ☏ 05 62 07 25 57 - www.tourisme-gascognetoulousaine.fr - from €18 per half-day.

Around the lake. This is a pleasant place to stop, in the Save valley. On the Place de l'Hôtel-de-Ville – the town hall takes its inspiration unabashedly from the Capitole de Toulouse, albeit without its columns – stands the house of Claude Augé, founder of the *Petit Larousse Illustré* encyclopedic dictionary. Check out its splendid glass roof, the sculptures on the facade and especially the Art Nouveau stained glass windows, including the famous Sower (La Semeuse) from a drawing by Eugène Grasset. The town's neoclassical Church of St-Martin was built between 1779 and 1784 by Jean Arnaud Raymond, an architect of the Languedoc States who admired the Italian style. A 19th century brick hall houses the Musée d'Art Campanaire (Campanology Art Museum). Those of a sportier bent can go directly to the lakeside of the outdoor activities centre to practice paddleboarding or water skiing.

A bed for the night. A 10-minute walk from the station, in the heart of town, the hotel-restaurant L'Echappée Belle is nestled behind an attractive Art Deco facade and has some lovely spaces set around a patio. Its menu is inventive, in the spirit of a contemporary brasserie.

A little further away, a 25-minute walk from the station, Le Pigeonnier de Guerre is a gîte offering a warm welcome to this farm which produces virgin vegetable oils from rapeseed, sunflower and safflower. Adorned with one of the most beautiful dovecotes in the region, it even has an outdoor jacuzzi for guests to enjoy. If

Auch. JackF/Getty Images Plus

you're put off by how long it takes to get to the hotel, the establishment also has rooms in the town, an 11-minute walk from the station.
Hôtel-restaurant L'Échappée Belle - 2 pl. Gambetta - ☏ 05 62 07 50 00 - www.echappee-belle.fr - 27 rms., 2 suites €95/€135 - 🍽 €15 - ✕ menus €23 (lunch)/€40.
Le Pigeonnier de Guerre guest house and gîte - rte de Grenade - ☏ 06 15 12 21 62 - www.terroir-gers.com - 5 rms. (as well as 3 rms. in town, 13 pl. Gambetta) €70/€85 🍽 - ✕ €22.

Rings a bell. Housed in the former grain market, with a beautiful timbered structure resting on octagonal pillars, this museum offers, on two levels, a panorama of the art of bell-making with more than a thousand bells. Bells from every age and every corner of the world are represented. On the ground floor, the "Foundry" space presents the techniques of bell-making. The "Revolution and Wars" section includes, notably, the three bells of the Bastille, dating from 1761. Further on, monumental timekeeping is represented by a town hall bell donated by Claude Augé, on which is inscribed "Je sème à tout vent" ("I sow to all winds"). See also the extraordinary clock with thirteen dials and four bell-ringers, a masterpiece made by a clockmaker from Meung-sur-Loire (mid-19th century) out of miscellaneous parts. On the first floor there are carillons and their keyboards, which visitors can sometimes play.
Musée d'Art campanaire - pl. de l'Hôtel-de-Ville - ☏ 05 62 07 30 01 - www.mairie-isle jourdain.fr - 10 a.m.-noon, 2-6 p.m. - closed Sun. and Mon. from late Dec. to early Jan. - €4.50 (children €2).

Dining. This shop, 11 minutes' walk from the station, stocks the products of local producers and offers platters to be tasted on the spot, including meat and an assortment of seasonal vegetables. There's a handsome cellar in the basement and a wide choice of Gascony wines and Armagnacs.
Le Comptoir de nos fermes - 13 pl. Gambetta - ☏ 05 62 07 27 93 - www.terroir-gers.com - 10 a.m.-12:30 p.m., Fri. 10 a.m.-12:30 p.m., 4-6 p.m., Sat. 10 a.m.-1:30 p.m., 3:30-6 p.m. - closed Sun.-Mon. - platters approx. €15/€25.

To the water! The 25-hectare outdoor activities centre, built around two lakes, offers a wide range of sports and recreational activities:

water-skiing, paddleboard, canoeing, tennis, fitness trail, etc. Swimming is not allowed, but the town has a swimming pool nearby.
Base de loisirs du lac - www.ccgascogne toulousaine.com.

Local colours. Celebration of Occitan culture guaranteed here: Gascon music, screenings and masses in Occitan, gastronomy.
Festival Escota é Minja - 1st w'end in Jul. www.facebook.com/escota.eminja.

Strolling by the river. The tourist office lists 4 hiking and biking trails around the town. The first (8 km, 2h) will take you through green valleys along the banks of the river Save.
"Le sentier du bout de la rivière" (The path at the end of the river") - to be downloaded at www.tourisme-gascognetoulousaine.fr.

❸ GIMONT-CAHUZAC

Good market. This bastide, founded in 1265 by the monks of Planselve, has a characteristic plan, closely matching the contours of a streamlined hill. The main street of Gimont, which marks its edge, passes in a straight line under the 14th century market. A very fine foie gras duck and geese market, one of the biggest in the department, takes place every Wednesday. Walk to its church, an example of Southern French Gothic with a single nave and a Toulouse-style brick bell tower.
Tourist office - 53 bd du Nord - 05 62 67 77 87 - www.tourisme-3cag-gers.com.

Dining and overnighting. 15 minutes from the station, the Étape Gimontoise offers studios and apartments in an old, tastefully restored presbytery.
Étape Gimontoise - 66 r. Nationale - reservations on booking.fr - 5 2-person apts. €70/€90 - €5.

For a picnic. 20 minutes from the station, near the wheat market, this small, unpretentious wine cellar and cheese shop offers sound advice, particularly on choosing your Armagnac. But you also have a great choice of irresistible cheeses.

Cave Saint-Éloi - 5 pl. St-Éloi - 05 62 67 86 04 - Tues.-Sat. 9 a.m.-12:30 p.m., 3-7:30 p.m., Sun. 9 a.m.-12:30 p.m.

❹ AUCH

→The station is on the other side of the Gers river, a 15-minute walk from the town centre.

Bike hire. A 25-minute walk from the station (but with delivery possible), there is a shop specialised in e-bikes.
Cyclomouv - 2 allée Jeanne-Daguzan - 05 36 03 00 32 - www.cyclomouv.com - closed Sun. - e-bike rental from €10 per 2h - fixed price €30 for drop-off and pick-up.

Town of treasures. Elegant and camera-friendly, with its cathedral and its Armagnac Tower high above the Gers river, the administrative capital of Gascony is full of attractions and has a laid-back vibe. From the medieval stepped streets to the monumental stairway that is its emblem, the town invites exploration and has many surprises in store. Indeed, one day might not be enough to fully enjoy this ancient Roman city and take in all its treasures : Renaissance stained glass windows in the cathedral, a rare collection of pre-Columbian art, circus festival, contemporary art, gastronomy, among other things. As well as good advice, the tourist office also offers, on the 3rd floor, a panoramic view of the beautiful Place de la République, the recently restored facade of the cathedral and, to the north, the town's sea of tiled roofs.
Tourist office - 3 pl. de la République - 05 62 05 22 89 - www.auch-tourisme.com.

A bed for the night. A 20-minute walk from the station, the Hôtel de France is an institution, next to the town hall, in the heart of the historic part of town. The rooms, some renovated, some old-fashioned, have antique furniture.
A little closer, just 15 minutes from the station, the Le Consulat B&B offers a handful of lovely rooms in a restored townhouse, the former Italian consulate, located in the centre of the old town.
Hôtel de France - pl. de la Libération - 05 62 61 71 71 - www.hoteldefrance-auch.com - 29 rms. €85/€132 - €15.

Chambre d'hôtes Le Consulat - 2 r. des Pénitents-Bleus - ☏ 06 16 84 56 42 - 3 rms. €77 🛏 - 2 nights min. in high saison.

Flamboyant baldachin. The construction of the cathedral, which began in 1489 with the apse, was not completed until two centuries later. Beyond the porch, the great organ of 1690 with its 360 pipes is the work of Jean de Joyeuse and the largest preserved example of a complete organ of the Baroque period. The choir, which is as large as the nave, contains two first-class works of art. The 113 oak stalls, including 69 high stalls under the canopy of a flamboyant baldachin, are populated with more than 1,500 figures. This gigantic masterpiece took more than fifty years to complete (around 1510-1552). Then look up at the stained glass windows. The chapels of the ambulatory were fitted with 18 stained glass windows completed in 1513 by the Gascon master glassmaker Arnaut de Moles (1460-1520). Each one illustrates a subject from the Old or New Testament and features full-length biblical figures as well as pagan sibyls that the Catholic Church had reappropriated.

Cathédrale Ste-Marie - pl. de la République - ☏ 05 62 05 04 64 - 9:30 a.m.-12:30 p.m., 2-6 p.m. - free entry.

Great pre-Columbian art. Housed in the former Jacobins convent, this museum, created in 1793, was completely renovated in 2019 to present, on three levels, evidence of the city's past, a Fine Arts section devoted to local artists, but above all a collection of pre-Columbian art, the second-largest of its kind in France after that of the Musée Quai Branly-Jacques Chirac in Paris. The first level contains a collection of more than 400 objects (gold and silverware, ceramics, cloth, wood), with significant representation of the Andean cultures. A small section is devoted to the Taino people of the Caribbean. The exhibition extends to the Hispanic period with a collection of Latin American sacred art that shows the persistence of pre-Columbian modes of expression in the representation of Christian scenes. Also on display is the museum's masterpiece, the exceptional *Mass of St. Gregory* (1539), a feather painting considered to be one of the first depictions of a Christian subject in the New World, and one of the last works of the Aztec civilization.

Musée des Amériques - 9 r. Gilbert-Brégail - ☏ 05 62 05 74 79 - www.ameriques-auch.fr - Apr.-Sept.: 10 a.m.-12:15 p.m., 2:30-6 p.m.; Oct.-Mar.: 10 a.m.-12:15 p.m., 2-5:15 p.m. - closed Jan. - €6 (under 18s free).

Dining. Located in the heart of the city, the Le Daroles brasserie serves traditional seasonal cuisine on a pleasant terrace, once frequented by the renowned French author, Stendhal.

At La Table d'Oste, you can enjoy local recipes in the pretty little rustic dining room (exposed beams, antique knick-knacks) or on the street-side summer terrace.

Le Daroles - 4 pl. de la Libération - ☏ 05 62 05 00 51 - www.ledaroles.com - lunch deal €11.90/€17.90, menu €27/€35.

La Table d'Oste - 7 r. Lamartine - ☏ 05 62 05 55 62 - closed Sun., Mon. lunch (Jul.-Aug. closed Sun.-Mon.) - market dish €12, menu €34/€38.

For a picnic. A foie gras producer has a shop in the town centre. Here you can find tinned and jarred preserves, wines, and armagnac to take home or to offer as souvenirs, as well as platters of charcuterie, hams and rillettes for tasting on the spot.

Le Comptoir de Tistou - 9 pl. de la République - ☏ 05 62 08 51 03 - www.foie-gras-ramajo.com - closed Sun.-Mon.

👣 **The 234 steps.** The monumental stairway (a 35 m climb) linking the historic town to the lower town was commissioned by a prefect of the Gers and a bishop in order to modernise Auch, which had just seen the arrival of the railway. To this end, the canon's house and its cloister adjacent to the cathedral were demolished to create the Salinis square (Place Salinis). The multi-level stairway, which alternates side ramps and central flights, is clearly inspired by the Baroque gardens of the Villa Garzoni (1652) in Tuscany. From Place Salinis, you can see as far as the Pyrenees when the skies are clear.

Fabulous Journeys

Auch, the beautiful Gascony town, with the family

The capital of Gascony is to be discovered from the vantage point of the banks of the Gers river, where it sits on high, resembling a fortress. And to get to it you need to pass via its monumental stairway. Halfway up the 234 steps you reach the statue of d'Artagnan and then, at the very top, you arrive beside the cathedral. Leave behind the city's landmark for a moment and head to the tourist office. From the 3rd floor, which doubles as a viewing platform, you will have a superb view over the town's rooftops and the cathedral. Auch has been awarded the "Famille Plus" label, and as such has plenty of ideas to occupy, entertain and educate youngsters. There's lots for them to choose from, such as a stained glass workshop at the cathedral, an exploration of the town with a digital tablet, or a "baby circus" workshop at CIRC, the circus innovation and research centre. While they're kept busy, you too can spend your time profitably taking in the cathedral's exceptional Renaissance stained glass windows (and carved wooden stalls), visiting the Armagnac Tower and the Treasure Museum, or calling in at the fascinating Museum of the Americas, which houses France's second-largest collection of pre-Columbian art. For the night, opt for a bed and breakfast, in town or in the surrounding area; for meals, you will be spoilt for choice in this capital of Gers cuisine.

2 days, 1 night - €226 for a family stay - to be done in spring, summer or autumn.
Contact: Auch tourist office.

THE GERS LINE

The statue of d'Artagnan sculpted by Firmin Michelet in 1931 and the Armagnac tower.
J.-M. Barrère/hemis.fr

THE CANAL DES DEUX-MERS LINE

Following the Canal des Deux-Mers and then the Garonne, the train line winds serenely through a green landscape of hills and vineyards, past picturesque medieval villages and spectacular engineering structures, in a region where good living is elevated to an art form. A delightful mix of terroir, natural and urban heritage, and museums.

★ MONTAUBAN TO AGEN - 4 DAYS

- To get to Montauban from Toulouse-Matabiau, direct route by liO train (27 or 40 min) or Intercity (24 min)
- Non-stop trip: 35 min
- Frequency : 11 liO trains/day in the wk., 7 at w'ends
- Timetables: www.ter.sncf.com/occitanie/se-deplacer/fiches-horaires
- Non-stop trip: from €5
- Onboard services: free carriage of bicycles
- For the return to Toulouse from Agen, direct liO trains (1h15) or Intercity (1h05)
- Connected lines: Lot and Dordogne line from Montauban

📷 Where best to sit to admire the landscape? On the left of the train in the direction of travel to Valence d'Agen for a view of the Canal des Deux-Mers, then on the right to Agen.

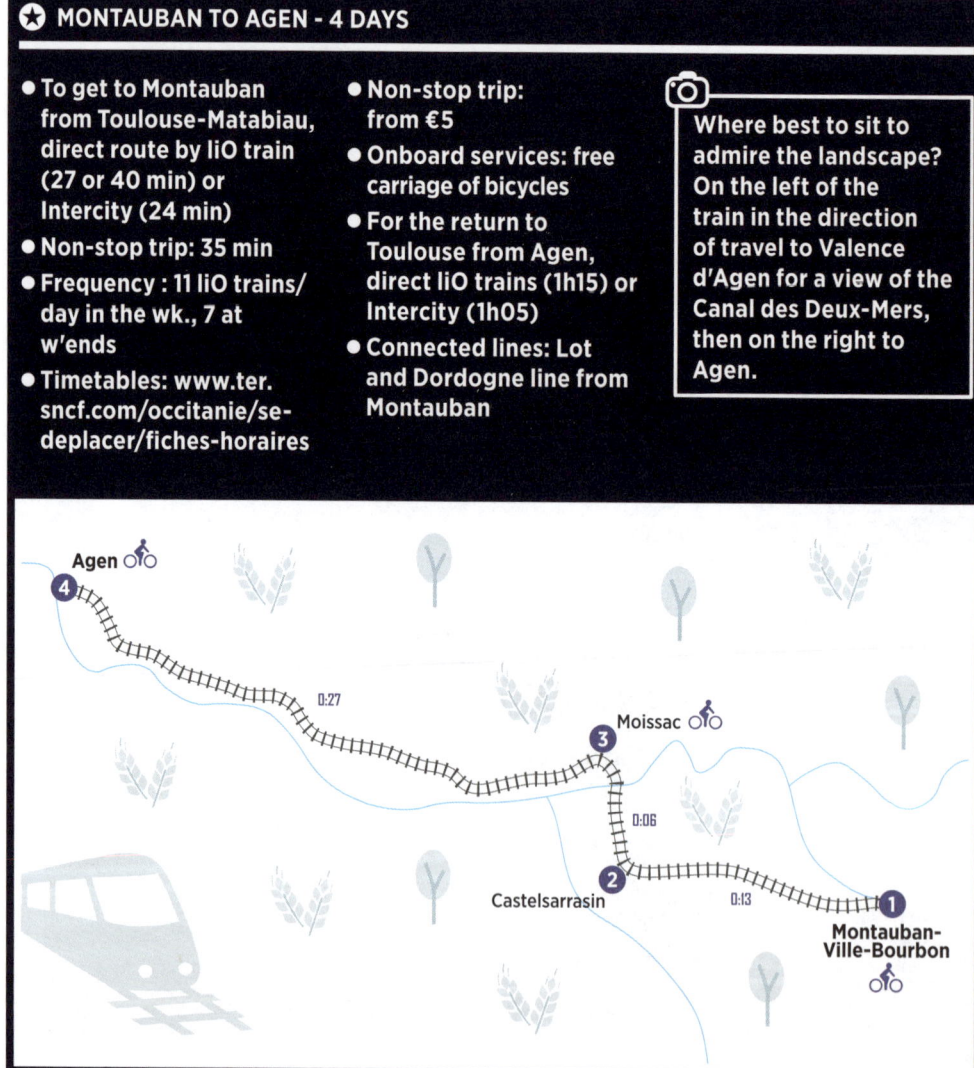

Moissac.

THE CANAL DES DEUX-MERS LINE

❶ MONTAUBAN-VILLE-BOURBON

See the Lot and Dordogne line p. 87.

❷ CASTELSARRASIN

An eventful history. This very old town is located in the heart of the Lavilledieu vineyards. Over the ages, it has gone through some turbulent times, including the Albigensian crusade in the 13th century and the Wars of Religion which saw the Catholic Castelsarrasin and the Protestant Montauban clash from 1560 onwards. An example of the Southern French Gothic style, the church of St-Sauveur, rebuilt in 1254, houses interesting Baroque furniture from the 17th and 18th centuries (the woodwork comes from the neighbouring Cistercian abbey of Belleperche). As for the shady banks of the canal, they are ideal for enjoying a walk and relaxing on fine summer days.
Tourist office - *3 allée de Verdun* - ☎ *05 63 32 01 39* - *www.ville-castelsarrasin.fr.*

A bed for the night. In the town centre, less than 10 minutes from the station, this beautiful Art Nouveau building exudes calm and serenity. Set around an inner patio, the elegant rooms are beautifully decorated and offer a haven of relaxation.
Hôtel Marceillac - *54 r. de l'Égalité* - ☎ *05 63 32 30 10* - *hotelmarceillac.com* - *12 rms. €83/€88* - ☕ *€9.*

Dining. An unpretentious address where the cuisine is very much centred on duck, in lip service to the region! Lovely private terrace, quiet and bedecked with flowers.
Le Patio - *60 r. de l'Égalité* - ☎ *05 63 32 63 50* - *closed Sun. eve.-Mon.* - *€15/€30.*

❸ MOISSAC

Bike hire. The Rand'eau leisure centre hires out hybrid bikes on the banks of the Tarn.
220 chemin de Rhode - ☎ *06 85 47 72 47* - *www.randeau.net* - *€17 per half-day.*

Beautiful stones and fine wines. You really should see, once in your life, the likeness in stone of the prophet Jeremiah, with his head

leaning on his shoulder. His statue has supported the tympanum of the portal of the marvellous abbey of Moissac since the 12th century. The small town branches out around it, on the right bank of the Tarn and on either side of the Canal de Garonne, amidst hillsides covered with orchards and vineyards. In summer, strollers make a beeline to the musical evenings and the Festival of the Voice, captivated by the melodies resounding off the old walls of the town.
Tourist office - 1 bd de Brienne - ☏ 05 32 09 69 36 - www.tourisme-moissac-terresdesconfluences.fr.

A bed for the night. A hotel facing the Pont Napoléon bridge, on the banks of the Tarn, 11 min. from the station. The trendy decoration features paintings, fine objects and antique furniture. Relaxation space with sauna, steam room and jacuzzi. The hotel bar proposes fast food at lunchtimes.
Le Pont Napoléon - 2 allée Montebello - ☏ 05 63 04 01 55 - www.le-pont-napoleon.com - 15 rms. €84/€96 - ☐ €9.50.

Romanesque masterpiece. As remarkable as is the tympanum of the portal of the marvellous Moissac abbey, whose golden age was in the 11th century, the building is also famous for its cloister dating from the end of the 11th century. Under the shade of a large cedar tree, it exudes an incomparable charm, thanks to its filigree arcades and the harmony of its marble, in white, pink, green and grey. The capitals are decorated with animals, foliage, geometric motifs and historical scenes inspired by the Bible. Simply sublime!
Moissac Abbey and cloister - ☏ 05 63 04 01 85 - www.abbayemoissac.com - Cloister: €6.50 (ages 12-18: €4.50).

Dining. A warm welcome with healthy cuisine, prepared with produce of local provenance. All served up in a charming setting (terrace, wooden tables) and at very reasonable prices.
Le Pigeonnier - 1 r. Poumel - ☏ 06 46 21 17 67 - Tues.-Fri. lunch - evenings on reservation - lunch deal: €15 - €12/€28.

Sweet snack. The cakes and other goodies of this pastry-chocolate-ice cream artisan enjoy a very good local reputation. The house

Agen Fine Arts Museum. J.-P. Garcin/Photomonstop

speciality is the Grain Doré de Moissac, a succulent chocolate containing a Chasselas grape macerated in an Armagnac liqueur. You can also get macaroons, walnut tarts and, for those blazing sunny days, tasty ice lollies.
Pâtisserie Moretto "Le Grain Doré" - 6 r. du Marché - ☏ 05 63 04 03 05 - 8h-12h30, 15h-19h - closed Sun. p.m. and Mon.

Opening up to the world's music. The town welcomes some top-notch artistes into the Abbey's cloister to give everyone, far from the commercial circuits, the possibility of discovering and sharing music from far and wide.
Festival de la voix - ☏ 05 63 04 01 85 - www.tourisme-moissac.fr/festival-de-la-voix - Jun.

❹ AGEN

 Bike hire. Café Vélo hires out bikes on the banks of the Garonne.
Café Vélo - 207 r. du Duc-d'Orléans - ☏ 05 53 96 15 51 - www.cafe-velo.net - daily Jul.-Aug.; Mar.-Jun. and Sept.-Oct.; closed Mon.-Tues. - MTB/hybrid bikes €19 and e-bikes €36 per half-day.

Medieval pearl. With its shady squares, its medieval streets lined with half-timbered houses and its wide boulevards, some of which have been made pedestrian-only, Agen has the true feel of the South of France. A hive of activity, the town is very welcoming with its assortment of nice shops and restaurants. Landscape developments along the Garonne and the Garonne canal have turned the river banks back over to pedestrians and cyclists, opening up the town to the surrounding nature. A good place to start is the Place du Dr-Pierre-Esquirol, location of the town hall (17th century), the Ducourneau Italian theatre, and the Fine Arts Museum *(see below)*. Take a trip back in time to the Middle Ages by strolling along Rue Beauville and around the Place des Laitiers, before visiting St-Caprais Cathedral, founded in the 11th century.

Tourist office - 38 r. Garonne - ☏ 05 53 47 36 09 - www.destination-agen.fr.

A bed for the night. Ideally located next to the train station (7 min. walk) and in the heart of the old town (and very quiet despite the boulevard), Stim'Otel offers comfortable, functional and well equipped modern rooms. At the Château des Jacobins, there is a real sense of the bourgeoisie of old: antique furniture, refined fabrics and nicely decorated rooms, impeccably maintained. This manor house, built in 1830 for the Count of Cassaigneau, is located 13 minutes' walk from the station.

Stim'Otel - 105 bd du Prés.-Carnot - ☏ 05 53 47 31 23 - stimotel.com - 58 rms. €75/€109 - ☕ €11.

Château des Jacobins - pl. des Jacobins - ☏ 05 53 47 03 31 - www.chateau-des-jacobins.com - 12 rms. €130/€140 - ☕ €12.

Amphoras and Corot. The collections of the Musée des Beaux-Arts (Fine Arts Museum) are housed in four private manor houses, built along the former line of the Agen ramparts, the only evidence of civil Renaissance architecture (facades visible from the Rue des Juifs opposite the main entrance). The museum houses fine collections of medieval and ancient archaeology. Renowned for its Spanish works of art of the 18th and 19th centuries, the museum also exhibits Flemish and Dutch still lifes, 18th-century paintings and examples of the Impressionist school.

Musée des Beaux-Arts - pl. du Dr-Esquirol - ☏ 05 53 69 47 23 - www.musee-agen.fr - closed Tues. - €6 (under 18s free).

Dining. You could walk right by L'Imprévu without noticing it, and that would be a real shame! In the modern dining room or on the terrace, enjoy well-made and nicely presented cuisine: anyone for a gizzard salad or burger and chips? And if you are a vegetarian, there's something for you too. Le Margoton is a pleasant locale in the old town: a convivial atmosphere and cosy decor based on traditional materials with a contemporary touch. Appetising cuisine in tune with the times.

L'Imprévu - 7 r. Camille-Desmoulins - ☏ 05 53 66 39 31 - www.resto-limprevu-agen.com - closed Sun.-Mon. - menus €15/€18 - à la carte €25.

Le Margoton - 52 r. Richard-Cœur-de-Lion - ☏ 05 53 48 11 55 - www.lemargoton.com - closed Sun.-Tues. lunch - menus €28/€35.

For a picnic. Agen is well known for its markets and its fine regional products, which form the perfect basis for some great picnics.

Covered market - pl. Jean-Baptiste-Durand - daily exc. Mon. and Sun. p.m.

Organic farmers' market - between Bd de la République and Pl. Castex - Sat. a.m.

Farmers' markets - pl. Jasmin - Sat. a.m.; pl. du 14-Juillet - Sun. and Wed. a.m.

Sweet snack. From breakfast to afternoon tea, this tea room offers light but tasty food, based on fresh and of course home-made products. Its famous cakes and a welcoming terrace make this a popular location.

Quarts Coffee-Kitchen - 63 r. Molinier - ☏ 05 53 96 63 74 - Wed.-Sat. 8:30 a.m.-6 p.m., Sun. 11 a.m.-1 p.m.

Aperitif time. This independent real ale bar is always busy. With its industrial decor, its large terrace and its delicious beers and ales, it is the meeting place for the youth of Agen.

L'Indé - 14 av. du Gén.-de-Gaulle - ☏ 05 53 68 65 66 - www.inde-agen.com - 9 a.m.-2 a.m.

Garonne parties on. In August, there's a festive programme for everyone in and around Agen in celebration of the Garonne: canoeing down the river, zip wire, farmers' market, concerts and fireworks.

A biking tour

The Garonne canal

113 km in 3 stages, from Agen to Toulouse.

Linking the Mediterranean to the Atlantic, the Canal du Midi and the Canal de la Garonne – grouped under the name "Canal des Deux-Mers" – have been developed into a wonderful cycle path. Between Agen and Toulouse, it offers a stress-free ride under the green canopy of plane trees, along the old towpath. Along the way there are picturesque medieval villages, vineyards and spectacular works of art to be encountered, in a region where good living is an art form.

Agen to Moissac - 44 km

On this stage, the longest of the entire route, but the easiest, your mission is to make your way to the Canal des Deux-Mers, north of Agen railway station. You ride along the banks of the Garonne and the canal. It's easy: all you need to do is follow the signposts for the V80. There are a succession of climbs and descents from kilometre 33.

Moissac to Grisolles - 39 km

In Moissac, you need to head towards the Avenue de l'Uvarium to pick up the Canal des Deux-Mers. You pass over the Tarn via the beautiful Cacor bridge-canal, which takes the Garonne canal over the river. Built in the mid-19th century, this bridge is one of the longest in France (356 m). It has fifteen arches, majestically combining Quercy stone and Toulouse brick. You then keep on riding to Grisolles. It's the most energetic stage of the route. It starts out easy, with a descent; but, very quickly, before the 5 km mark, it starts to climb and keeps on climbing for around 15 km (with a tough passage between km 21 and km 24). Once this difficulty is behind you, you ride on the flat, and can just admire the bucolic scenery.

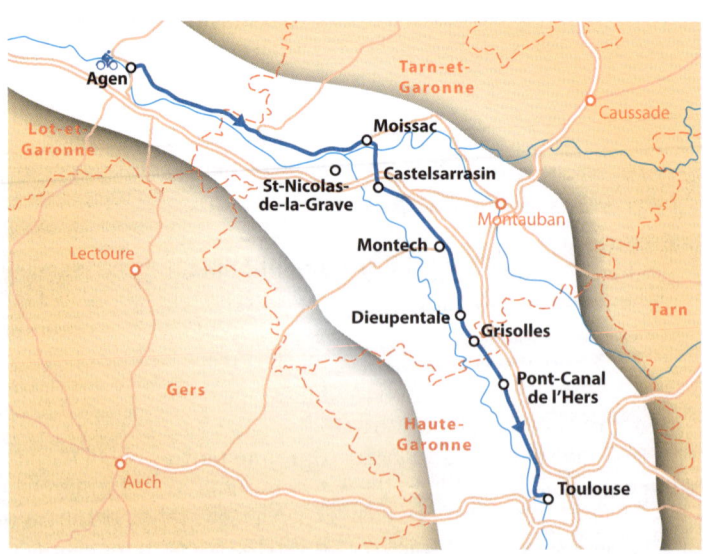

Cacor bridge-canal. F. Guiziou/hemis.fr

Grisolles to Toulouse - 30 km

There are no complicated passages or rough surfaces on this last section. From Grisolles, continue on the Canal des Deux-Mers cycle path, which continues through the dense industrial area at the entrance to Toulouse. There, at Ponts-Jumeaux, you join the Canal du Midi, which takes you to Matabiau station (take extra care from the Ponts-Jumeaux onwards, as you are travelling on shared roadway). The only slight difficulty is that this section of the stage is a steady climb towards Toulouse. But it's good for the lungs and the legs!

PRACTICAL INFO

- **Bike hire at Agen**
  Le Café Vélo – see p. 176.
- **Where to stay?**
  In Moissac: see p. 176.
  In Grisolles: Le Relais des Garrigues - rte de Fronton - 📞 05 63 67 31 59 - www.relaisdesgarrigues.fr - €80 - ☕ €8 - ✖ closed Sun. eve. - €15 (lunch), €25/€28 (evening).

- **Useful to know**
  This route can be travelled in both directions. We have opted for the finish in Toulouse, to enjoy all the "pink city" has to offer, but in this direction the route is predominantly uphill. For an easier ride, follow the route in the downhill direction, from Toulouse to Agen.

THE TARN LINE

The train leaves Saint-Sulpice and heads for Lavaur and the promise of another town steeped in history and character. Along the way, the landscape softens into the rolling hills of the Land of Cockaigne. The line offers views over the Agout valley from on high and soon Castres comes into view, with its mosaic of red-tiled roofs. You then leave the town to head for Mazamet. This is the end of the line, where everyone alights on the Tarn side of the Montagne Noire (Black Mountain).

⭐ ST-SULPICE-SUR-TARN TO MAZAMET - 4 DAYS

- Non-stop trip: 1h10
- Frequency: 11 liO trains/day
- Timetables: www.ter.sncf.com/occitanie/se-deplacer/fiches-horaires
- Non-stop trip: €14.20
- Onboard services: bicycle transport authorised
- Connected lines: Bastides and most beautiful villages line from St-Sulpice

📷 Where best to sit to admire the landscape? On the left-hand side of the train in the direction of travel.

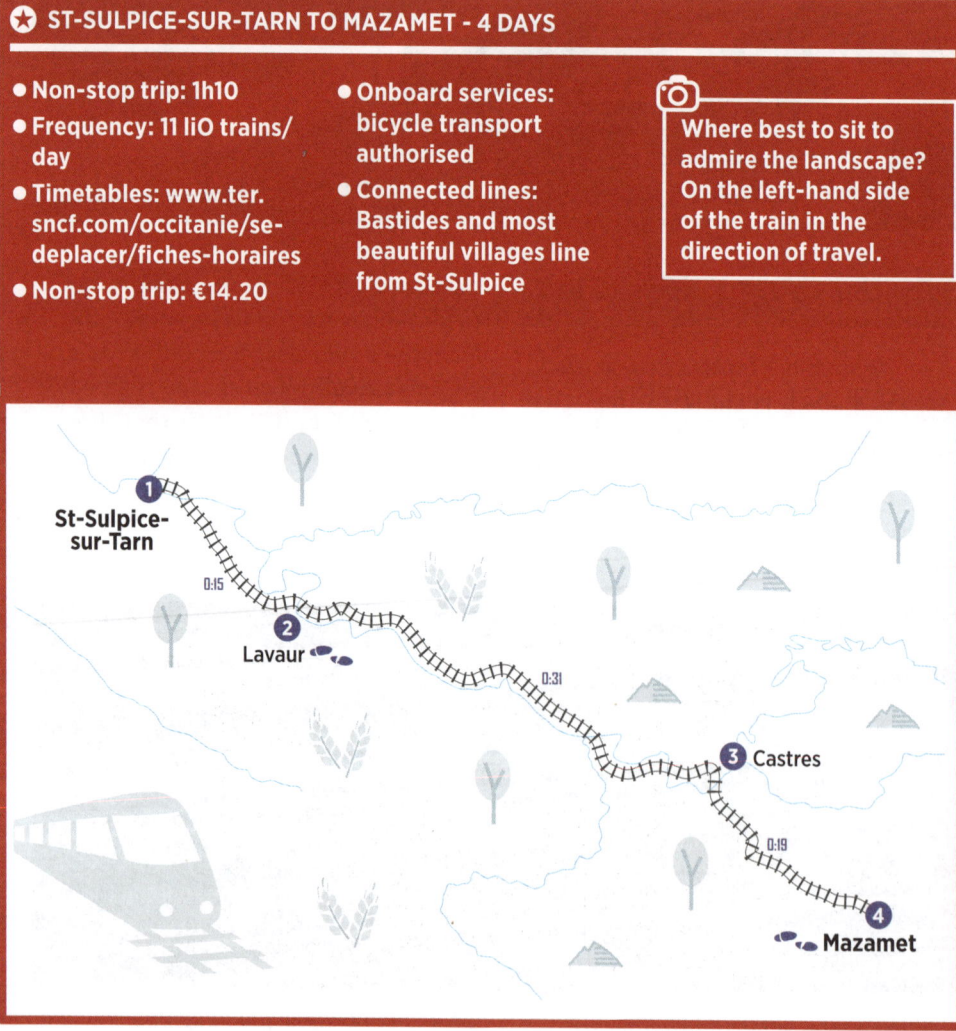

Mazamet footbridge.
Gael Fontaine/Getty Images Plus

1 ST-SULPICE-SUR-TARN

See the Bastides line p. 97.

2 LAVAUR

Town of character. Capital of the Pays de Cocagne ("Land of Cockaigne"), Lavaur retains, in its old quarters, the charm of a small sun-drenched Languedoc town. Defended by the Castle of Plo, of which just a few sections of the walls remain, it offered refuge to the Cathars, who were nevertheless unable to escape Simon de Montfort. Its Gothic Cathedral, dedicated to St. Alan of Lavaur, succeeded a first Romanesque building destroyed in 1211, to be rebuilt in brick in 1254. In the choir, the white marble altar table from the 11th century (Moissac school) comes from Sainte-Foy, the oldest church in the town.

Tourist office - quai la Tour-des-Rondes - 05 63 58 02 00 - www.tourisme-tarnagout.com.

A bed for the night. Just a 10-minute walk from the station, this cosy, family-run hotel offers nicely decorated rooms. On sunny days, the garden is the perfect place to relax, especially if you have just enjoyed the restaurant's excellent cuisine. Its signature dish? The "fromage en 2 façons" ("2-style cheese"). Bar and tea room.

L'Inattendu - 6 r. Escoussières-de-Naridelle - 05 63 79 11 41 - www.inattendu-lavaur.fr - 6 rms. €85/€115 - lunch deal €20/€29, menu €26/€35.

Dining. This handsome restaurant occupies a space created out of stone, brick and wood. There aren't many tables and booking is advised as the place is very popular. Chalkboard menu featuring tasty home cooking using fresh produce. Friendly welcome.

L'Assiette au comptoir - 19 bis r. Carlesse - ✆ 05 63 42 60 30 - noon-1:30 p.m. (Fri. 7:45-9:30 p.m. too) - closed w'ends - lunch deal €14/€16 - menu €24.

Walking in Cathar country. The tourist office offers hiking circuits for downloading. A very easy walk, for example, is the 3 km loop "Lavaur, cité cathare" (Lavaur, city of the Cathars) (1h30), which passes by the cathedral and old pigeon lofts, these rural constructions that were once the preserve of the nobility, and typical of the Tarn.
Tarn Walks and Hikes - www.tourisme-tarn agout.com/respirer/randonner.

❸ CASTRES

➔ The station is a little out of the way, a 15-minute walk from the town centre.

Handsome tableau. Along the pilgrimage trail to Santiago de Compostela, Castres has extended its mosaic of red tiled roofs right along the banks of the Agout, a tributary of the Tarn. Its pastel-coloured tanners' houses paint a changing picture, whose charm foreshadows the allures of the old centre, with its townhouses and the Goya Museum. Now entirely pedestrianised, the Place Jean-Jaurès pays tribute to the town's most famous dignitary and offers a pleasant space in the heart of the town. Along the way, you will discover the medieval homes of the weavers, dyers and tanners who worked on the banks of the Agout and brought prosperity to Castres. A perfect balance between architecture, gourmet food and festivities, life in Castres has plenty to keep tourists occupied!
Tourist office - 2 pl. de la République - Castres - ✆ 05 63 62 63 62 - www.tourisme-castres.fr.

A bed for the night. Right in the centre, a 12-minute walk from the station, the Hôtel La Renaissance offers rooms with a personal touch behind its 17th century half-timbered facade. In the same street, the Europe Hotel has modern and comfortable rooms with original decoration and offers copious buffet breakfasts.

Castres.
J.-J. Gelbart/AFCC/CRT Occitanie

Hôtel La Renaissance - 17 r. Victor-Hugo - ☎ 05 63 59 30 42 - www.hotel-renaissance. fr - 20 rms. €90/€120 - ⛌ €10.
Europe Hôtel - 5 r. Victor-Hugo - ☎ 05 63 59 00 33 - www.hoteleuropecastres.com - 36 rms. €76/€172 - ⛌ €12.

Museum of the Master. Focusing on Spanish painting, the Castres Art Museum is most famous for its exceptional collection of works by Goya, bequeathed in 1893 by the son of the Castres painter, Marcel Briguiboul. Among the Goya masterpieces on show are the impressive *Junta of the Philippines* (1815) and the *Portrait of Francisco del Mazo* (circa 1815-1820). The superb collection of Spanish paintings, from the 14th century to the present day, also includes works by Sebastián Muñoz (*Martyrdom of Saint Sebastian*, c. 1687), Velázquez (*Portrait of Philippe IV*, c. 1634), Cano, Murillo, Sorolla, Bueno, Picasso, etc. It is the second largest such collection in France after the Louvre.
Goya Museum - Museum of Spanish Art - ☎ 05 63 71 59 30 - www.ville-castres.fr - closed for works, reopening scheduled for mid-April 2023, contact for details.

Dining. Just a stone's throw from the Goya Museum, Aux Couleurs Gourmandes is a small restaurant with all it takes to please: simple, tasty food, with close links to local producers. Also not far away, La Part des Anges is another restaurant favouring generous and creative cuisine, market-fresh and seasonal.
Aux Couleurs Gourmandes - 23 r. Milhau-Ducommun - ☎ 0982512381 - www.auxcouleursgourmandes.fr - closed Sun.-Mon. and Tues.-Wed. eve. - menu €29.50, lunch menu €13.50.
La Part des Anges - 5 bd Raymond-Vittoz - ☎ 05 63 51 65 25 - www.lapartdesangescastres.fr - closed Sun.-Mon. - €21/€43.

Sweet snack. For four generations, the Signovert family has been making homemade delicacies: Castres nougatine, an almond nougat coated with royal icing; Dutch frangipane, with royal icing and roasted almonds, etc. The choice of pastries, to be enjoyed in the tea room, is impressive.
Signovert - 5 r. Émile-Zola - ☎ 05 63 59 21 77 - 8:30 a.m.-12:30 p.m., 2:15-7:15 p.m. - closed Mon. and Sun. p.m.

④ MAZAMET

At the foot of the Black Mountain. Mazamet's natural charm can be discovered along its many hiking trails. You can also admire its large 19th century bourgeois mansions, one of which houses the Museum of Catharism, in the Hotel Fuzier. Here you are taken on a discovery of this religion which found refuge on the Tarn side of the Montagne Noire (Black Mountain), in the villages and castles of Occitan country.
Tourist office - 7 pl. Georges-Tournier - ☎ 05 63 61 27 07 - www.tourisme-castresmazamet.com.

A bed for the night. A 6-minute walk from the station, right in the town centre, an early 20th century mansion offers simple, well-equipped rooms, along with a restaurant and cuisine tailored around fresh local produce. For a spot of pure indulgence, La Villa de Mazamet (3 minutes from the station) offers spacious and sophisticated rooms, also within the walls of a very fine mansion (dating from 1935).
Hôtel-restaurant Mets et Plaisirs - 7 av. Albert-Rouvière - ☎ 0563615693 - www.metsetplaisirs. com - closed Sun. eve. and Mon. - ✖ - 12 rms. €60/€70 - ⛌ €9 - half-board possible - menu €24/€70.
La Villa de Mazamet - 4 r. Pasteur - ☎ 05 63 97 90 33 - www.villademazamet.com - ⛴ - closed Nov.-Mar. - 5 rms. €120/€160 ⛌.

Dining. In pleasant surroundings, you are offered a nice choice of pizzas, salads, pastas and grills.
La Scala - quai Charles-Cazenave - ☎ 05 63 98 12 52 - 12h-14h, 19h-22h - closed Sun.-Mon. - lunch deal €13 - pizzas €10/€12.50.

👣 **Dizzying escapade.** For thrill-seekers, we strongly recommend walking from Mazamet to Hautpoul on this long monkey bridge over the Arnette valley. It offers exceptional views, 70 m above the ground. But if you are afraid of heights, you'd better give it a miss!
Mazamet footbridge - 4 km to the south via the D54 (12 min by taxi, Taxi Mazamet ☎ 06 09 62 10 14) and the first road on the right - Set off from the car park, at 93, rue de la Resse, and follow the path of the Cormouls Houlès gardens (30 min.) or the Chemin de la Jamarié (15 min. but steeper).

THE TARN LINE

A biking tour

The Passa Païs

76 km in 2 stages, from Mazamet to Bédarieux.

Mazamet to St-Pons-de-Thomières - 35 km

The Passa Païs traverses a large tract of Occitanien country, as its Occitan name suggests. This greenway in the Haut-Languedoc runs along the old railway line between Mazamet and Bédarieux. The route starts from the village of Mazamet, at the foot of the Montagne Noire, and crosses three valleys: the Thoré, the Jaur and the Orb. The track generally runs alongside the D612, and is surfaced essentially with compacted sand and asphalt, making it an ideal greenway for non-motorised vehicles. Cyclists are carried along between undulating pastures and villages of charm. At the end of the stage, why not pay a visit to the Grotte de la Fileuse de verre ("Glass-spinner's cave") in Courniou, which is beside the trail just before arrival at St-Pons-de-Thomières.

St-Pons-de-Thomières to Bédarieux - 41 km

Our second stage crosses the Jaur and Orb rivers. You leave St-Pons-de-Thomières along the D907, before returning to the greenway about 600 m further on. Here again you can ride safely on a site especially designed with bikes in mind. The distant views of the Monts de Somail hills and the Caroux massif accompany cyclists all along the route. At Mons-la-Trivalle, you rise some way above the landscape as the path takes you over an "Eiffel-type" bridge, a viaduct that spans the Jaur at the entrance to Olargues. The more intrepid traveller may be tempted by a diversion to the Héric gorges and the eponymous village perched in the heights. At the entrance to Nissergues, the route follows 1.5 km of paved road (the D35E35) shared with cars, but with little traffic. Then you are back on the banks of the Orb. The stage terminates with your arrival in Bédarieux, cycling along the river.

Caroux plateau.
Sophie Pirkin/CRT Occitanie

PRACTICAL INFO

- **Bike hire**
Near Mazamet: 2x2 Roues - Zac de la Castagnalotte, à Bout-du-Pont-de-L'Arn (15-minutes' bike ride from Mazamet) - 06 18 34 02 71 - rental of hybrid bikes (€15 per half-day) and e-bikes (€45 per half-day) - open Mar. to end Sept. - possibility of delivery on arrangement.
At St-Pons-de-Thomières: Station U – 64 av. de la Gare - 04 67 97 13 55 - hybrid bike and MTB hire (€10 per day) and e-bikes (€25 per day).

- **Where to stay?**
At St-Pons de Thomières: Le Somail - rte de Castres - 04 67 97 00 12 - hotel-restaurant-lesomail.com - 11 rms. €30/€65 - €6 - open every day, €14/€32 (eve.).
At Bédarieux: see p. 109.

- **For getting back**
Once in Bédarieux, you join the Aubrac line (see p. 108). Either continue north to St-Flour or get off at Béziers.

- **Useful to know**
The liO 762 coach links Castres to Bédarieux via Mazamet, but also passes via St-Pons-de-Thomières where it is easier to hire a bike. The coach can carry bikes in the luggage compartment in each direction.
Info: www.lio-occitanie.fr.

Beginning of the journey in Ax-les-Thermes station.
Guillaume Payen/CRT Occitanie

Thematic excursions by rail

Stade Toulouse rugby supporters at Ernest-Wallon stadium (Toulouse)
A. Spani/hemis.fr

THEMATIC EXCURSIONS BY RAIL

RUGBY TOWNS

Once Upon a Time in the West – or rather in the South-West – a territory discovered a passion for the oval ball which continues unabated to this day. With Toulouse hosting five matches of the Rugby World Cup due to take place in France in autumn 2023, the entire region is rooting like never before for the national side. This chapter invites you to extend the "rugby experience", again by rail, by taking in eight emblematic towns whose teams play in the Top 14 or Pro D2 leagues. From a visit to the Ernest-Wallon stadium, home of Stade Toulousain, to the GGL Stadium of Montpellier Hérault Rugby, via souvenir shops and bars run by stars of the past, at each stage you will find addresses dedicated to this sport for some unforgettable off-the-field entertainment. Lots to enjoy before, during or after the World Cup. Immediate boarding, on liO train of course!

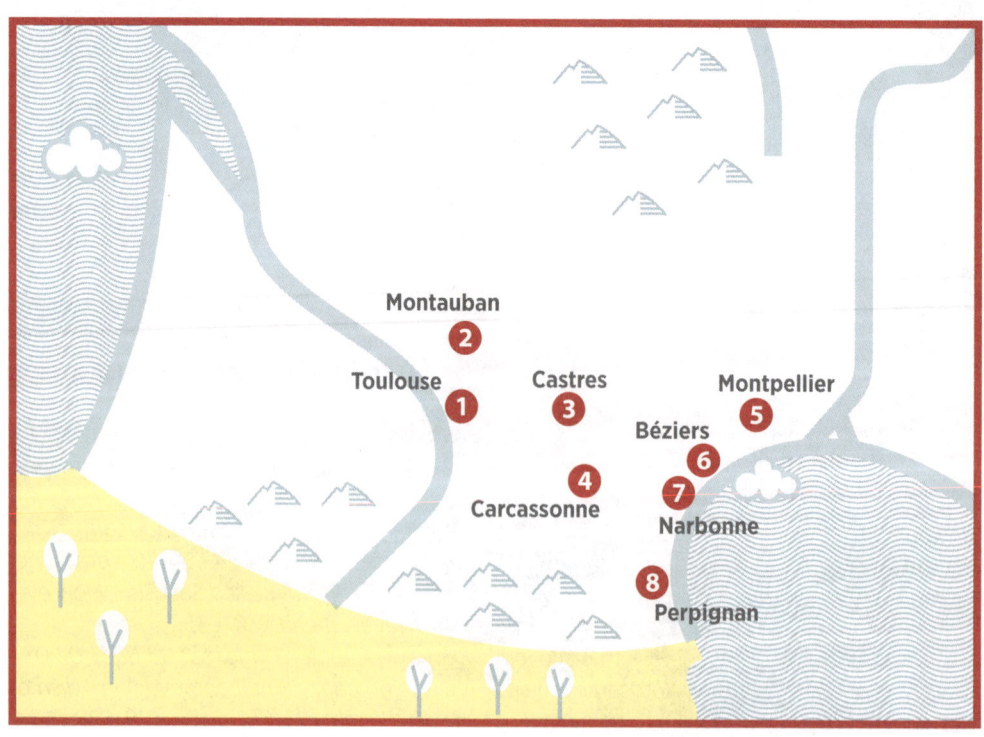

The Brennus Shield on the Place du Capitole.
Stade Toulousain/CRTL Occitanie

① TOULOUSE

The club and its stadium. Founded in 1907, Stade Toulousain plays its home games at the Ernest-Wallon stadium. Coached by Ugo Mola, the "Black-and-Reds" proudly wear the colours which, historically, symbolise law, but also the city itself for, in the Middle Ages, Toulouse was represented by the red of the Counts of Toulouse, who ruled the south of the city, and the black of the abbots of St-Sernin, who administered the north. With its 21 titles, Stade Toulousain holds the record for winning the most French rugby union championships. It has lots of internationals in its ranks, including fly-half Romain Ntamack, and scrum-half Antoine Dupont.
Stade Toulousain - www.stadetoulousain.fr.

Behind the scenes at the stadium. The most successful rugby club in France and Europe invites its supporters – but also the merely curious and fans of rugby in general – to discover its history and environment. You can even sit on the bench, feel what it's like to be a player, and take part in a virtual training session on a fun course.
Tours of the Ernest-Wallon stadium - 114 r. des Troènes - www.stadetoulousain.fr/visites-ernest-wallon - €14 (ages 7-18: €11) - 1h30 - online bookings only.

Dining. Hard to get any nearer the action: the Brasserie du Stade welcomes you to the heart of the Ernest-Wallon stadium. This elegant address offers a sophisticated seasonal menu. Signature dish of chef Martin Page-Relo: pan-fried foie gras with grapes and armagnac.
In a vast room with Gascon decor, the J'Go, right next to the market hall, also champions both its own team of restaurateurs and the local arable and livestock farmers and market gardeners.
La Brasserie du Stade Toulousain - 114 r. des Troènes - ℘ 05 34 42 24 20 - brasserie.stadetoulousain.fr - closed Sat.-Sun., Mon. eve. and Fri. eve. - menu €30/€35.
J'Go - 16 pl. Victor-Hugo - ℘ 05 61 23 02 03 - www.lejgo.com - lunch and evening - dish of the day (lunch) €13/€14, dishes €19/€28.

After the match. Unsurprisingly, the pink city is not short of places to go to celebrate the exploits of the "Black-and-Reds". A pub with an easy-going atmosphere and a retro feel, the Danu screens all the big sporting events. With a more British ambiance, the London Town is also an institution in Toulouse. Lastly, you can always be sure of a great atmosphere in the Rouge et Noir, bar that is always buzzing on match days.
The Danu - 9 r. du Pont-Guilheméry - ✆ 05 61 62 58 79 - www.thedanu.fr.
The London Town - 14 r. des Prêtres - ✆ 05 62 26 53 10 - www.londontownpub.fr.
Le Rouge et Noir - 3 r. du Pont-Saint-Pierre - ✆ 09 83 39 38 36.

Shopping. Fancy picking up a jersey, a scarf, a pennant or maybe even a tea cloth in the colours of this legendary club? There are two shops you can go to for your purchases, or buy them online.
La Boutique du Stade - at the stadium or at 73 r. d'Alsace-Lorraine - boutique.stade toulousain.fr - closed Sun.

BRENNUS SHIELD PLACE DU CAPITOLE

Whenever Toulouse wins the famous Brennus Shield - the trophy awarded to the team winning the French rugby union championship, the Top 14 - the whole jubilant city, attired in the red and black of Stade Toulousain, seems to descend the next day on the Place du Capitole. This is where the players, after a victory procession through the city, present the Shield to the gathered throng from the Town Hall balcony. A moment not to be missed!

Fiesta time! For the Toulouse Rugby Festival, in June, the Place du Capitole stages a celebration of the sport and is transformed into a vast rugby pitch.

➔ Would you like to see more of Toulouse? Go to p. 84.

At the Toulouse Rugby Festival. Dominique VIET/CRTL Occitanie

2 MONTAUBAN

➔ To get to Montauban-Ville-Bourbon railway station: direct Intercity and liO trains (25 min journey) from Toulouse.

The club and its stadium. Welcome to Sapiac Stadium, home of US Montauban. The team has been playing in green and black since 1920, in memory of the club's 55 players who died on the battlefields of the First World War. The club, founded in 1903, won its only French championship title in 1967 and two Division 2 titles in 2001 and 2006. It currently plays in the second division (Pro D2).
US Montauban - www.usmsapiac.fr.

Shopping. At the US Montauban store you can find replica kit and other accessories in black and green at the shop or online.
USM Boutique - 188 r. Léo-Lagrange - 05 63 66 78 21 - shop.usmsapiac.fr.

➔ Would you like to see more of Montauban? Go to p. 87.

3 CASTRES

➔ To get to Castres railway station: direct liO trains (1h13 journey) from Toulouse.

The club and its stadium. All year round, the beating heart of Castres is coloured blue and white for its team, Castres Olympique, whose home is the Pierre-Fabre Stadium. Founded in 1907, the team has won the French first division championship a total of five times, last picking up the famous Brennus Shield as champions in 2018. Runners-up in 2022, the club includes in its ranks the centre, Adrien Séguret, and the tighthead prop, Aurélien Azar.
Castres Olympique - castres-olympique.com.

Shopping. Jackets, polo shirts, balls and a children's range are available at the Castres Olympique store or online.
Castres Olympique Boutique - 19 r. Frédéric-Thomas - 05 63 73 46 93 - castres-olympique.com/boutique.

➔ Would you like to see more of Castres? Go to p. 182.

4 CARCASSONNE

➔ To get to Carcassonne railway station: direct Intercity (42 min journey) and liO trains (1h10 journey) from Toulouse.

The club and its stadium. The Stade Albert-Domec Stadium is the rugby stadium of Carcassonne. Built in 1899, it is one of the oldest stadiums in France. US Carcassonne owes its creation to Émile Génie and Antoine Tallavignes, two young men from bourgeois families who had discovered rugby during their secondary school studies in Toulouse. The first players got to choose the team's colours, yellow and black, which are also the town's colours. US Carcassonne embarked on their 12th consecutive season in Pro D2 in 2023.
US Carcassonne - www.uscarcassonne.com.

Shopping. To pick up replica kit, jackets or body warmers for men, women or children, in the shop or online, head for the US Carcassonne store.
US Carcassonne Store - at the stadium or at 32 r. Antoine-Marty - 04 68 47 18 52 - www.uscarcassonne.com/boutique.

➔ Would you like to see more of Carcassonne? Go to p. 149.

5 MONTPELLIER

➔ To get to Montpellier-St-Roch railway station: Intercity trains (2h07 journey) from Toulouse.

The club and its stadium. The Yves-du-Manoir complex was built in the Ovalie district as the home of Montpellier Hérault Rugby club. The GGL Stadium, its main stadium, is the venue for national and international competitions. Created in 1986 from the merger of two clubs, the team has been playing in the Top 14 since 2003. The team, which plays in sky blue and navy blue shirts, won the French championship in 2022. Its back-rower, the Englishman Zach Mercer, was voted best player in the Top 14 Championship in the same year.
Montpellier Hérault Rugby - www.ggl-stadium.com.

RUGBY TOWNS

Occitanie: land of rugby

"When Perpignan's team goes to play in Montauban / It obviously gets beaten by Montauban's team / And when Montauban's team goes to play in Perpignan / It obviously gets beaten by Perpignan's team... » These lyrics (somewhat lost in translation!) of the comic singing group, les Frères Jacques, in their song *C'est ça l'rugby* ("That's rugby for you") from the last century speak volumes of the attitude to rugby in these parts.

With its solid foundations in the south of France, rugby is something that marks out the people of Occitanie: a subtle blend of sporting determination and the sense of celebration, it perfectly illustrates the region's philosophy.

Birth of a sport

A passion once was born for the oval ball. In 1823, at Rugby School in England, William Webb Ellis broke the rules of football by picking up the ball and running with it. Rugby was thus born, a game with certain similarites to a game played in the Middle Ages in France: la soule. Some decades later, rugby was successfully established in the south of France, where it became a major sport in the region. It was Winston Churchill who famously said that rugby is a "hooligans' game played by gentleman". Finding a foothold in villages and small towns where each team defends its colours, rugby generates a real sense of solidarity. The pleasure of togetherness is just as joyously celebrated over the odd pint after the match.

Rugby fever!

With more than 70,000 registered players in nearly 400 clubs, Occitanie is the leading regional league in France for rugby union. At the same time, more than 20,000 young people are being introduced to rugby in the hundreds of rugby schools scattered throughout the territory. Occitanie is also the French region with the most professional clubs in the top flights with, in 2023, 4 teams in the Top 14 (first division) and 5 teams in Pro D2 (second division).

Rules of the game

In rugby union (played with 15 players, unlike rugby league, which fields 13 per side), the goal consists in scoring points by carrying or kicking the oval ball. A match consists of two 40-minute halves, with a maximum 10-minute half-time break. A try (worth 5 points) is scored when a player touches the ball down over the opponents' goal line; kicking the ball over the bar (3 m off the ground) and between the posts is worth 3 points. A converted try (touchdown plus kicked goal) is worth 7 points (two extra points for the successful kick at goal). A player is penalised by the referee for passing the ball forward or knocking it on, leading to a scrum, a spectacular set-play in rugby: the forwards of the opposing teams wrap heads, arms and shoulders in a pushing contest to win the ball on the ground. Another key moment for winning possession of the ball is when the ball goes out of play along the touchline and is thrown in by one of the forwards of the two teams forming two parallel lines.

The top teams

A star team in the world of rugby, Stade Toulousain regularly occupies top spot in the French rugby elite league, the Top 14: it has won the French championship trophy, the famous Brennus Shield, 21 times, including four times in a row between 1994 and 1997. The most recent of the major club competitions, the European Cup, was launched in 1996, and has been won five times already by Stade Toulousain. The famous *Midi Olympique* sports' weekly has in the past regaled its readers with the exploits of rugby heroes such as Robert Barran, Yves Bergougnan, Jean-Pierre Rives and Christian Califano. Today, still, the team continues to provide the French national side with its players of talent.

A sport for all

The spirit of rugby is particularly open and tolerant, encouraging anyone and everyone to practise the sport. Hence the development of women's rugby, with three regional clubs in Élite 1 (the top division), and three in Élite 2 (the second division). Gaëlle Hermet, who currently plays for Stade Toulousain, was also captain of the French women's rugby team in the 2018 Six Nations Championship. Boosted by the good results of the regional teams and their media coverage, the number of registered women players is growing fast, with more than 80 women's clubs in the region.

The other rugby in Occitanie

A less popular sport in France as a whole, rugby league is played by 13 players per side and has some 50,000 registered players in France, particularly in Occitanie, and above all in and around Toulouse, Carcassonne and Perpignan. Rugby league is a major sport in England, Australia and New Zealand in particular. Only two French teams, both in Occitanie, play at the same elite level as the top English teams and, indeed, compete in the same international league structure as these English teams: the Catalans Dragons of Perpignan and Toulouse Olympique XIII.

An emblematic sport of the region.
CRTL Occitanie

Dining. Inspired by the concept created in Narbonne by a clan of rugby players, cousins Kélian and Guillaume Galletier, players of the Montpellier Hérault Rugby club, have opened an annex in their own town. In their butcher's shop in the Halles du Lez market halls, the meat passes directly from the shelves to your plate, as grills for you to enjoy.
Chez Bébelle - Halles du Lez, 1348 av. de la Mer-Raymond-Dugrand - 🕿 04 67 15 02 78 - www.chez-bebelle.fr/montpellier - closed Sun.-Mon. - dishes €10/€21.

After the match. This bar-restaurant was opened by former Montpellier international François Trinh-Duc. Great atmosphere guaranteed!
La Chistera - 2 bis r. d'Obilion - 🕿 04 67 55 39 51 - www.la-chistera.com.

Shopping. In the shop or online, you can order a personalised jersey with your name and the number of your choice from the Montpellier Hérault Rugby store.
MHR Store - 500 av. de Vanières - 🕿 04 67 47 27 69 - www.montpellier-rugby.com/boutique.

➔ Would you like to see more of Montpellier? Go to p. 44.

⑥ BÉZIERS

➔ To get to Béziers railway station: Intercity and liO trains (1h29/1h54) from Toulouse or TGV and liO trains (49/55 min) from Montpellier.

The club and its stadium. Founded in 1911, AS Béziers Hérault is the third-most successful club in French rugby with 11 French championship titles between 1961 and 1984. The Raoul-Barrière stadium hosts the games of the red-and-blues, currently playing in the second division (Pro D2).
AS Béziers - www.asbh.net.

Dining. Located in the stadium itself, the atmosphere is all rugby, with quality cuisine and a warm welcome assured. On top of which are large bay windows overlooking the pitch and a great view of the playing surface!
Brasserie Côté Vestiaire - Raoul-Barrière Stadium - avenue des Olympiades - 🕿 04 67 00 15 15 - lunchtimes only - closed Sat.-Sun. - menu €18.80.

Shopping. Fans of AS Béziers can go to the club shop to buy souvenirs and kit in the club colours (red and blue) or order them online.
ASBH Official Store - 6 r. du 4-Septembre - 🕿 09 70 75 73 21 - www.asbh.net/boutique.

➔ Would you like to see more of Béziers? Go to p. 50.

⑦ NARBONNE

➔ To get to Narbonne railway station: direct Intercity and liO trains (1h13/1h33) from Toulouse or TGV and liO trains (1h06/1h15) from Montpellier.

The club and its stadium. Founded in 1907, Racing Club Narbonnais (RC Narbonne or RCN) spent a total of 85 years in the top flight between 1919 and 1946 and 1949 and 2007, before being relegated to Pro D2. The "Orange and Blacks" play their home games in Narbonne, at the Parc des Sports et de l'Amitié.
RC Narbonne - www.rcnm.fr.

Dining. Chez Bébelle, an original meat bar, was launched by André Belzons, a former RCN player, and taken over by his son Gilles, captain of the "Orange and Blacks" and a French international in the 1990s.
As for Chez Franck, this is another Narbonne institution, managed by former rugby player Franck Tournaire, a native of the town and a former international with Racing Narbonne.
Chez Bébelle - halles de Narbonne, 1 bd Dr-Ferroul - 🕿 06 85 40 09 01 - www.chez-bebelle.fr/narbonne - closed Sun.-Mon. - dishes €13/€25.
Chez Franck - 37 av. d'Espagne - 🕿 04 68 41 59 32 - www.chezfranck11.fr - closed Sun. - lunch deal €15/€20.

After the match. Fans like to meet up in this Irish pub run by former Australian RC Narbonne player, Anthony Hill. Hot atmosphere guaranteed!
O'Brians - 9 bd Gén.-de-Gaulle - 🕿 04 68 75 96 57 - www.facebook.com/obrianspubnarbonne.

Shopping. The Narbonne-based designer Stéphanie Marinesse makes unique, rugby-themed clothing. Her most notable creations are a collection of "femme de rugbyman" ("rugby player's wife") T-shirts sold under the brand "15 Août" (15 August).

If wine is more your thing, the Domaine de l'Hospitalet should be right up your street. Born in Narbonne, Gérard Bertrand started playing rugby in the town before ending his sporting career as captain of the Stade Français club in Paris. He took over the family wine estate from his father, and has been running it since 1995. It also has rooms and three gastronomic restaurants.

15 Août - 14 r. de l'Ancien-Courrier - 07 70 63 48 68 - www.15aoutofficiel11.fr.

Domaine L'Hospitalet - château de l'Hospitalet - rte de Narbonne - 04 68 45 28 50 - www.chateau-hospitalet.com.

➜ Would you like to see more of Narbonne? Go to page 53.

8 PERPIGNAN

➜ To get to Perpignan station: direct Intercity trains (2h31) from Toulouse or TGV trains (1h30) from Montpellier.

The club and its stadium. Originally founded in 1902, the current club is the result of a merger between two clubs in 1933. USAP (Union Sportive Arlequins Perpignan-Roussillon) won the French championship four times between 1938 and 2009. The team plays at the Aimé-Giral stadium, in the heart of Perpignan. Its players, in their sky blue, blood and gold livery, remained in the elite of the French championship until their relegation to Pro D2 in May 2014. Twice second division (Pro D2) champions, in 2018 and 2021, USAP is now back in the top flight (Top 14).

USAP - www.usap.fr.

After the match. The Arena Bar is the fans' bar with up to three simultaneous match broadcasts every week!

Arena Bar - 22 bd Georges-Clemenceau - 04 68 64 37 80 - www.arenasport.bar.

Shopping. The USAP club has two shops, at the Aimé-Giral stadium and in the town centre. In addition to the traditional jerseys and balls in the colours of Perpignan, there are some great vintage posters for sale. Online purchases possible.

USAP club stores - at the stadium or on quai Vauban - 04 68 63 89 70 - boutique.usap.fr.

➜ Would you like to see more of Perpignan? Then go to p. 56.

RUGBY WORLD CUP 2023

The Rugby World Cup will take place in France from 8 September to 28 October 2023. The Stadium in Toulouse will host 5 matches:
- Japan-Chile on 10/09 (Pool D)
- New Zealand-Namibia on 15/09 (Pool A)
- Georgia-Portugal on 23/09 (Pool C)
- Japan-Samoa on 28/09 (Pool D)
- Fiji-Portugal on 8/10 (Pool C)

Info.: rugbyworldcup.com.

Perpignan stadium.
Mairie de Perpignan/CRTL Occitanie

THEMATIC EXCURSIONS BY RAIL

UNESCO WORLD HERITAGE SITES

In Occitanie, there is no shortage of unmissable tourist sites. These include sites on the UNESCO World Heritage List, an inventory representing the diversity of the world's cultural and natural heritage. This listing testifies to a genuine commitment to preserving the sites concerned for the benefit of humanity and future generations. In Occitanie, five sites, one "cultural landscape" and two "serial properties" are listed: the Episcopal City of Albi, the City of Carcassonne, the Canal du Midi, the Pont du Gard bridge, the Cirque de Gavarnie, the Causses and the Cévennes, the Vauban fortresses and the Santiago de Compostella (Way of St. James) pilgrimage trail. You can discover them by train or other public transport in the region since, in Occitanie, all paths lead to the region's heritage!

The locations of the sites listed below are shown on the map on pages 200-201. They are also described in the pages dedicated to the railway lines. For each of them, we indicate below how to get there by liO train or, if applicable, by liO coach. For further details about the sites, please refer to the stated description page.

❶ TOULOUSE

Since the discovery of the tomb of Saint James the Great in Compostella in the 9th century, pilgrims have set out in great numbers to venerate the relics of the apostle . Rubbing shoulders with all kinds of travellers along the usual communication routes, the pilgrims have always made a point of visiting the local shrines and sanctuaries. Over time, renowned Christian sanctuaries such as Paris, Tours, Le Puy, Vézelay and Arles have become established as points of departure for the Way. These departure towns and the routes linking them form the modern network of paths on the Way of St. James. Toulouse, like the seven other sites listed below, is a stage on one of the pilgrimage routes leading to Santiago de Compostela. Hence the listing of its Basilica of Saint Sernin as a UNESCO World Heritage Site.

See description p. 84.
➔ Toulouse is accessible by train from the main towns and cities of France (TGV and Intercity).

❷ AUCH

The Sainte Marie cathedral of Auch is listed as a "serial property" on the Santiago de Compostela pilgrim trail.
See description p. 172.
➔ Auch is accessible by liO train from Toulouse (Toulouse-Auch line).

❸ RABASTENS

The Notre-Dame-du-Bourg church is listed as a "serial property" on the Santiago de Compostela pilgrim trail.
See description p. 97.
➔ Rabastens is accessible by liO train from Toulouse or Rodez (Toulouse-Albi-Rodez line).

*Cloister of Moissac Abbey.
J. Garcia/hemis.fr*

UNESCO WORLD HERITAGE SITES

❹ MOISSAC

Moissac Abbey and its cloister are listed as "serial properties" on the Santiago de Compostela pilgrim trail.
See description p. 176.
➔ **Moissac is accessible by liO train from Toulouse or Montauban (Toulouse-Montauban-Agen line).**

❺ CAHORS

The Valentré bridge and Cahors Cathedral, considered one of the paragons of domed churches in the South-West, are listed as "serial properties" on the Santiago de Compostela pilgrim trail. *See description p. 90.*
➔ **Cahors is accessible by liO train from Toulouse (Toulouse-Cahors-Brive line).**

❻ ROCAMADOUR

A place of spiritual pilgrimage in its own right, the religious citadel is listed as a "serial property" on the Santiago de Compostela pilgrim trail. *See description p. 21.*
➔ **Rocamadour is accessible by liO train from Rodez or Figeac (Rodez-Figeac-Brive line).**

❼ FIGEAC

The Hospital St.-Jacques Santiago is listed as a "serial property" on the Santiago de Compostela pilgrim trail.
See description p. 22.
➔ **Figeac is accessible by liO train from Rodez (Rodez-Figeac-Brive line).**

❽ CONQUES

The Abbey Church of St. Foy and its portal illustrating the Last Judgement along with the treasure and its statue-reliquary of St. Foy are listed as "serial properties" on the Santiago de Compostela pilgrim trail.
See description p. 107.
➔ **Conques is accessible by liO coach from Rodez (line 223).**

⑨ CAUSSES AND CÉVENNES

The Causses and the Cévennes are listed as UNESCO World Heritage sites as part of the "Mediterranean Agro-Pastoral Cultural Landscape". *See description p. 31.*

➔ **Florac**, which can be considered a gateway to the Causses and the Cévennes, is accessible by liO coach from Mende (line 251), itself accessible by liO train from Nimes (Nimes-Clermont-Ferrand line) and Montpellier (Montpellier-Mende line).

⑩ PONT DU GARD

A marvel of antiquity, a grandiose structure built in the 1st century, the Pont du Gard Roman bridge, encrusted in a superb setting, would in itself justify a trip to the region. As for the Gard, a tributary of the Rhône that gave its name to a department, it has the rare distinction of not actually existing, at least under that name. The Gardon (Gard is the Occitan name), and its many tributaries of the same name - notoriously prone to flooding - retain the name Gardon all the way to the river mouth. *See description p. 120.*

➔ **The Pont du Gard is accessible by liO coach from the new bus station in Nimes (line 121).**

⑪ ALBI

Albi is a city of great charm and rare harmony, known for its exceptional urban ensemble of the Episcopal City, grouped around the Cathedral Basilica of Saint Cecilia and the Palais de la Berbie, and classified as a UNESCO World Heritage Site. The lively streets with their old houses decked in red, the museums, gardens, churches, and the Tarn river flowing at the foot of the ancient fortifications all contribute to the town's mellow atmosphere, where the memory of the painter Toulouse-Lautrec still lingers. *See description p. 104.*

➔ **Albi is accessible by liO train from Toulouse or Rodez (Toulouse-Albi-Rodez line).**

Albi Cathedral (choir and rood screen). F. Leroy/hemis.fr

12 CANAL DU MIDI

The long blue line of this exceptional canal conceived in the 17th century by Pierre-Paul Riquet now stretches 240 km between Toulouse and the Thau lagoon. Whether making your way along its sweeping curves by boat, on foot or by bicycle, you will discover magnificent landscapes, vast plains, hills, vineyards and lagoons, and be able to admire more than 300 structures that make it a unique masterpiece of civil engineering.
See description p. 152.
➔ **Several towns along the canal can be reached by liO train from Toulouse or Narbonne (Toulouse-Carcassonne-Narbonne line).**

13 CARCASSONNE

A sheer marvel! You cannot fail to admire this site, which stands out imposingly above the wine-growing plain and against the backdrop of the Corbières Massif! Listed as a World Heritage Site since 1997, the historic fortified town of Carcassonne remains etched in the memory of all those who have walked its narrow medieval streets, protected by its impressive double walls.
See description p. 149.
➔ **Carcassonne is accessible by liO train from Toulouse or Narbonne (Toulouse-Carcassonne-Narbonne line) or from Montpellier (Toulouse-Montpellier-Marseille line).**

14 VILLEFRANCHE-DE-CONFLENT

Fortified from the outset and completed in the 17th century by Vauban, Villefranche is a marvel of military architecture, whose ramparts and Fort Liberia are on the UNESCO list of World Heritage sites as "serial properties", as part of the Vauban fortifications. In the heart of the longest valley in the department, the former capital of ancient Conflent contains some real heritage gems.
See description p. 64.
➔ **Villefranche-de-Conflent is accessible by liO train from Perpignan (Perpignan-Villefranche-Vernet-les-Bains line).**

15 MONT-LOUIS

Atop a hill, Mont-Louis is the highest fortified town in France. Created in 1679 by Vauban to defend the new frontier created by the Treaty of the Pyrenees signed between France and Spain (1659), the town was intended to act as a gatekeeper. The stronghold comprises a citadel and a new town below, entirely enclosed within the ramparts. Having never been besieged, the town and citadel remain completely preserved. Like the works of Villefranche-de-Conflent, the citadel of Mont-Louis is part of Vauban's fortifications as a "serial property", for which it has been listed as a UNESCO World Heritage site since 2008.
See description p. 68.
➔ **Mont-Louis is accessible by the Train Jaune (Yellow Train) from Villefranche (Villefranche-Latour-de-Carol line).**

16 MONTE PERDIDO - GAVARNIE

This sublime mountain landscape, which culminates at the summit of Monte Perdido, at 3,352 m altitude, presents two very distinct aspects. On the northern, French side there are three magnificent cirques to admire; on the Spanish side, the southern slopes are split by two of the largest and deepest canyons in Europe. And everywhere you look in these breathtaking landscapes, you will find traces of the agricultural societies of the past and of Pyrenean pastoralism. This natural heritage site has been UNESCO-listed since 1997.
See description of the Cirque de Gavarnie p. 167.
➔ **Gavarnie is accessible, in summer only, by liO coach from Lourdes (line 965).**

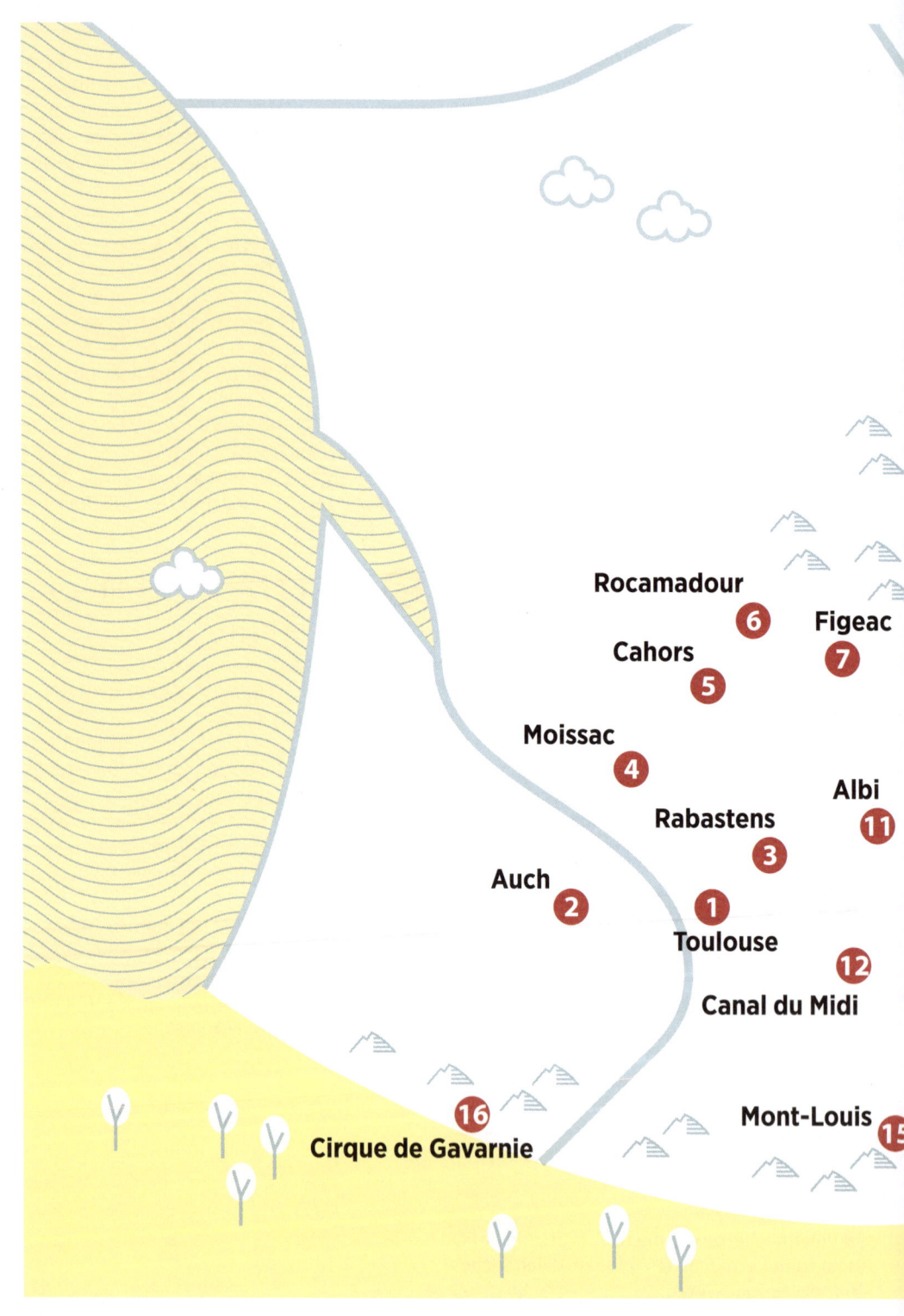

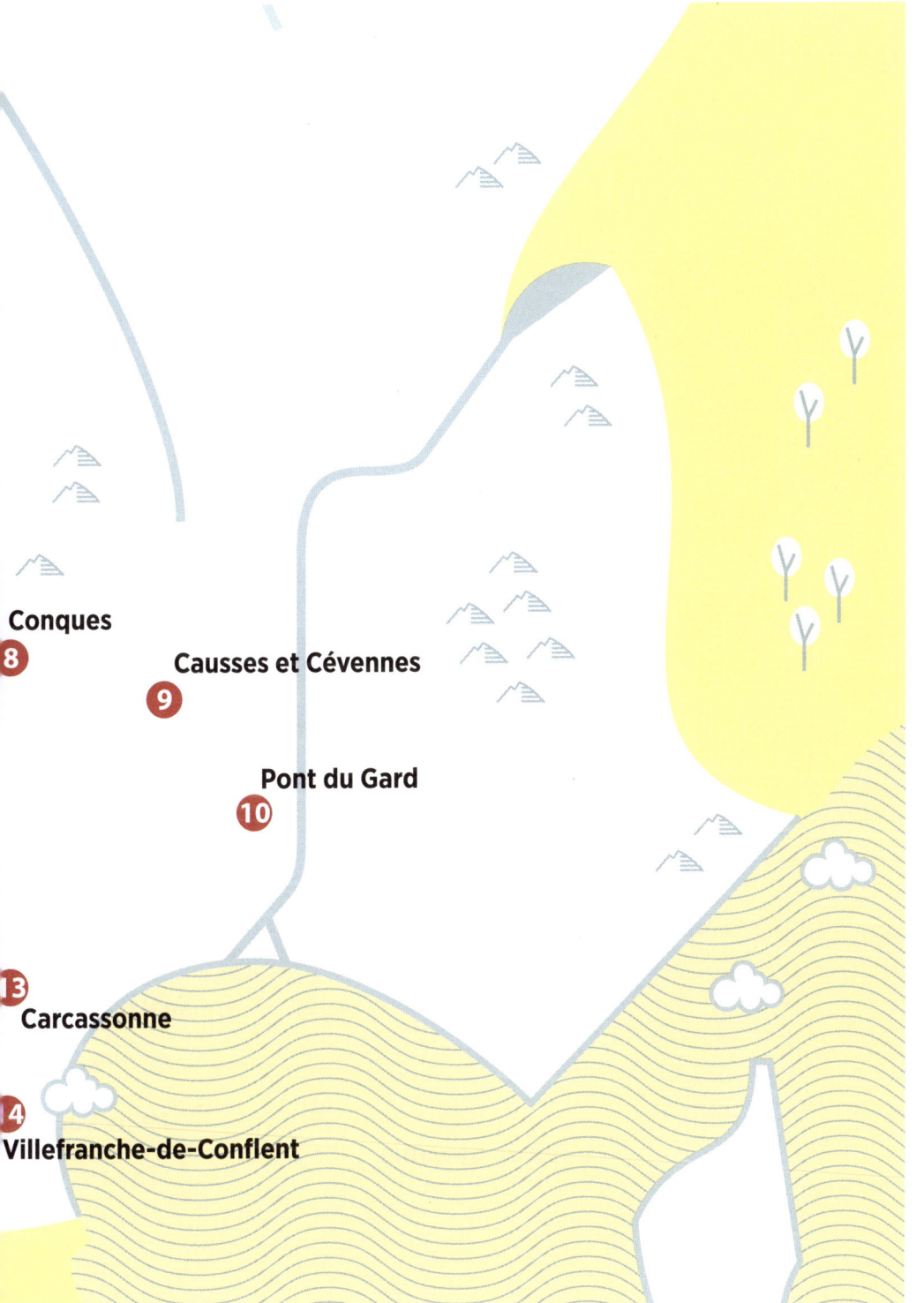

NOTES

NOTES

Red & Yellow,

VISIT FENOUILLEDES AND PAYS CATALAN BY TRAIN!

 tourism-mediterraneanpyrenees.com

INDEX

A

Agde	49
Agen	176
Aigues-Mortes	130
Albi	103
Alès	38
Andorra, Principality	76
Anduze	41
Argelès-sur-Mer	135
Assier	22
Aubin	25
Auch	171
Aumont-Aubrac	115
Avignon	121
Axat	58
Ax-les-Thermes	77

B

Bagnères-de-Luchon	160
Bagnols-sur-Cèze	123
Banyuls-sur-Mer	139
La Bastide-Puylaurent	29
Beaucaire	119
Bédarieux	109
Béduer	92
Béziers	50
Bolquère	69
Bourg-Madame	72
Bram	149
Brive-la-Gaillarde	17

C

Cagnac-les-Mines	105
Cahors	89
Cajarc	92
Camargue	128
Capdenac	23
Capvern	162
Carbonne	156
Carcassonne	149
Carmaux	104
Cases-de-Pène	59
Cassagnas	31
Castelnaudary	147
Castelsarrasin	175
Castres	182
Caussade	88
Cazères-sur-Garonne	157
Cerbère	141
Cévennes Train	41
Chanac	32
Cirque de Gavarnie	167
Collioure	137
Conques	107
Cordes-sur-Ciel	99
Cransac	25

E

Elne	135

F

Le Fauga	156
Figeac	22
Florac	31
Foix	81
Font-Romeu	70
La Franqui	53
Frontignan	45

G–H

Gaillac	98
La Garde-Guérin	37
Gavarnie	167
Génolhac	36
Gimont	171
Gourdon	91
Gramat	21
Le Grau-du-Roi	131
Grisolles	178
L'Hospitalet-près-l'Andorre	76

I–L

Ille-sur-Têt	61
L'Isle-Jourdain	169
Laguépie	95
Lalbenque	89
Langeac	36
Langogne	35
Latour-de-Carol-Enveigt	73
Lavaur	181
Leucate	53
Lexos	95
Lisle-sur-Tarn	98
Lourdes	165
Luc	37
Lunel	43
Luzenac	78

M

Marseillan-Plage	48
Martres-Tolosane	157
Marvejols	32
Maury	59
Mazamet	183
Mende	30
Mérens-les-Vals	76
Millau	112
Moissac	175
Monestiés	105
La Mongie	164
Montauban	87
Mont-Louis	67
Montpellier	44
Montréjeau	161
Montricoux	94
Muret	155

INDEX

N

Najac	100
Narbonne	53
Nimes	39

P

Padirac	20
Pamiers	83
Perpignan	56
Pic du Midi de Bigorre	164
Le Pont-de-Montvert	31
Pont-Saint-Esprit	124
Port Barcarès	144
Portbou (Spain)	142
Porté-Puymorens	75
Port-Vendres	138
Prades	63
Puilaurens	59

R

Rabastens	97
Remoulins	126
Rivesaltes	55
Rocamadour	19
Rodez	26
Roquefort-sur-Soulzon	110

S

Saillagouse	71
Saint-André-Capcèze	37
Saint-Antonin-Noble-Val	94
Saint-Chély-d'Apcher	116
Saint-Flour	116
Saint-Gaudens	158
Saint-Jean-du-Gard	41
Saint-Julien-d'Arpaon	31
Saint-Laurent-d'Aigouze	129
Saint-Martory	158
Saint-Pons-de-Thomières	184
Saint-Sulpice-la-Pointe	97
Sainte-Léocadie	72
Salses	55
Sète	46
Sévérac-le-Château	113
Souillac	93

T

Tanus	106
Tarascon-sur-Ariège	78
Tarascon-sur-Rhône	121
Tarbes	162
Le Thort	37
Thuès-Carança	67
Toulouse	84
Tournay	162
Train Jaune (Yellow Train)	66
Train Rouge (Red Train)	58
Turenne	18

U–V

Uzès	127
Varaire	92
Varilhes	83
Vias	50
Villefort	36
Villefranche-de-Conflent	64
Villefranche-de-Rouergue	101
Villeneuve-lez-Avignon	122
Vinça	63

Collection managed by Philippe Orain

Publishing Director	Hélène Payelle
Editorial Secretary	Iris Dion
Redaction	Céline Chaudeau, Joanna Dunis, Arnaud Goumand, Émilie Morin, Léonie Piraudeau, Emmanuelle Souty
Translation	LanguageWire
Contributors	Costina-Ionela Lungu, Theodor Cepraga (**Cartography**), Véronique Aissani, Carole Diascorn (**Cover**), Marion Capéra, Marie Simonet (**Iconography**), Sabine Mannequin (**Objective Data**), Hervé Dubois, Pascal Grougon (**Prepresse**), Dominique Auclair (**Production Manager**)
	Maps : ©Michelin 2023
Acknowledgments	Occitanie Regional Tourist & Leisure Board
Graphic Design	Laurent Muller (cover and interior layout), Michelin Éditions adaptation
Advertising Sales and Partnership	contact.clients@editions.michelin.com *The content of any advertising pages contained in this guide is the sole responsibility of advertisers.*
Contacts	Your opinion is essential to improving our products Help us by answering the questionnaire on our website: editions.michelin.com
Published in 2023	

MICHELIN Éditions
A French stock company with capital of 487,500 euro
57 rue Gaston-Tessier – 75019 Paris (France)
Registered in Paris 882 639 354

No part of this publication may be reproduced in any form whatsoever without the prior permission of the publisher.

© 2023 MICHELIN Éditions - All rights reserved
Registration of Copyright: 05-2023 – ISSN 0293-9436
Typography/Photoengraving: MICHELIN Éditions, Paris
Printer: Grafotisak, Grude (Bosnia-Herzegovina)
Printed in Bosniae-Herzegovine: 05-2023

Printed on sustainably sourced paper

YES, ECO-FRIENDLY TRAVEL IS POSSIBLE!

Cars and planes account for three quarters of the greenhouse gas emissions caused by tourism in France. How about travelling differently in the south-western region of **Occitanie**?

TOURISM IN FRANCE IN NUMBERS:

89.3 million **tourists**, with **10.4%** in Occitanie

11% of greenhouse gas emissions, of which **77%** are related to transport
Source : 2021 ADEME study (2018 figures)

40%
32%

Check out **impactco2.fr** to choose the least polluting means of transport

by foot
GR®, Saint James Way (Camino de Santiago) pilgrimage routes, etc.

by bike
Zero pollution!
- **20 cycling routes**
- **50 greenways**

by train
8 X less pollution than driving
14 X less pollution than flying

by coach
5.5 X less pollution than driving

Transport in Occitanie:
- more than **280 train stations**
- **550 trains/day**
- **5,000 buses/day**

GREENER ACCOMODATIONS?
Find lodgings with the sustainability certifications listed at agirpourlatransition.ademe.fr/particuliers/labels-environnementaux

ECO-FRIENDLY ACTIONS EVERY STEP OF THE WAY!
- **Consume local and seasonal products** when shopping and in restaurants.
- **Sort your waste,** limit how much you produce, and never leave anything behind in nature!
- **Save energy,** especially when it comes to heating and air-conditioning.
- **Save water:** take short showers, etc.
- **Respect plant and animal life** by staying on marked trails and avoiding motorised activities.

TO GO FURTHER
- agirpourlatransition.ademe.fr/particuliers
- occitanie.ademe.fr

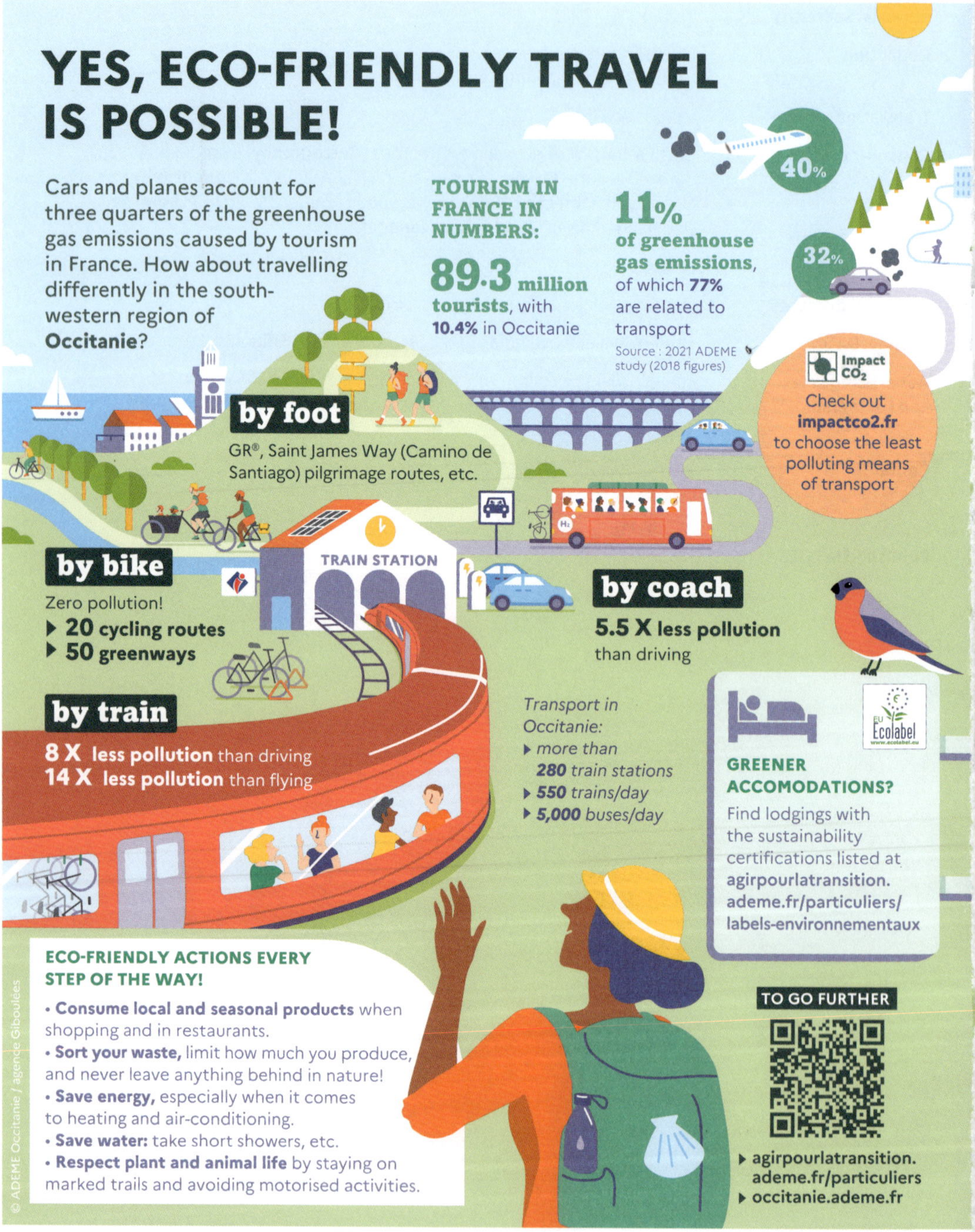